Herping Texas

Myrna and David K. Langford
Books on Working Lands

Herping Texas

The Quest for
Reptiles and Amphibians

Michael Smith and Clint King

TEXAS A&M UNIVERSITY PRESS
College Station

Design: Barbara Haines

This paper meets the requirements of ANSI/NISO Z39.48-1992 (Permanence of Paper).
Binding materials have been chosen for durability.
Manufactured in China through FCI Print Group

Library of Congress Cataloging-in-Publication Data
Names: Smith, Michael, 1951 April 18– author. | King, Clint, author.
Title: Herping Texas: the quest for reptiles and amphibians / Michael Smith
    and Clint King.
Description: First edition. | College Station: Texas A&M University Press,
    [2018] | Series: Myrna and David K. Langford books on working lands |
    Identifiers: LCCN 2018006359 (print) | LCCN 2018010303 (ebook) | ISBN
    9781623496654 (ebook) | ISBN 9781623496647 | ISBN
    9781623496647 (flexbound with flaps: alk. paper)
Subjects: LCSH: Herpetology—Texas.
Classification: LCC QL653.T4 (ebook) | LCC QL653.T4 S65 2018 (print) | DDC
    597.909764—dc23
LC record available at https://lccn.loc.gov/2018006359

To all young herpers and naturalists
who follow their dreams
into the field

CONTENTS

ACKNOWLEDGMENTS

This book would never have been possible without the understanding and patience of our families during our many absences in the field for the past ten years or so. Jo, Geoff, Amber, and Zev have taken all this in stride and never kicked us out for being hopeless herp vagabonds. We appreciate their support and forbearance.

When we finally managed to assemble our notes and articles into some sort of coherent form, Rick Pratt (director of the Port Aransas Museum and Farley Boat Works) was that pivotal person who got it into the right hands, through author and photographer David K. Langford. We will be forever grateful that they saw value in those initial ideas and helped connect us with Texas A&M University Press.

The director of TAMU Press, Shannon Davies, is another pivotal person without whom the book in front of you might just be stacks of notes and papers. Her belief in the idea behind the book and her support were priceless. We then had the pleasure of working with an editorial team including Stacy Eisenstark, Katie Duelm, and Alison Tartt, who have definitely made us better writers and shown great patience with us through the long process of manuscript preparation.

We had been writing about reptiles, amphibians, and other wildlife for some years prior to working on this book, in an e-publication called *Texas Field Notes*. Some of that material found its way into the pages of this book. We are grateful for the guidance and support of Rob Denkhaus, Suzanne Tuttle, Andy Gluesenkamp, Carl Franklin, John Placyk, Travis LaDuc, and Malcolm McCallum while we were writing *Texas Field Notes*.

Although many of our travels were to publicly accessible places such as preserves and parks, there were times that we benefited from visiting private lands. Many thanks to John Herron, Max Pons, and Chris Pipes at The Nature Conservancy in Texas, and thanks to Jim Costabile, Mark Grosse, Rob Morris, Dave Fitzgerald, and Lyman and Janette Arthur for allowing access to their land.

Many people have accompanied us in the field over the years, and their observations, insights, and companionship are of incalculable worth. The joys, successes, bittersweet failures, target species found, herp-less nights, and an endless succession of inside jokes and road trip memories are a vital part of what it means to be a field herper. We name a few friends here, at the risk of leaving out even more, and we apologize in advance to anyone we fail to mention. Many thanks to the late Steve Campbell, Ryan Blankenship, Tim Cole, Mark Pyle and family, Carl Franklin, Tim and Luke Sellers, Michael Price, Justin Garza, Scott Robinson, Steve Levey, Casey Garcia, Shelsea Sanchez, Jan and Cheyenne Williams, and Symantha Gray.

Other people have helped greatly through such things as reading parts of the manuscript, providing information, or going into the field with us at other times. We thank Roy and Ruth Engeldorff, John Chmielewski, John Karges, Troy Hibbitts, Terry Hibbitts, and Neil Ford. We have also benefited from encouragement and support from others who are not named here, but who are nevertheless appreciated.

A final thanks to all the reptiles, amphibians, and other native Texans of both the warm-and cold-blooded persuasions who have been the backbone and driving force behind our many adventures afield. The brief sharing of their lives, sometimes involuntary as it may have been, has brought us great joy. These moments were well worth the sleep deprivation, weariness, scratches, stings, and sore muscles. We wish these creatures and their progeny well, both now and in the future, and vow to continue to fight to preserve them and their habitats for future generations.

Herping Texas

Introduction

Michael Smith

Toward the end of March a few years back, a group of us took a walk through a bottomland forest at the Fort Worth Nature Center and Refuge. We were documenting all the species of reptiles and amphibians in the large refuge on the edge of Fort Worth. In early spring in North Texas, new green growth appears in a landscape in which the trees have bare branches and the ground is, for a little longer, mostly a brown collage of last year's leaves. The warmth of the sun felt good; the hot and sticky days of late spring and summer would not arrive for some time. We saw cricket frogs around the little streams and rivulets of water draining to the marsh. Crayfish burrows were everywhere, and we found some parts of crayfish exoskeletons in a couple of places, victims of birds or raccoons or some other predator with a taste for "mudbugs." Farther on, where the forest meets the edge of the marsh, one member of the group picked her way amid the deadfall and started to brace herself against a tree trunk. She was surprised to find that while she had been looking for reptiles and amphibians on the ground, the action was at eye level—on that very tree trunk. We heard the commotion and converged to see a western ratsnake (previously known as the Texas ratsnake) motionless on the tree trunk in beautiful dark kinks and curves, stopped in its downward progress by our intrusion. The snake raised its head, sized up the situation, and held still. Black blotches were vaguely evident against a lighter but dark-smudged background. Between the scales were yellows and hints of salmon pink shading to orange. Here and there were flecks of white. The overall impression, however, was of four feet of satiny, nearly black snake clinging to the irregularities in the bark. After being surrounded by humans taking pictures for a couple of minutes, the snake decided that its best escape was back up the tree, and turned to climb. As it did so, I gently took its body and lifted it off the tree. Seeing nothing coming at it and having no target in front of it to strike at, the snake simply accepted this and allowed itself to be examined. What a marvelous animal! They are not highly prized by naturalists, both because they are very common and because they typically bite

Western (Texas) ratsnake

when handled. However, in the complexity and variability of pattern and in their strength and agility in climbing, they are magnificent.

Why do we go looking for these animals?

Why would anyone go looking for snakes, lizards, and other reptiles and amphibians, just for the enjoyment of seeing, photographing, or holding them? Why would we spend days searching for reptiles, hiking through the desert or crawling through a thorn thicket, just for a few minutes of observation and some photos to take back home? For some readers, these may seem to be silly questions—it may already be obvious to you why we do this. For others, the questions may need answering. We go looking for reptiles and amphibians for the same reasons that a person spends the day standing in a river and casting the line in, feeling the river current and waiting for the sudden pull of a trout on the line. It is for much the same reason that another person goes to a museum and stands in the hushed stillness, getting lost in a painting. Our trips into the field are one way of interacting with something that engages the senses and the spirit, feeding a part of us that needs to experience fascinating and beautiful aspects of the world around us.

We may be looking for some species in particular, but "getting there" is most of the fun. Walking through a mature forest in southeast Texas immerses you in a sensory wonderland of breezes soughing through pines, birds

Common five-lined skink in the Big Thicket

calling, the colors and textures of trees, water, ferns, and the leaves and pine needles carpeting the ground. Seeing the glossy, striped form of a common five-lined skink in a patch of sunlight on a tree trunk is one of the highlights of such a walk, but it is not the whole point. This is a treasure hunt where everything around us is treasure. It is a symphony in which we may be partial to the beautiful notes of the woodwinds, but the real work of art comes from all the instruments together. It is true that the animals themselves are beautiful and fascinating in their own right, and some people just want to see the animals. However, placing them in the natural context of woods and fields makes seeing them much more satisfying. And what if we don't find any reptiles or amphibians? We do complain loudly about getting "skunked" on field trips, but the truth is that, for most of us, walking through the forest or wading through the marsh is satisfying in itself.

We have spent many days in the field together, and many of our stories are told by both of us, either blending what each of us remembers or alternating between our individual perceptions. Some stories are from trips we took with others or on our own. In each case, we indicate who is speaking when it is not both of us together.

We hope that reading about our trips to the prairies, woods, deserts, and mountains will communicate something of our love for these places and leave you with a desire to visit some or all of them. It is hard for us to imagine

Coastal marsh at Texas Point National Wildlife Refuge

Cross Timbers woodland at the Fort Worth Nature Center and Refuge

that you could visit Big Bend, Palo Duro Canyon, or the Big Thicket and not fall in love with these places. We have fallen in love with countless wetlands, forests, and fields in the state, and we are hopelessly caught up in the desire to see them survive unspoiled into the next century. Not all of them will, but those places that do continue will do so because people knew them and cared enough to protect them.

What are "herps" and what is "field herping"?

In the field of biology, reptiles and amphibians are "herpetofauna." The first part of the word comes from the Greek word "herpeton," meaning a creeping thing. The word "fauna" comes from Latin and means "animal." It is easy

In the Sabine National Forest

Palo Duro Canyon

to shorten "herpetofauna" to simply "herp" or "herps." (One has to be careful that it's not confused with the viral illness herpes, which derives from the same Greek source!) And so if you go out looking for herps—reptiles and amphibians—you are "herping." Those who are very involved in looking for, studying, or keeping herps are often referred to as "herpers." This may seem more familiar to you if you think about those who are interested in birds. Such a person is casually referred to as a "birder" and the activity they pursue is called "birding."

Chihuahuan Desert habitat in Big Bend National Park

Herpers are an incredibly variable group. Some are primarily interested in keeping reptiles and amphibians at home and may have an extensive captive collection and breed a number of species. To make it clear when someone is going out looking for herps living in the wild, we add the word "field," as in "field herping." Many field herpers are interested in the natural history of reptiles and amphibians, and their focus may be mostly or entirely on finding them in the places where they live and then photographing them. Although the authors keep some herps at home, our focus is mostly on natural history and on seeing them in the wild.

Reptiles and amphibians are two very different groups of animals, and so it is a little odd that they are lumped together under one branch of science. This originated in the eighteenth century when the biologist Carolus Linnaeus developed a system for classifying living things. He had little regard for herps and lumped them together, calling them "amphibians."[1] The two groups have been stuck together ever since, despite their differences. What does continue to unite them is that both amphibians and reptiles are the only land-dwelling vertebrate animals that are cold-blooded. That is, both groups are "ectotherms," meaning that they get heat from their surroundings. While mammals and birds ("endotherms") generate their own heat using the energy of metabolism, reptiles and amphibians get warmth from the sun. They keep their body temperature within a workable range by shifting into warmer or cooler places. In order to get warm enough to move around and meet their needs, herps may have to emerge from cover and bask in the sun for a while;

then later on, when it gets too hot, they have to find shelter. On the other hand, because they do not have to use their energy to generate heat, reptiles and amphibians have much lower metabolism and can generally get by on less food.

Professional and amateur herpetology

Field herpers are not necessarily trained biologists. The scientific study of herpetofauna is called herpetology, and it is a branch of biology that uses scientific and experimental methods to understand reptiles and amphibians. The authors of this book are naturalists, and we might be called amateur herpetologists, but we do not have formal training in herpetology. The history of herpetology includes many contributions from those who were not formally trained in biology. One of the most widely respected is Laurence M. Klauber, who was an electrical engineer with an interest in the reptiles of southern California where he lived. First through volunteer activity, then as the curator of reptiles at the San Diego Zoo, he became an authority on rattlesnakes. Ultimately, Klauber published a two-volume set titled *Rattlesnakes: Their Habits, Life Histories, and Influence on Mankind*, which is still a prized addition to any herpetologist's library.

Many of the names most recognized by hobbyists and naturalists are of people who have worked in zoos and have written books or field guides. Among these is Raymond Ditmars, who was long associated with the Bronx Zoo and wrote a number of popular books in the early twentieth century. Another significant name is Carl Kauffeld, a curator at the Staten Island Zoo. Kauffeld wrote two books that have been very influential with field herpers: *Snakes and Snake Hunting* and *Snakes: The Keeper and the Kept*. In the 1950s Roger Conant (who was with the Philadelphia Zoo) authored a classic field guide to reptiles and amphibians of the eastern United States. This Peterson field guide is the one that several generations of us have carried with us, dog-eared, and read over and over. In later editions Joseph Collins and, more recently, Robert Powell, joined Conant as coauthors, and the book is still probably the best field guide for herps from Texas eastward.[2]

There are also well-known herpetologists who are more closely associated with experimental and field research. Harry Greene, recently retired from Cornell University, has written several popular books, including the beautifully written and illustrated *Snakes: The Evolution of Mystery in Nature*. And J. Whitfield ("Whit") Gibbons, now retired, was prolific as a scientist at the Savannah River Ecology Lab and as a popular writer and educator. Gibbons authored such books as *Their Blood Runs Cold* and has written many conservation-related columns and newspaper articles. He was central to the formation of Partners in Amphibian and Reptile Conservation, which brings together various groups to help protect herps and their habitats.

Texas—a herp "hot spot"

According to James Dixon, in the third edition of his *Amphibians and Reptiles of Texas*, the state has 284 species and subspecies of amphibians and reptiles,[3] which makes Texas a hot spot for field herping in the United States. Texas is home to nearly 1,200 species of vertebrates (fish, herps, birds, and mammals) in a state with a land area of 261,797 square miles. That is a lot for a naturalist to see and study! The state can be divided into a number of natural regions, each of which has its own distinct geography, plants, and animals. For our purposes, we have divided this book into the following areas: the plains and canyons of northwest Texas; the oak woodlands and grasslands in the north-central part of the state; the Piney Woods of East Texas; the marshes and prairies along the Gulf Coast; the South Texas thorn scrub and the Rio Grande Valley; the Edwards Plateau; and the deserts and mountains of the Trans-Pecos. These areas are based on ten ecoregions (map) that can be found in maps such as those available from Texas Parks and Wildlife Department.[4]

Some of the reptiles and amphibians are specific to particular parts of the state. Examples include the desert box turtle and the Chihuahuan greater earless lizard in the Trans-Pecos, Berlandier's tortoise (previously known as the Texas tortoise) and the Texas indigo snake in the thorn scrub, the Houston toad in the Piney Woods, and the plains gartersnake in the Panhandle. Others are generalists whose ranges cross one or more boundaries, such as the western ratsnake, the American bullfrog, the red-eared slider turtle, or the little brown skink. Knowing about the different ecoregions may sometimes but not always allow us to predict where a species will be found. Such knowledge always enables us to understand these animals better. Our discussion of Texas field herping is organized according to these ecoregions.

Herping and the conservation ethic

The authors live in a huge state with a wide variety of habitats, but Texas' population is growing and its natural areas shrinking. As of 2016, Texas had 27.86 million residents, according to the US Census Bureau.[5] While the trend is for people to congregate in cities, our state has plenty of low-density cities and towns dotting the landscape, with exurban sprawl covering much of the eastern half of the state.[6] Six of the fastest-growing towns in the United States with populations over 50,000 were located around major Texas cities.

The ecoregions of Texas are crisscrossed and fragmented by over 675,000 lane-miles of roads. Since the prevailing economic view is that continuous growth is necessary and desirable, it is hard to see where this will all end. Not all wildlife species can coexist with humans and live within farmland or urban areas. At some point, natural areas can become so squeezed, fragmented, and changed by human use that they cease to exist. This has almost happened to our native prairies. The original prairies were far different from the pastures and fields of Johnson grass (a nonnative species) that we are so used to seeing. Real prairie, when you look closely, supports a great diversity of native grasses and forbs and is maintained by periodic fires and a certain amount of grazing. Wildlife species living on the prairie often have large home ranges, traveling considerable distances to forage for food and find shelter or mates. Once the prairie is fragmented by roads, the turtles, snakes, small mammals, and other species are confined to smaller habitat patches or killed on the roads. Once fire is prevented from burning off woody growth, shrubs and trees start to take over. And of course, much of the prairie has been replaced by pastureland, cropland, malls, and residential development. Alteration and loss of habitat is occurring in all the ecoregions of Texas. And although much still remains, we need to actively conserve the natural and wild places or else, at some point, almost all of it will be changed and much will be lost.

Most of us who go field herping would say that too much has already been lost and that we must find a better way of balancing the needs and activities of people against the needs and existence of wild places. Like birders, hunters, anglers, and hikers, we see these undisturbed places as necessary for an adequate quality of life, without which the world would be much poorer. Not only that, but the world would be more fragile and less able to support whatever was left, because diversity in nature provides stability and a variety of resources to all species, including our own. The more an area is stripped of biodiversity, the more vulnerable a place is; in an acre filled with nothing but apple trees, a disease like fire blight is a world killer. If, instead, that acre had a hundred species of plants, a disease of one of the species would be less devastating.

We need nature, but beyond that, we should consider whether it is wise to let unrestrained growth needlessly destroy other lives with whom we share the planet. Maybe the value of nature goes beyond our needs. Perhaps we should spend a little more time considering the idea of stewardship, in which we are entrusted with the care of something that is not ours and that we did not make. Field herpers often appreciate the value of nature, seeing the places and the animals as a gift that we must appreciate and have the wisdom to leave alone, for the most part. As field herpers, we are likely to see our-selves as part of the overall picture, knowing that we have some impact on the places we visit and striving to make sure that those impacts leave no last-ing damage.

In the early days of herping, reptiles and amphibians were often taken as if there were an inexhaustible supply. Carl Kauffeld wrote, in *Snakes and Snake Hunting*, that he had occasionally collected too many snakes, express-ing regret for this. He argued that herpers might do what birders had done, forming a sort of Audubon Society and seeking to offer snakes some protec-tion. Kauffeld wrote: "Among reptile lovers the policy of observing instead of collecting should be promoted first, last, and always, as the means of gaining the greatest benefits from a hobby which can have rich returns—the appre-ciation of the creature in its undisturbed habitat—a worthy end in itself, which the devotees of bird observing have developed into a skillful pursuit from which they derive the greatest satisfaction."[7]

It is unfortunately true that some herpers still consider populations of reptiles and amphibians to be inexhaustible. After a herper has caught and examined a specimen and maybe photographed it, the next thing to do is to let it go, right where it was found. This can be difficult, and many a snake hunter has rationalized that it won't hurt anything to keep *this* particular one, while believing that people in general should not overcollect. You can be sure that we have used this same rationalization, and it is true that for the great majority of species, collecting a few specimens for personal use is unlikely to have any negative effects. Nevertheless, it is a sign of maturity when a herper can examine a beautiful and desirable specimen and then let it go—or merely observe it from nearby without catching it at all.

One collector taking one animal is probably no big deal, but multiply that by hundreds of visitors and you can see how populations might be harmed. Notice that our stories lean heavily on taking photographs instead of taking animals. Over the years we have learned that herps are often more beauti-ful in that moment of discovery than they are later on, at home, in a box. We hope you will consider just observing and just photographing, leaving the reptiles and amphibians where you found them.

Scientific names of reptiles and amphibians

In the stories we tell in this book, we refer to reptiles and amphibians by their common names—with few exceptions. All species of animals, and all other organisms as well, have scientific names that are more precise ways to refer to what is being described. Scientific names mostly use Greek or Latin words that describe something about the organism. For example, map turtles are in the genus *Graptemys*, which comes from the Greek words for "writing" and "turtle." The patterns on their shells have intricate lines suggesting a map or the lines of a written word. Scientific names have been a way for everyone to understand which animal we are referring to. Different people might refer to a plains hog-nosed snake as a spreading adder, a spread-head snake, a Texas rooter, or other names, but scientifically it has only one name: *Heterodon nasicus*. We do not use scientific names throughout the text for two reasons. First, we want these pages to be friendly and accessible to those who are interested in Texas wildlife but are not herpetology specialists; second, we are in a period in which many scientific names are changing so rapidly that it can be hard for anyone to keep up with them. For a current authoritative list of the scientific names of reptiles and amphibians, we refer the reader to the names list published by the Society for the Study of Amphibians and Reptiles.[8]

A herpetological tour of Texas

What we offer in the following chapters is to take the reader on a herpetological tour of Texas. For some readers who have already "taken the tour," it will evoke memories of finding a particular snake in the Big Bend region or hearing a frog chorus in East Texas. For others, it will be an introduction to animals that are often overlooked and even shunned. It is an opportunity to see them from a new perspective in their natural habitat. We hope to pass along a greater understanding of these remarkable creatures. Hardly any group of animals is more misunderstood and needlessly feared than reptiles, although only a few pose any risk to people and many are breathtakingly beautiful. Seeing them in the wild is the best way to get to know them, we think. How better to witness their uniquely adapted bodies and fascinating behaviors—from the spikes adorning the heads of horned lizards to the dramatic cobra-like bluffing and death-feigning of the hog-nosed snakes? Watching the American alligator in coastal marshes, seeing a big western diamond-backed rattlesnake in the desert, and listening to a beautiful green treefrog as it clings to a reed in a marsh and calls during the night—these experiences bring both the animal and its habitat to life.

After reading our adventures, we hope you will want to go field herping. If you are new to this, we have a short chapter toward the end of the book with helpful information about choosing places to go, laws that apply to field herping, and venomous snakebite. We hope you will consider those issues before venturing out.

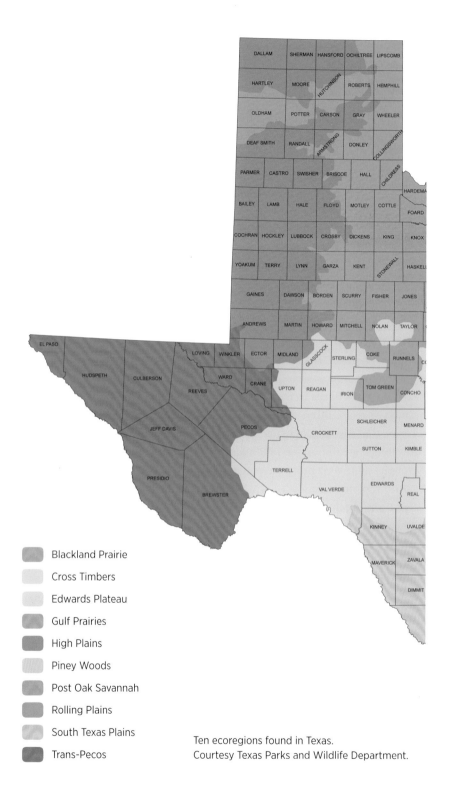

Blackland Prairie

Cross Timbers

Edwards Plateau

Gulf Prairies

High Plains

Piney Woods

Post Oak Savannah

Rolling Plains

South Texas Plains

Trans-Pecos

Ten ecoregions found in Texas.
Courtesy Texas Parks and Wildlife Department.

GOULD
ECOREGIONS
OF TEXAS

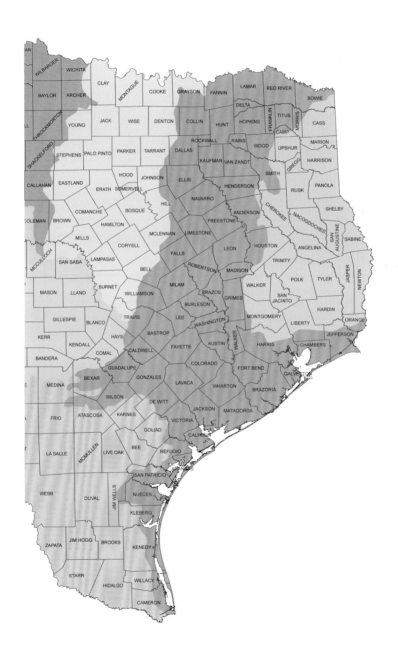

1 The Big Thicket

THE BIG THICKET IS A REGION in the southeastern part of Texas where huge forests of pine and hardwood trees grow in deep, sandy soil; creeks and bayous meander through places where cypress and tupelo trees stand in dark-stained water; and savannah wetlands grow thick with ferns and pitcher plants. Species such as southern crawfish frogs and red-bellied snakes live here. All of this makes it hard to believe you are in the same state renowned for cacti and grasslands.

There are estimates that the Big Thicket once covered over three million acres in southeast Texas.[1] Lumbering, farming, oil drilling, and various other influences chipped away at it until in the 1920s it was clear that if some of the Big Thicket were not protected, it could disappear. There was some support from one timber company: Temple Industries had stopped clearcutting and spraying herbicides and had even quit harvesting in the area of the proposed preserve.[2] Finally, legislation introduced by Congressman Charlie Wilson of Lufkin was passed, establishing the Big Thicket National Preserve, 84,550 acres administered by the National Park Service. The preserve is a patchwork of units scattered around the region, protecting various ecosystems representative of the Big Thicket. Through the additional efforts of Congressman Wilson, 10,776 acres were added to the preserve in 1993, for a total of 105,684 acres. The area is listed as an International Biosphere Reserve and a Globally Important Bird Area. It is located where the subtropical climate shades into a temperate one, and it receives a great deal of annual rainfall. Its location also marks the boundary of the eastern forests, which give way to the prairies and cross-timbers to the west. So the Big Thicket is a kind of transition zone, and it contains a magnificent assortment of plants and animals.

Three kinds of trees—the beech, magnolia, and pine—grow together in the Big Thicket and help define this area. Growing amid these trees is a profusion of vines, orchids, holly, briars, palmetto, royal ferns, cinnamon ferns, and other plants. Not every place in the Big Thicket is impenetrable forest. The savannah wetlands are open areas that may have fields of pitcher plants

Kirby Trail, Turkey Creek unit, Big Thicket National Preserve

Pitcher Plant Trail, Turkey Creek unit, Big Thicket National Preserve

Pitcher plant leaves form a vertical tube with a flap over the top. Insects fall into the tube and dissolve, providing nutrients for the plant.

that send up vertical leaves forming tubes in which insects become trapped and their nutrients absorbed. This and another carnivorous plant, the sundew, are common in these savannahs. In the floodplains and sloughs, bald cypresses and water tupelos stand in the water and tower overhead, while snapping turtles and (in some places) gators make use of the dark waters below.

No hoops, no stingers, just a beautiful black snake / SMITH

On one of our trips, we drove a back road on our way to the Jack Gore unit of the Big Thicket National Preserve. Just after dark, we stopped for a moderate-size dark snake undulating across the dirt roadway. Given where we were, the odds favored this chunky dark snake being a watersnake or a northern cottonmouth, which would have been a perfectly good find. However, this was a day to beat the odds. The snake crossing in front of us was a western mudsnake. In a series of visits to this region with the Dallas–Fort Worth Herpetological Society, we've been lucky to find four or five of these glossy black snakes with their brilliant salmon-red pattern along the belly and sides. They are not so common, though, that we take them for granted. A mudsnake is always an exciting find for us.

Western mudsnake seen in the Big Thicket

The western mudsnake is semiaquatic, spending most of its time in swamps, sloughs, and ditches where it finds sirens and amphiumas, which are the snake's favorite prey. Amphiumas, eel-like salamanders, are found in muddy wetlands with lots of emergent vegetation, so it's a good bet that you'll find mudsnakes nearby. In Texas the mudsnake's range includes the Big Thicket northward to the Red River and westward to the Brazos River in east-central Texas and along the Texas coast to around Victoria. In coastal areas they may be found in brackish marshes, and they reportedly eat fish in those areas.

There are a couple of misconceptions associated with this physically powerful but completely harmless snake. The first is that the snake is equipped with a poisonous stinger in its tail. The truth is that mudsnakes have a hard, pointed scale at the tip of the tail that they use to get prey better positioned for swallowing after they've seized it in their jaws. If captured by a human, this three- or four-foot snake wraps the lower part of its body around the captor and pushes the tail tip against the person's arm or hand. The snake is strong, and the sharp tail tip would no doubt startle anyone who is not expecting to be poked. However, there is no stinger and no poison.

The other misconception is one I read about years before I ever saw a mudsnake, and I could never figure out how it might have gotten started since it is so improbable. As this story goes, the snake takes its tail in its mouth and rolls downhill like a hoop, straightening itself out to sail through the air, its supposed "tail stinger" extended forward. The truth is, mudsnakes are not particularly graceful on land and could never roll like a hoop. It is possible that someone came upon a mudsnake swallowing a large amphiuma and mistook the dark body of the salamander grasped in the snake's mouth as part of the snake. The snake and amphiuma would no doubt be writhing and twisting on the ground. Perhaps this is one explanation for how this story emerged.

Ten thousand frogs—or so it seemed / SMITH

There are twenty kinds of frogs and toads found in the Big Thicket, and sometimes it seems like you may be hearing almost all twenty types at once. In May 2003, on my first trip to the Big Thicket, I pulled up to a pond nestled in the pines. The sun had just set, and a little after 9:00 p.m. several frog species had begun calling. Listening in the warm East Texas darkness, I untangled each of the voices from this amphibian concerto. First, there was the "grick-grick-grick-grick" of Blanchard's cricket frogs, sounding almost like stones being clicked together. Choruses of cricket frogs rose and fell in waves, as more little frogs joined in, and then fell off. At a lower register were calls from green treefrogs, "wank-wank-wank," vaguely reminiscent of ducks quacking. These frogs also call in large numbers, with voices overlapping in thick choruses. Emerging from this background was the "doink" of the green frog (previously known as the bronze frog), a banjo-plucking character spending a leisurely evening on his front porch. Often several green frogs would be calling, but rarely in numbers that would result in overlapping calls or choruses. Other solo voices came from the various southern leopard frogs calling from the water's edge, producing a chuckling call and occasionally a sound that is best compared to the rubbing and twisting together of a couple of balloons. At the lower registers, the bass viols of this concerto, if you will, were several American bullfrogs. Forget the "jug-o-rum" stories you've heard; these amphibians produce a harsh hum that rises to a peak and then subsides. It vaguely suggests the sound you would make if you imitated a large truck driving by you at highway speed: "r-r-r-r-m-m-m-m-m." Several overlapping calls create a sonorous droning sound. In addition to the droning, the quacking, the banjo-plucking, the chuckling, and the sleigh-bell quality of the massed cricket frog voices, a few Gulf Coast toads were chorusing. While frogs tend to have short, repeating notes—the gricks and quacks and doinks—toads have extended trills. The Gulf Coast toad trill has a resonant quality like a wooden ratchet being turned rapidly for about five seconds or

Green treefrog, a beautiful frog with a "quacking" voice

so. Altogether, it was magnificent! I stayed for a while at the pond, the voices blending and weaving in and out of each other, creating a fascinating and pleasing tapestry of sound.

And what was all this about? What possesses these amphibians to use up their time and energy creating these choruses? It's all about frog romance. Male frogs gather at suitable breeding spots—ponds, bogs, even roadside ditches—and advertise their presence to females. The ladies approach, and the male gets onto the female's back with his front legs grasping her, and he hangs on as she lays eggs. This position, called "amplexus," allows him to fertilize the eggs as the female lays them.

On the trail of the hog-nosed snake / SMITH

We had a particularly memorable visit in the spring of 2009, at the start of the Dallas–Fort Worth Herpetological Society's annual field trip to the Big Thicket. Clint and I arrived at the Big Thicket National Preserve headquarters and got the permit that allowed us to temporarily collect and photograph specimens to contribute to a survey of the plants and animals of the preserve. Our next stop was the Kirby Trail, which threads northward through the Turkey Creek unit, a narrow strip of protected land in Hardin and Tyler Counties. The Kirby Trail winds through a tall forest of pines, oaks,

American beeches with their smooth, ashen trunks, and tall southern magnolias with their broad, waxy leaves. Interwoven into all of this are hollies, azaleas, and other shrubs and plants. As the trail gently drops into bottomland, there are shallow pools of water, dark as tea from the decaying leaves that drop into it, and at the water's edge there are little mud chimneys made by crayfish. There is so much to see, so many details of color and texture in the dappled sunlight, that a slow, meandering pace is the only way to take in the experience. A couple of lizard species—the common five-lined skink and the broad-headed skink—prowl the tree trunks and branches, skittering away as you get close. Still another lizard, the green anole, shares this territory. Male anoles defend their little patch of the thicket by extending a dewlap out from the throat, exposing red skin between the scales, and bobbing their heads. The leaf litter, downed trees, and hollow stumps conceal more lizards, frogs, toads, and a number of snake species.

I had high hopes of seeing one species in particular, the eastern hog-nosed snake, a stubby little snake with an upturned scale at the snout and a dramatic flair for self-defense. They are powerfully built for digging but terribly awkward when trying to put on a burst of speed. While they have enlarged teeth in the back of the upper jaw and a mild toxin that subdues toads, the principal items on their menu, hog-nosed snakes are harmless to humans and larger predators. To defend themselves, they need a better strategy than biting or crawling away. Nature has given these snakes a defensive display so grotesque as to be clownish when you understand that this is really a harmless little bluffer that never actually bites in self-defense. When first disturbed, the snake takes a deep breath and spreads the ribs of its neck, cobra-like. With head and neck flattened, a pattern on the neck is exposed that includes two dark patches that may function like eyespots. Some animal species use pairs of black spots that mimic eyes on a gigantic head, possibly scaring a predator away or at least misdirecting the attack. The hog-nosed snake turns its flattened neck toward the intruder in a way that makes the snake look larger and emphasizes these bold patches. The snake exhales a lungful of air to produce a loud hiss, and it often lunges forward or jerks its body while hissing, even though the mouth does not open in an attempt to bite. Nevertheless, it is convincing enough as a counterfeit strike to startle the predator or human observer. It is also convincing enough to earn this little reptile various common names like "hissing adder" and to convince people that it is dangerous and must be killed on sight. After hissing, flattening, and giving several false strikes, if the intruder has not retreated, then the snake moves on to "act two." It suddenly contorts its body as if having a seizure, writhes on the ground open-mouthed and with its tongue hanging out,

Eastern hog-nosed snake cruising through leaf litter

and lies on its back as if it has suddenly died. If picked up, it does not move. On the other hand, if turned over, it promptly rolls onto its back, which is evidently the prescribed way of being dead. It may be that an attacker, faced with a now-dead snake, will stop attacking and the snake may get a chance to escape. If left alone for a minute or two, it raises its head to look around, and if there is no attacker, it turns back over and crawls away.

Perhaps because of this fascinating behavior, or the variety of colors that individual hog-nosed snakes may possess (shades of brown, gold, orange, or even red), or their short faces and upturned noses that many people anthropomorphically think of as "cute," hog-nosed snakes are widely admired by herpers. And I had gone forty years or so without seeing one alive in the wild. Clint, on the other hand, grew up catching them in his yard. These snakes are more common in places with loose, sandy soil and plenty of toads, and so there are places within its range where the hog-nosed snake is—or used to be—common, and other places where they are not found. I came close to seeing one in the mid-1960s when someone ran over one with a mower near my back yard. I remember looking at the two halves of what-could-have-been and wishing I could stitch the snake back together. Over the years, I had seen a couple that had been run over on the road, but never a live one.

The same hognose, feigning death

My luck finally turned in 2009, when I finally saw a live hog-nosed snake in the wild. As Clint and I walked through the Turkey Creek unit of the Big Thicket, a plague of mosquitoes was challenging our peaceful enjoyment of the forest and attentive search for herps. Our exhalations of carbon dioxide were sending up a flare for the Kirby Trail squadron of the Mosquito Airborne. Clouds of bloodsuckers scrambled from tree cavities and hollow logs on a mission to drain the herpers. Nevertheless, we continued along the trail, recording the localities of skinks and anoles and batting away the mosquito attacks. And then the clouds parted, Heaven opened up, and Clint said, "Hognose!"

There it was! Cruising through the scattered leaves and pine needles on the forest floor, right up to the trail's edge, was an eastern hog-nosed snake. Alerted by our movement, the snake froze in position. Its two-foot-long, grayish-brown mottled pattern, with a shading of orange along the lip scales, fit in well with the forest floor. Had it become motionless a few seconds earlier, a little farther back into the forest, we would never have seen it. Having caught sight of my elusive Holy Grail of snakes, I fell to my knees, and I expect Clint presumed I was giving thanks. I was, but I had gone to my knees to get out the cameras and preserve this moment. Clint pulled out his camera as well, and we moved in slowly and carefully to fill the frame with close-ups.

After a few photos, we wanted to examine this snake. It took a deep breath and began the hognose Dance of Danger, flattening and hissing and jerking its head. After this did not result in our leaving, the snake moved on to the Dance of Death. After a couple of twisting spasms, it rolled onto its back, mouth hanging open in the dirt. By this time I was videotaping, catching the dramatic action of a snake lying still. Clint and I both wanted to capture the moment when the snake peeked around and rolled back upright. And so we waited and waited, as mosquito squadrons continued their attacks and we sat motionless, not wanting to frighten the snake. In due time the snake looked up, waited for what seemed an eternity to see if anything moved, and then righted itself. Slowly it glided over leaf litter and under deadfall and moved on into the forest.

An invisible cottonmouth / KING

It was a bright and promising morning during the spring of 2009 as I walked casually along the Pitcher Plant Trail in the Big Thicket. Heavy seasonal thunderstorms the night before had hit the area, but the morning's sunrise was hard at work drying it all up, providing the perfect recipe for high reptilian activity. Michael and I had arrived in the area the night before and had met up with other members of the Dallas–Fort Worth Herpetological Society at the head of the trail a little after nine o'clock the next morning. Our expectations rose with the sun, which shone its way through the tangle of briars at trailside, providing a patchy, dappled play on the thick mixture of leaf and pine detritus of the forest floor that blankets this immense section of East Texas.

We had traversed about a half mile of the trail, with a few of the younger members taking the lead, their keen eyes picking out common five-lined and broad-headed skinks warming up on fallen logs in preparation for the day, and prairie lizards and green anoles bobbing and displaying and fighting for territory on sun-exposed pine trunks. As we crossed over a small bridge, one of the kids pointed across the shallow bog at a large snake stretched out on a half-submerged stump.

I quickly identified the serpent as a harmless broad-banded watersnake, one of the most common snakes native to the Big Thicket. Unlike its cousins, the diamond-backed and yellow-bellied watersnakes, which share the same habitat and are somber in coloration, the broad-banded watersnake can be a colorful creature, ringed in wide chocolate- to mahogany-colored bands broken by lighter orange or cream-colored ones. This one was a prime and

Broad-banded watersnake with typical yellow, orange, and brown patterns

stunning example of its kind, and I proceeded to remove my shoes and slip as silently as possible into the water, snake hook at the ready. The snake was a good ten feet away, but I moved like a shadow, and when I had advanced to within about four feet of it, I ducked down ever so slowly and dropped my hand under the water. Easing forward those last couple of feet, I brought my hand back up underneath the log and quickly wrapped my fingers around the snake's body.

A triumphant shout rang up from the throng of young herpers gathered on the trail to watch the supposed veteran snake-grabber stalk and catch his elusive aquatic prey. Brandishing the writhing and musking prize aloft like the Olympic torch, I proceeded to remove myself from the muck and mire of the bog and show the snake to my audience, educating them on the watersnake at hand and describing how to differentiate it from the highly venomous and equally common northern cottonmouth, which shares space with the watersnake throughout the Big Thicket.

As I described the characteristics of the cottonmouth, one of the kids said, "Like that?"

I froze and followed his pointing finger back behind me into the bog, and, sure enough, not two feet to the left of the very spot where I had been standing lay an adult northern cottonmouth, its dark, muscular trunk camouflaged perfectly with the water-logged pine stump it was basking on. It was close enough to us so that we could observe the thick, triangular head adorned with a dark stripe angling down from beneath the eye to the back of the jawline, which is one of the field markings that distinguish it from its nonvenomous counterparts.

Northern cottonmouth

The snake had remained motionless, so I had never noticed it, as my eyes were fixed solely on catching the watersnake. I sat there dumbfounded on the bridge, staring into the water at the venomous pit viper that had so generously neglected to act aggressively toward the oblivious snake-hunter who now found himself feeling far less field-seasoned than usual.

I photographed the watersnake and released it back into the water, then moved the children along the trail, taking care to direct them well out of the path of the still-sunning cottonmouth, which watched us go with all the indifference of the very log it lay on. I tipped my hat to and thanked it silently for letting me pass by in its territory.

For a snake with such an ill reputation, the cottonmouth is more often than not a placid and easygoing animal, almost always choosing to remain still and out of sight when encountering potential predators. Nevertheless, people fear them as the bane of practically every river, pond, lake, and other body of water in the country. There are countless tales of cottonmouths chasing bathers out of the water or dropping into fishermen's boats from overhanging trees, causing unimaginable havoc. So loathed is this creature that all snakes discovered in the water are immediately suspected of being the dreaded cottonmouth, and many harmless semiaquatic species are promptly executed.

In all truth, the northern cottonmouth can be an abundant species, and as I learned on that sunny spring morning on the Pitcher Plant Trail, people should watch out for them when wading through bodies of water in regions where they occur. In fact, cottonmouths are probably more common in the swamps and bayous of East Texas than anywhere else in the state and should not be ruled out as a potential hazard to woodsmen and naturalists in the area. However, I have had the good fortune of meeting dozens of these swamp denizens over the years in all types of habitats and have yet to be struck at, much less chased, by a single one of them. Almost all specimens either remained completely motionless until I had passed, or they crawled leisurely away. Even when riled into a defensive stance by my snake hook as I positioned some for photographs, the most I ever got out of them were a vibrating tail and a gaping mouth. This latter behavior is the most common defensive mechanism of the cottonmouth and involves the snake opening its mouth to expose the cottony white interior, which gives the species its name. This display is usually enough to discourage even the boldest attacker, myself included, and the snake is then free to go on its way.

In a study of cottonmouth defensive behavior, Whit Gibbons and Michael Dorcas put the snake's notorious reputation to the test, seeking out forty-five wild cottonmouths in South Carolina and doing one of three things.[3] They stood beside the snake with a boot touching it. Alternatively, they stepped on the snake with just enough force to restrain it. With other snakes, they picked it up with a set of tongs outfitted with a glove and a shirt sleeve to simulate a human arm and hand. When they stood in contact with the snakes, some tried to escape and others gave a defensive display, but none bit the boot. Defensive displays included tail-rattling, musking, gaping, or striking without biting. Of those that were stepped on, most gave a defensive display, and only one of twenty-two snakes bit the boot. Of those that were picked up, only 36 percent bit the artificial hand!

These results should not under any circumstances lead anyone to take stupid chances with cottonmouths. None of the above reports is any kind of guarantee that a particular cottonmouth won't bite, and the venom is pretty nasty. However, what these reports do help establish is that the cottonmouth is not vicious. A couple of things that may contribute to its nasty reputation is that it may be less likely to immediately run away than the nonvenomous watersnakes, and frightened humans probably mistake its mouth-gaping display for an attempt to bite. The stories about them dropping into boats simply reflect the habit (which they share with the nonvenomous watersnakes) of resting on low branches over the water, and when a boat comes by and startles them, their first instinct is to drop down and swim away.

Driving through sand and clay, finding an alligator snapper / SMITH

The Big Thicket is, in part, a geological gift that comes from millions of years in which the rivers have carried sediment southward from the interior of North America and sea levels have risen and fallen. The upper coastal plain of Texas is largely sand and clay, dating from the Pleistocene (two million years ago). However, those sands and sediments go much deeper, as much as 40,000 feet, and date back much earlier, according to Darwin Spearing's book, *Roadside Geology of Texas*.[4] Traveling through the area, we find areas of sand through which rainfall quickly disappears and clay that holds water in shallow bowls known as baygalls. Thus, in the Roy E. Larsen Sandyland Sanctuary of the Nature Conservancy, cacti and yuccas grow in deep sand in open places dotted with pines and oaks. The soil dries quickly after rainfall, allowing these plants to thrive. In other areas the clay traps the water in bogs and ponds where bald cypress trees and tupelos filter the sunlight, and ferns, orchids, and thick stands of azalea and holly grow below.

The coastal plains sediments create interesting driving experiences on unpaved backwoods roads. The road that forms a boundary for the Turkey Creek unit has patches of deep sand through which cars can navigate, but they do so with a certain amount of "swimming" and drifting through the sand. Roads with clay surfaces can be very treacherous after rains. On one trip, a friend and I tried our luck on Segno Fire Lane Road, running alongside the Big Sandy Creek unit, after heavy rains the previous day. My all-wheel-drive vehicle managed fairly well, crawling along at walking speed and straddling the top of the road in the center. As I questioned the wisdom of what I was doing, driving white-knuckled at less than ten miles per hour, a local resident in a pickup truck approached us coming the other way. I moved a little to the right to accommodate him, hoping I would not slide sideways into the ditch. We soon decided not to attempt the whole length of the road and turned around. If a three-point turn is one in which you turn, stop, back up, and finish the turn, we must have executed about a twenty-seven-point turn, moving a few inches at a time. Be warned: during and after rains, these back roads can become flooded and impassable.

My first trips to the Big Thicket were with Steve Campbell, cofounder of the Dallas–Fort Worth Herpetological Society and a talented naturalist. On a warm, sunny day when the road was much easier to drive, Steve and I visited Big Sandy with memorable results. This is a more upland place than some of the other places within the preserve, with loblolly pines mixed with beech, magnolia, sweetgum, and oak trees. Red clay alternates with sand through much of the area. With more than 14,000 acres, there is room for much diversity of habitat, and in places there are cypress sloughs or low areas with thick understory, making for a dark and jungle-like walk along the trail. Big Sandy Creek winds its way at a leisurely pace through the unit, fed by multiple little tributaries half hidden by dozens of plant species.

Juvenile alligator snapping turtle from the Big Sandy unit, Big Thicket National Preserve

Underneath, the alligator snapper has a small bottom shell (plastron).

We stopped where Segno Fire Lane crosses one of these tributaries on an old wooden bridge. The quiet waters are a dark tea color from all the leaves that fall into the pools and release their tannin. Deeper than a foot or so, it is hard to see what moves about in those waters. As I looked around at one end, Steve walked across the bridge to investigate the other side. I began to hear victory "whoops" and self-satisfied laughter. Steve emerged from the woods and onto the road with a little treasure. He had spotted a small turtle whose shell resembled a chunk of dark, waterlogged tree bark, and managed to sneak up on it and snatch it out of the water. This was a juvenile alligator snapping turtle, uncommonly seen in Texas. This turtle grows larger than its cousin, the snapping turtle (until recently known as the common snapping turtle), and has a fascinating adaptation for luring prey into its massive jaws. On the floor of the alligator snapper's mouth is a small appendage that can twist back and forth. When the turtle sits at the bottom of a pond or slough, with jaws open wide, this lure looks like a worm resting in the hollow of an old chunk of wood. Any fish approaching close enough to investigate will trigger the jaws to snap shut, and the snapper will have its meal.

The alligator snapping turtle is found in East Texas, with the western limits of its range found in Harris, Freestone, Rains, and perhaps Collin Counties. It spends almost all of its life submerged in rivers and sloughs, from the time that the hatchling leaves the nest to find the water until reaching maturity, when the female emerges to dig a nest for the next generation. As this behemoth sits at the bottom of quiet waters, it catches fish but also eats a wide variety of other things, from fruits and nuts that drop into the water to crayfish, other turtles, snakes, and other things unlucky enough to encounter this giant chelonian.

It is truly a giant; in fact, the alligator snapper is the largest freshwater turtle in the Western Hemisphere. The largest on record is said to have had an upper shell—the carapace—measuring 80 centimeters (about 2.6 feet). Average carapace lengths are more like 50 centimeters (19–20 inches) for males and 43 centimeters (just under 17 inches) for females, according to a report by Robert Reed and others in 2002.[5] Since the alligator snapper has a long tail, roughly as long as the carapace, this means that these turtles may be over four feet in total length. Imagine such a dark hulk walking along the bottom of the bayou, enormous head and hooked jaws first emerging through the murk, followed by powerful legs and a huge rough shell, and trailing a long tail with a row of knobby tubercles along the top.

How long does it take to grow such a giant? One report (cited by Reed and his colleagues), suggested that these turtles attain maturity after fifteen to seventeen years. The scutes or plates on the lower shell, or plastron, are often examined so that growth rings can be counted, much as annual rings are counted on trees. Based on these estimates, alligator snappers examined in field studies may be thirty-nine to forty-five years old. An individual at the Philadelphia Zoo reportedly lived for seventy years.

Predators, including raccoons, savor turtle eggs. Once hatched, the mortality rate for baby turtles is very high. A hatchling alligator snapping turtle has few defenses and is just the right size to be eaten by many of the animals living around it. The only workable life history for an animal such as this is to live for a long time as an adult to breed and lay eggs many times in order to replenish the population. However, people have historically trapped a great many alligator snappers for food to the point that many populations disappeared. The alligator snapping turtle is now protected in Texas and most states, though not in Louisiana, and it is possible that the protections will be too little, too late. Reed and his colleagues estimated that decreasing the adult female population by as little as 1 percent annually would result in the gradual decline of this species.

Racers on the roadway / SMITH

Together with a couple of friends, I drove the two lanes of FM 943 through the southeast Texas forest on a sunny April afternoon in 2007, past tall pines, sweetgums, and thick understory that formed impenetrable walls of vegetation on either side of the road. Meanwhile, we scanned the pavement for reptiles, knowing that any such animals would likely be "DOR" (dead on the road). One common species, the tan racer, is a nervous and active snake that is often run over as it cruises from one patch of forest to another during the day. Sure enough, we spotted the broken body of another tan racer on the pavement ahead. We stopped and examined the lithe and muscular body with smooth, tan scales on the back and pale, whitish scales down the belly. It was an adult female about three feet in length.

I would take this specimen for the museum collection at the University of Texas at Arlington, but I hated putting this slender and graceful serpent into a plastic bag. I would much rather have seen her for a moment alive, slipping from pavement through roadside grasses like a bolt of lightning and into the safety of the forest. Like other racers and coachwhips, these snakes are alert and visual, with large, bright eyes set beneath a small ridge that gives them a stern expression—like that of a hawk. They scan their surroundings and detect movement of lizards or other small creatures, and they are swift and agile predators. Such an animal deserves better than to be run down on the road.

As I was considering all this, someone called out, "Hey, here's another one." Amazingly, another racer was right here at the roadside, and although it quickly slipped behind some vegetation, I was determined to find it if possible. In several trips to the Big Thicket, I had seen a number of tan racers dead, but none alive. An opportunity for a good photo would be a real gift. However, this snake was either well hidden or long gone. I began to think about our luck in seeing this second snake; maybe this was not a coincidence. It was spring, and the snake that was killed was a female. Male snakes

Tan racer

have been known to pursue mating opportunities with a boldness that would never be seen at other times of the year.

And, sure enough, at that moment I spotted him again, to my left, emerging from the forest. There was not a moment to be lost, and I jumped on him. It is hard to describe tackling a three-foot snake, taking care not to literally fall on him and hurt him, but getting up close and personal so as to not miss the chance at capture. I grabbed him as he turned back for the trees, nearly escaping. We wrestled in the dirt for a few moments, with me grabbing at the snake and the snake biting at me. I felt his six rows of tiny, needle-sharp teeth in my T-shirt and once in my beard. Racers have no venom; they chase down, subdue, and swallow prey by sheer speed and strength. When threatened and unable to escape, they strike fiercely and repeatedly, startling a predator enough that it may release the snake. However, they are unable to do any real damage to a large animal or human, leaving only tiny and superficial scratches.

After a minute or so, the snake calmed some and stopped striking. It was a male, and so my hypothesis about why he persistently stayed in the area seemed to be confirmed. As I held him supported mostly underneath, with no obvious target to strike at, he simply waited for an opportunity to escape. The snake rested like three feet of restless energy, not struggling but with muscles tensed and ready. With such a snake, the trick is to provide just enough restraint to prevent a sudden thrashing escape while not squeezing or hurting it. Retrieving a pillow case from my backpack, I placed the racer in the bottom of the bag while gathering the neck of the bag with my other hand, to prevent his jumping back out like a suddenly released coiled spring. A single overhand knot in the bag, and he was secured for a later photo opportunity.

Black coachwhips / SMITH

On another trip in 2015, heading northward on the red clay road, through forests and thickets, Clint and I both spotted a long black ribbon of scales stretched across half the roadway. I instantly sped up, pulling closer as the slender black snake on the road began to double back. At about twenty feet away, I stopped as Clint ejected himself from the car and sprinted toward the disappearing eastern coachwhip. As the snake's lithe form slipped into the thicket, Clint closed the distance and literally dove into the wall of possumhaw, blackberry, and tree saplings where the beautiful midnight-black coachwhip had disappeared.

Although he could not have been more than a few feet within the thicket, Clint was hidden behind a wall of green. I asked if he needed help (wondering how I was going to push through that tangle of leaves and branches). His reply was a little garbled, but it sounded like he was okay and wasn't asking for help. Within a minute or so, he returned with no coachwhip. He said that the snake, which we had wanted to photograph but would not have collected, was velvety black from head to tail. He had nearly captured it. At the last moment he had tripped on a root and had gone face down in the leaf litter, smacking his forehead, which made the disappearing coachwhip tail swim before his eyes. Amazing speed and gracefulness, together with a maze of sheltering branches, had saved the day for this snake.

This was completely different from an experience with a Big Thicket coachwhip from eight years before. On that occasion, Clint, Ryan Blankenship, and I were working our way through a roadside pile of trash. Under an old couch Clint and Ryan surprised an eastern coachwhip that was about four or five feet long. This one bore the typical pattern for its subspecies. Its head and forebody were a velvety jet black, but toward the tail it shaded into brown, ending in a pattern that looked remarkably like a braided whip. They captured the snake, and after some gentle handling, it calmed down enough to be posed for photographs. Most coachwhips lunge away the moment they are no longer restrained and perhaps attempt a few well-aimed strikes at the nearest person's face. However, occasionally a coachwhip decides to stop moving, almost playing dead, until it is left alone. This one sat placidly for photos, its large, hawk-like eyes watching our every move. When we released it, the snake simply sat where we put it. Eventually we stretched it out, stepped back, and waited. After a short hesitation, the snake came alive and shot into the nearby underbrush.

Planning a visit

If you plan to visit the Big Thicket, please leave the place the way you found it. Fallen logs create their own delicate microenvironment, which would be greatly disrupted if they were turned over or torn up. If field herpers visit an area with the goal of finding as many species as possible, they may tear through an area with the destructive force of a group of feral hogs, destroying habitat and gobbling up specimens. A better goal is to take your time and see herp species in the context of their surroundings, going for quality over quantity. You can make your way carefully along the trails, pausing to look at everything and take in the big picture. In areas where it is permissible, lift some logs or bark and look beneath, and then put them back just where they were. Collecting within the preserve is not allowed, so be content to take photos and memories only.

2 The Piney Woods

Much of East Texas is dominated by forests of pine and hardwood, although people have cleared many places for ranching and farming. The pine trees grow among other trees such as beech, sweetgum, oak, and hickory, labeled as "hardwood" because the wood of many of these species is harder than that of pine. The forests thrive in the wetter climate and deep, sandy soil of East Texas around places like Jefferson, San Augustine, and Nacogdoches. The Piney Woods landscape includes plenty of lakes and ponds, and among the East Texas rivers that wind through the forest are the Trinity and the Neches. Upland forests are more often dominated by pines such as short-leaf and loblolly, and in places the longleaf pine can still be found. Hardwood species are more typical of the bottomlands along rivers, lakes, and creeks. The Piney Woods is the region where you would most expect to see the alligator snapping turtle in creeks and ponds. It offers shady, moist habitat for a variety of salamanders. Upland habitats with openings in the forest are places where eastern coachwhips and buttermilk racers might be found. Summers are hot, the understory vegetation is thick, and the ample rains keep things humid. As the average rainfall decreases to the west and the soil changes, the Piney Woods come to an end, shading first into oak savannah and then into prairie.

Caddo Lake in drought and wet years / SMITH

On the shores of Caddo Lake, across the channel from a thick line of cypress trees, I walked into the headquarters of Johnson Ranch to rent a canoe. I mentioned to the gentleman behind the weathered old counter that Clint and I had rented a canoe here several years ago, during a drought when the lake was a lot lower. I noted that the water was higher now with the rains from last year and this spring.

"It was up to the ceiling of this place a little while back," he said, with no trace of drama. I supposed he had seen lots of changes in lake levels over the years and simply accepted the bad with the good. The place looked like it had been drowned a time or two, with ancient gray boards and old bait tanks as well as piles of life jackets and some paddles leaning against the corner at the other side of the room. A few steps outside, a marine fuel pump stood ready to gas up the many bass boats that prowl this lake. I wondered how the clunky old fuel pump had withstood the flood.

Back in September of 2011, the drought had shrunk Caddo so that local folks claimed they had never in their lifetimes seen the lake so low. Caddo is not a deep lake to begin with, averaging eight to ten feet according to the Texas Parks and Wildlife Department. It is a twisting maze of bayous and sloughs, with larger (and deeper) open areas as well as quiet backwaters. Arriving after dark, Clint and I had walked down to where the lake should have been and found a shed with a few boats resting on the mud. I played the flashlight off several short docks and into the night. Where was the lake? Down about four feet, we could see some lotus struggling to get by on residual moisture below the drying mud's surface. Beyond were a few pools and ribbons of water where a sizable inlet of the lake should have been.

The next day we got a canoe at the Johnson Ranch and set out to explore the bayous. The tall cypresses, draped with Spanish moss, stood in the quiet water among the lotus, looking like everyone's picture of what a southern swamp should be. The Spanish moss is really a type of bromeliad with long, grayish, curling leaves that give the tree branches the familiar bearded look. That day, we pulled the canoe up onto an area that was at least temporarily dry land and explored on foot through the cypresses and out into open areas where Clint found a Fowler's toad under some fallen branches. Some people refer to this as the "East Texas toad," and its status (as a hybrid, a subspecies of Woodhouse's toad, or a Texas population of Fowler's toad) has been debated for years. Some individuals have a rusty-reddish wash over the top parts of their bodies, and this was one of those. We admired it, photographed it, and returned it to its shelter.

We also found green treefrogs in the cypress along the water's edge. These small frogs are a creamy lime green, with a white stripe down each side. Many of them have a very few tiny gold speckles randomly appearing on their backs. They are among Texas' most attractive amphibians, although in some circumstances, such as when it is colder, they may take on a more olive coloration. Green treefrogs are generally found close to permanent water and are good climbers. During the day, they sleep, practically glued to a leaf or the stem of a reed or cattail using their adhesive toe pads. Against a green leaf or reed, they are beautifully camouflaged. They are active at night, searching for insects to eat. In spring and summer great choruses of calls from hundreds of males may be heard across marshes and ponds, sounding like the

An inlet into the cypresses at Caddo Lake

nasal quacking of a large group of ducks. These males are calling for females, whose eggs they will fertilize when the eggs are deposited in shallow water.

That was Caddo in 2011 during a drought that plagued all of Texas. Just five years later, after two wet springs, we were ready to see what Caddo had to offer. After my conversation with the man behind the counter at Johnson Ranch, we got an old orange canoe and a couple of paddles and prepared to shove off into the lake. I have limited canoe experience, and it takes a minute for me to get settled so that I can maintain balance in the canoe and not feel like every movement will roll us over into the water. Once that equilibrium is achieved, a canoe is the ideal way to see the lake—quietly, slowly, and close to the water.

We prowled along the edges of the watery forest, peering back into realms of green floating vegetation lit by dappled sunlight slanting down between the columns of bald cypress. Occasionally a blue heron flapped majestically by, and we saw a big white egret standing on a fallen branch among the cypresses, intently watching a spot in the water where something was on the verge of being speared and eaten. We edged along under the Spanish moss, among the tree trunks, watching for a basking watersnake or a treefrog half hidden in the vegetation. What we did see, of course, were turtles here and there, balanced precariously on logs or snags just above the water. Quite possibly all of them were red-eared sliders; it was hard to tell from that distance. These and other semiaquatic turtle species climb onto logs, old stumps, and anything else sticking up out of the water to bask. Turtles bask to raise their body temperatures in the sunlight. In the process their shells dry off, sometimes limiting the growth of algae on their shells and discouraging some aquatic parasites. Basking also warms the little reptiles and allows them to absorb ultraviolet light, which is essential for their metabolism. Sometimes turtles even climb onto each other when basking at a particular spot, resulting in a pile of shells like carelessly stacked dishes looking as though the slightest wind could send them all tumbling into the water. They manage to stay in that position, but if they want to survive, they must remain alert to possible predators. When a human approaches, first one and then another slides off into the water until the whole group is submerged and out of danger.

Paddling around the edges of the cypress, after 50 or 100 yards we would reach a bend in the waterway and cross the open water to the next stand of trees. One of these times, we spotted a fellow traveler, of the reptile variety, a couple of hundred feet ahead of us, making his way to the next area of forest. His head was just above the water, and we got a peek at the long, scaly back and powerful, undulating tail of an American alligator, probably about eight feet in length. Now we were onto something good! Without discussion or hesitation, hoping to get a further glimpse or maybe a photo of this alligator, we paddled toward the area where he had submerged.

Were we now being foolhardy? Should we have headed in the opposite direction? As Clint is fond of saying, nobody accuses either of us of having the highest level of good sense. However, we also know some facts about alligator behavior, which inform what we do when we find one. The American alligator is ordinarily shy and, except when guarding nests or young, is unlikely to attack unless harassed. It was midmorning, not nighttime, when gators are more actively hunting, and we were bigger than what such a reptile would ordinarily go after for food. If we had seen it again or begun to catch up with it, we would not have tried to close the distance between us. And we were not positioned in a way that the gator might feel cornered or trapped.

Several factors make an alligator encounter more dangerous: First, if an alligator has often seen people at close range, it usually becomes habituated to their presence and less shy. Even worse, if people have fed the alligator, it can cause the animal to approach people because it associates them with food. Additionally, alligators will often react to a disturbance in the water with interest, as it might involve the movement of a prey animal. Nighttime encounters might be more dangerous since gators tend to forage for food at night. If we keep our distance, don't feed them, and don't go swimming with them at night, alligators pose little risk to us.

Remnants of the munitions plant in the woods at Caddo National Wildlife Refuge

"Ghosts" in the forest of Caddo Lake National Wildlife Refuge / SMITH

Just south of Caddo Lake is an area of thick pine and hardwood forest that has seen a great deal of history before being acquired by the US Fish and Wildlife Service and protected as Caddo Lake National Wildlife Refuge. In the middle 1800s it was home to the Starr Ranch, and a historic old home from the ranch still sits on a point of land jutting into Caddo Lake; its lawn is kept clean, but the house behind the big screened-in porch awaits restoration. In 1942 the Longhorn Army Ammunition Plant, with buildings and crisscrossed streets, was established in this forest to make TNT for the war effort. In subsequent years the place made rocket motors, then pyrotechnic ammunition for the Vietnam War, and finally closed after 1997. Shortly thereafter, it was transferred to the US Fish and Wildlife Service to become a wildlife refuge, but over fifty years of manufacturing explosives and rockets leaves a lasting mark. Parts of the refuge were designated as an Environmental Protection Agency Superfund site after the plant closed, and the EPA website shows that there is "insufficient data" to determine whether groundwater contamination is stabilized or there is the potential for human exposure to hazards in several locations at the old plant.

Never ones to let a Superfund designation deter us, Clint and I visited the refuge in 2011 and again in 2016. You will never visit a wildlife refuge with so many roads—from small paved two-lane roads to abandoned concrete lanes where the forest is gradually taking over, like on the set of a postapocalyptic town where no car ever drives. In some ways this makes for easy hikes through the woods. Grab your camera and stroll down an arrow-straight little lane for a quarter mile, watching the forest on either side. In places you have to step under or around a small tree that is bent completely over the road. In one place a sweetgum started toward the sky and then bent over in a long arc, with the top touching the other side of the lane. It was not broken, just bent over. We saw trees like this in several places within the refuge. Getting off the road and stepping between the trees, you enter a tangled woodland described by the Fish and Wildlife Service as "one of the highest quality old-growth bottomland hardwood forests remaining in the southeastern United States."[1] Near the lakeshore are places designated as "wetlands of international significance." All this magnificence stands shoulder to shoulder with areas fenced off with Do Not Enter signs. Particularly on our 2011 visit Clint and I noticed areas of the refuge where a petrochemical smell, vaguely like a pesticide, hung in the air. And then you round a corner and, nestled amid the trees, concrete walls or buildings come into view, like a scene from some old *Twilight Zone* episode. Half-skeletons of buildings are overgrown with vines, and vertical slabs stand among the trees like dominoes that should have fallen decades ago. In one place a series of concrete frames stands in the forest on tall pillars like stilts, ghosts of a time when tanks or storage containers with a devil's brew of ingredients fed a deadly production line. And just as we contemplated all this, we heard thunder approaching, and a slightly chill wind blew away the muggy warmth that had enshrouded this place. Clouds were moving in, and it was either shelter in one of the concrete tombs or head for the car. We chose the latter.

Giant spiders, feral hogs, and murder in the Sam Houston National Forest / KING

The Sam Houston National Forest is located just south of Huntsville, Texas, in the swampy pine-dominant country that forms the southern border of Lake Livingston. On hills and ridges grow huge loblolly and shortleaf pine trees, the signature trees of a forest that occupies 163,037 acres of the state. In some low places there are wetlands heavily influenced by cypress trees, which tower over the tannin-soaked bogs and bayous in the interior of this immense forest. Here saw palmetto and various ferns and orchids grow from the carpet of mixed leaves and needles on the forest floor.

My wife and I were walking a trail in the stagnant humid air that hangs like a sweaty cloak over any typical June day in East Texas. While a hefty dose of DEET kept most of the mosquitoes and deerflies at bay, a few of the braver ones would occasionally dive in and sneak a quick piercing bite in some unsprayed crevice, causing us to wince in sudden alarm. To be honest, my wife was not in the best of moods on this particular trip. We had spent the two previous nights in less-than-comfortable quarters, largely due to my failure to get proper hotel accommodations. In the wake of Hurricane Katrina everything that hadn't been blown to bits was completely full. Even Van Choate's Cajun Cookery in Orange, Texas, near the Louisiana border had been reduced to a pile of rubble behind a twisted, makeshift chain link fence that read "No Trespassing." So we had spent the first night in the parking lot of a Louisiana truck stop and the next in the confines of my single-cab truck off State Highway 105 east of Cut N' Shoot, Texas, in a tiny roadside park. In the morning a sign posted on a tree not two feet from the passenger window stated that someone had been murdered there earlier in the year and local police were looking for details concerning the affair. The only thing missing from this unnerving scene was a bloody hockey mask dangling from a bare pine limb. Needless to say, we didn't stick around to look for further evidence.

Now, two hours later, we were deep in the Sam Houston National Forest, and we hadn't found squat. In fact, the only signs of wildlife we had seen were in the form of giant golden silk spiders, which resemble larger versions of the familiar black and yellow garden spider that frequents overhangs and porch eaves throughout the state. The golden silk spider is an arachnophobic's nightmare. It builds huge, thick-stranded webs that stretch across entire trails, from the lowest-lying tree limb to the ground, and it sits in the center of the web and waits patiently for its prey. The webs are a magnificent sight, provided one sees them before walking through them. Otherwise, the sticky silken threads wrap around an unsuspecting hiker's face like some grim mask, gluing the eyelids closed. It is about this time that the thin, tufted black legs of this enormous arachnid begin to make laps around the face as the bewildered spider searches for its former position at the web's center, which at this point is lying directly between the hiker's mouth and nose.

We had already walked into three or four of these, and needless to say my wife was only getting angrier. When the muffled grunt of feral hogs met our ears while we paused beside a rotten pine log to scrape off spider silk from our arms and faces, it broke the camel's back.

"That's it!" she cried. "We're done here! This is ridiculous! Giant spiders! Poison oak! Murderous hillbillies running rampant! Deerflies with ten-penny nails for mouthparts that defy repellant! Hurricanes have blown the whole place into a pile of matchsticks! And now we're being stalked by wild boars! And for what? To find a snake that will probably kill you if it bites you, which at this point in our journey is almost sure to happen! Surely you can just photograph someone else's coralsnake, or go somewhere else to find one! We're out of here!"

"Ye of much complaint and little faith!" I rebuked her. "The Sam Houston National Forest is a naturalist's playground! It's where herpers hope to go when they die! A Mecca for . . ."

"Okay," she said. "I'll compromise. We can finish herping the Sam Houston National Forest, but we're doing it from inside the vehicle! And if your precious coralsnake happens to be crossing the road and our paths converge—and God willing it will—then you can go home triumphant. Otherwise, you're going home in two more hours, no matter the outcome!" To which I replied (as most husbands who long ago figured out the secret to a happy marriage would), "Yes, ma'am. But of course."

On our way out of the forest I pulled over to roll some choice logs that were screaming "snake." It was in this pile that I first became acquainted with the walkingsticks of the genus *Anisomorpha*. Walkingsticks are long, stilt-legged insects and excellent twig mimics. Shorter and stockier than the more typical northern walkingsticks, this chiefly eastern species is most often seen in pairs, with the smaller male clinging tightly to the more robust female's back. Clad in varying tones of camouflaging grays and browns, they are all but invisible, both in the canopy where they feed as well as the forest floor. Their most remarkable feature is perhaps their ability to spray a noxious, milky cocktail of chemicals known as terpenes from the end of the abdomen. This chemical compound is so irritating that it can cause temporary blindness in large mammals, including humans. These and a few green anole lizards were the only creatures moving in the log pile.

Our time was running pitifully short, as was my wife's fuse, so we turned off the Forest Service road and onto the main highway, a hilly farm-to-market with dense pine trees growing on either side. As we topped the hill, the glossy, tricolored scales of a Texas coralsnake glistened in the sunlight in sharp contrast against the black asphalt. Success at the last minute! How often it has saved me in the field.

An East Texas coralsnake / SMITH

On the last day of April, after hiking in the Angelina National Forest until dusk, Clint and I drove several roads through the stands of pine and sweet-gum. Recent rains had the creeks running, and low places in the forest were flooded. The roadside ditches were full, and the frogs were taking full advantage of the shallow pools to lay eggs where no fish would eat them. The frog calls were sweet music, but we were hoping that the snakes would be moving, either hunting or seeking high ground. In fact, this would be an evening to remember, because our road would soon lead us to one of our favorite snakes.

Two prairie lizards in the Angelina National Forest

The road started as one of the irregularly paved paths through the East Texas woods, with trees and understory plants growing close to the edge. Soon the pavement gave way to hard-packed soil and sand, pockmarked here and there by shallow holes filled with water. In pool after pool, concealed under mats of last year's fallen pine needles or among the grasses and sedges growing out of the water, narrow-mouthed toads sang a nasal, buzzing drone. Cope's gray treefrogs trilled in their faster, less musical call, which distinguishes them from their nearly identical gray treefrog cousins. Somewhere a brightly ringed serpentine form wound its way through the vines, fallen leaves, and deadfall branches, edging nearer to our road.

Earlier in the day, we had hiked for several hours, reveling in the experience of the pines, sweetgums, and other hardwood trees and the dappled forest floor, which, in wetter areas, was covered in cinnamon ferns. We walked upstream from a small lake, seeing prairie lizards and green anoles in low branches and tree stumps. Near the water cricket frogs hopped from hidden places and were promptly lost again in the vegetation. On one big pine tree trunk, we watched two prairie lizards bobbing their heads in a display that says, "I'm the boss here," while also scampering around the trunk to stay out of our reach. On another trail Clint discovered the red cap of an *Amanita* mushroom. There are many species, including the fly agaric mushroom, which contains psychedelic substances. Many, but not all, of the *Amanita* species are poisonous.

Although we were not seeing a wide variety of herps, our hike was enormously helpful as we familiarized ourselves with the habitat we were search-

Texas coralsnake on a road in the Angelina National Forest

A closer view of the coralsnake. The black snout, yellow band across the back of the head, followed by a black band, is typical.

ing. There have been too many times when I have driven roads at night, seeing snakes or frogs and wondering what the habitat to either side of the road was like. Having walked in the Angelina National Forest during the day, we felt that we could place the animals seen on the road into the context of their habitat. Our understanding of what we saw was greatly improved.

Now it was time to drive down some of the back roads. By 7:20 p.m., we were making our way along the dirt road in the gathering gloom when up ahead a serpent-like form broke for the edge of the road. In the flowing curves of the snake's body, we could make out a ringed pattern. The spacing and width of the light and dark rings was informative—broad black rings, separated from broad red ones by narrow yellow ones.

"Coral!" Clint called out.

It was indeed a Texas coralsnake, a venomous snake we respect but do not fear. We were out of the car immediately, with the intention of temporarily corraling this beauty for some photos. Clint quickly noted that the snake was female, based on a short and quickly tapering tail. We also saw that she was quite chunky, with the lower half of her body looking distended, likely with a clutch of eggs that she would soon lay in a rotting log or in some protected place beneath the sandy soil.

With its slender, glossy body and bright yellow, black, and red rings, the Texas coralsnake is a treasured find. Although it has a dangerous neurotoxic venom, it is shy and not aggressive toward humans. It is so beautiful and bright that it is a startling sight when seen against almost any natural background. Startling is what a coralsnake would want to be if the little reptile were able to think about its options for surviving among big animals that might step on it and others that might want to eat it. Not terribly fast and having a small head and mouth, it would be lousy at fleeing and not particularly good at fighting. The bright colors might startle a predator, buying an extra moment or two for the snake to get away. Additionally, this bright pattern may function as a warning. If an animal were bitten and survived, it would probably avoid the brightly colored snake in the future. Whether the pattern works by startling an animal or warning of its venomous bite, this combination of colors is evidently useful. In fact, the harmless and unrelated milksnakes use the same color scheme in a slightly different sequence to their own advantage as coralsnake mimics.[2]

Lessons in mimicry in the Sabine National Forest / KING

The first day of May in 2016 found Michael and me beneath the statuesque pines in the Sabine National Forest on the Texas-Louisiana border. A dense forest comprising over 160,000 acres, it is dominated by evergreens such as loblolly, shortleaf pine, and, in times past, longleaf pine. The elongated emerald leaves of the southern red oak emerge from the canopy, their branches reaching for the sunlight that sneaks in between the needles. Sweetgum, American beech, and maple are also sparsely placed in this scene, providing a healthy mixture of hardwoods. Representing the Texas Piney Woods in all its glory, the Sabine is the easternmost of the state's national forests.

As we wound the car over the paved trails that catered to the RV campers, the road took us around to the back side of a lake, where we parked and proceeded to comb an embankment at the water's edge. Here we found small fist- to football-size stones piled loosely atop each other. It appeared that they had been intentionally placed here along the banks as riprap. It looked like a great little nook for a snake or lizard to be sunning, but aside from the sun-dried cast skin of a long-departed eastern coachwhip, we found nothing.

Uphill from the lake Michael and I parted directions. This is a common occurrence in our wanderings afield. It is not intentional; instead it is the result of my tendency to lock eyes on the tree trunks, rotting logs, and piles of deadfall around me while everything else fades into a blurry background. Then I look up to find that I have once again drifted into complete isolation in the forest. It is easy to get lost in places like this. Standing beneath the shade of a million seemingly identical trees with a million more seemingly identical logs and stumps to further distort your general sense of direction, one can all too easily begin to feel that twinge of nervousness set in, creeping up the nape of the neck on the centipede feet of hypothetical paranoia-laced questions. "Am I lost?" "Which direction did I come from?" Peering into the upper canopy beneath a shielding hand to check the position of the sun is a meager remedy at best. The pines are so thick, growing so closely together, that their towering tops form a giant enclosed huddle, as if they are purpose-fully trying to conceal the secret of where to go. Some of these pines are over 200 years old.

A rainstorm had visited several days earlier, and with the late-morning sun beginning to part the stubborn clouds that gave way only reluctantly, there was an edge of expectation in the air that seemed to provide an extra boost of vivacity to everything. Birdsong echoed through the woods, each species' distinctive notes bringing the understory and canopy to life.

I broke from the tree line unexpectedly as I topped the hill and found myself staring down a steep slope littered with pine needles. Lichen-covered wedges of rock peeked through here and there. As I began my descent, I wondered if any of the handful of local salamander species were tucked away beneath the rocks. Undoubtedly there were, although the odds of turning over just the right rock among a thousand others seemed unlikely enough that I didn't see much reason in wearing my back out this early in the day.

East Texas is well known for its humidity. Eighty-five degrees at 80 percent humidity can make it feel as if you are walking around in a sauna, and temperatures above ninety seem downright unbearable. To further enhance the hiking experience, swarms of bloodthirsty deerflies descend on the hapless explorer like a rain of tiny piercing darts, and the hotter and stickier the air feels, the worse they seem to get. But we were well armed with DEET, having learned our lesson some years ago in the Big Thicket.

As I reached the bottom of the hill, my breath ragged and heavy from the thickness of the air, I stepped out onto the pavement of the park road, where an old bearded man with no shirt saw me and began to head in my direction in a determined stride. Before he had even fully approached, he called out, "What are you doing?"

I gave the standard reply of "Looking for snakes," and he immediately pointed in the direction of a narrow trail some sixty yards to our right. "I

A hillside in the Sabine National Forest

don't know much of anything about snakes," he said, "but I saw one down that trail earlier."

I thanked him for the tip and took a short walk over to the trailhead. It was an unpaved, thin strip that ran down through the pine and sweetgum trees to the southwest shore of the lake, where a congregation of red-eared sliders and river cooters had gathered on snags of waterlogged timber. The high-domed carapaces of the cooters, along with their larger size, distinguished them easily. Closer to the shore, stands of reeds grew in six inches of rich, organic-smelling water. I toyed with the dip net here, but it was a long-poled, cumbersome beast that scooped up mud and muck in great globs; aside from the odd mosquitofish or crayfish, I mostly pulled up algae and drowned sticks from the primordial soup.

A strange call emanated from the reeds on a nearby bank as I balanced on a massive fallen pine trunk half submerged several yards from shore. It was a short snoring sound, falling in pitch. I knew it was of a froggy persuasion, but I could not identify exactly which species. It sounded teasingly like the elusive southern crawfish frog, a species I have desperately wanted to see for some years. Residents of crayfish burrows, southern crawfish frogs spend most of their lives hidden beneath the muck of shorelines and water-choked grasses of timber-rich floodplains, emerging only during periods of heavy rainfall. These chunky frogs, with a reticulated pattern that reminds me of shifting squares of light at the bottom of a swimming pool, are notoriously

Rough greensnake

difficult to see in their natural habitat. While many herpers are great at locating the frogs as they call from hidden places in that realm between overhanging plants and dark water, I am not one of them. To add to this maddeningly fruitless task, the frogs are usually shy and clam up just as you begin to think you can tell the direction from which an individual is calling. After a short time I left the frogs to their guttural snoring calls amid the reeds and headed back to the trail to find Michael.

A thin green vine that abruptly ended in a sharp taper made me pause at trailside. My eyes, long accustomed to picking out scaly patterns from various plants, quickly spotted the posterior portion of a small rough greensnake as it transitioned from the trunk of a pine tree to a tangle of poison ivy and greenbrier. Looking every bit like one of the greenbrier branches, I marveled at its ability to render itself invisible as its forked orange tongue detected my presence and it began to sway its tiny tapered head in an effort to convince me it was nothing more than a section of flora swaying in the breeze. The snake allowed me to approach within several inches—so close that I could see its gold-rimmed irises shift as it watched my every move. Eventually the snake convinced itself that I could not see it, and it remained still long enough for me to get some good shots of it in situ.

No sooner had I abandoned the greensnake to its search for soft-bodied caterpillars than another snake showed up, this one on the ground. A solid brown trunk of keeled scales froze as I approached, but with my next footfall this eastern hog-nosed snake performed the opening act of its fanciful display of bluff. I was amused but not concerned by its feigned strikes. Field her-

Eastern hog-nosed snake. One of the enlarged teeth is easily visible toward the back of the upper-right jaw.

pers know that, despite the hognose's enlarged rear teeth (the scientific name for this group of snakes is *Heterodon*, meaning "different-toothed"), the snake really never bites in defense and its toxic secretions would not be dangerous to people, even if it did bite.

Photos ensued, which resulted in more badgering as I jostled the determined-to-scare animal into position for the perfect shot. To make matters worse for the hognose, Michael's keen nose for *Heterodon* had picked up the scent of musky victory in the stifling air, and he had followed his flaring nostrils through the forest like Toucan Sam on the trail of a bowl of Fruit Loops. In a short time his camera joined my own, and the snake seemed to sense that it was going to have to pull a new trick out of its grab bag of scare tactics if these two persistent humans were ever to be sent back to whatever metropolitan habitat they had come from.

The hognose raised it head, stopped flattening its neck, and simply gaped up at us, much as a cottonmouth would have done. But it was unresponsive and mostly limp except for the upturned head, while a cottonmouth seems more aware of the movement of its adversary as it holds its mouth open, showing the white interior. Nevertheless, the resemblance seemed obvious. The fact that this particular specimen was similarly colored only seemed to enhance this already impressive display. Of course, this only ended up in an additional series of photos. We got close enough to see the glisten of the saliva off the enlarged rear teeth of the open-mouthed snake. Knowing that the hognose seldom if ever actually bites in self-defense, we took photos of us putting our hands "dangerously" close to this imitation pit viper for the benefit of fellow herpers back home. The end result was a very safe encounter, but one that looked like the type of irresponsible behavior occasionally posted online by reckless folks posing with a cottonmouth. The only thing left to do was send the pictures out in text messages to friends and wait for the flood of responses. It seemed in this forest of mimics we had set up one of our own: two safety-conscious field naturalists giving the appearance of two very foolish ones.

However, none of my friends fell for this ruse. They all instantly identified the snake, as if they hadn't even noticed that we were trying to pass it off as its venomous counterpart. Either that or they played it off well. You guys know your snakes too well. Get your nose out of the field guide and go live a little.

3 The Gulf Coast Prairies and Marshes

ALL UP AND DOWN THE TEXAS COAST, the theme of the landscape is similar. Flat land gradually slopes to the Gulf of Mexico, starting with coastal prairie and becoming marshland as fresh water from river deltas partially inundates the land. Geologists tell us that the shoreline of Texas has been building for millions of years as rivers bring sediment and gravel down to the Gulf. The relatively flat coastal plain is the result of all those tons of sediment, brought from far inland and added to the landscape along the coast. The prairies along the coast tend to be open and flat, but there are places where live oak woodlands grow. Near the shore, salt water and fresh water mix, creating saltmarsh ecosystems that are among the most biologically productive places on earth. Various grasses, sedges, and reeds grow in shallow water and soil, sometimes stretching as far as the eye can see. Some of them are adapted to withstand the slightly salty or brackish water resulting from river water meeting the salt water of the Gulf. They must be adaptable, because when the rivers flood, the water is mostly fresh, but in times of drought or when there is a storm surge, the salinity greatly increases. These salt marshes are teeming with a variety of species that not only exist here but depend on the nutrient-rich, brackish wetlands.

Encounter with a seasick alligator:
how I caught crabs at Sea Rim / KING

Overcast clouds hung over Michael and me like a mob of ever-threatening henchmen, ready to unload another assault of raindrops onto us at any moment. The temperature had remained in the low sixties all day. We had waited out the morning and some of the afternoon at our hotel, crossing our fingers for a rebellious ray of sunshine to pierce the depressive gray sky. The sun may as well have been a star in another galaxy for all the good it seemed to be doing us on this dreary Monday on the upper end of the Texas coast. Nevertheless, we were down here for better or worse and were dead set on making the best use of our time, inclement weather or not, and so the early afternoon saw us pulling into the parking lot at Sea Rim State Park headquarters.

I am ever the optimist because even in less than ideal conditions herps can be found, provided their seeker possesses an iron will and an overly enthusiastic stamina. After checking in at the ranger's station, we walked down the short winding boardwalk past a flock of birders with their binoculars trained on a pair of double-crested cormorants, perched miserably atop a docking post several yards from the shoreline and looking as if they too hoped for a little sunshine. Under normal conditions the sandy beach would be no place to find herps, but both of us had heard stories of the spectacular speckled kingsnakes with the bright orange bellies that turned up beneath the driftwood from time to time here. So we set out with high hopes, flipping chunks of the sand- and water-worn timber. I was not used to flipping up crabs, and after several minutes of finding no herps, these common beach crustaceans aroused my curiosity. Up until then, my ignorance was born from the blissful ideology that "what you don't see need not concern you." Now that I was seeing them, I made a mental note to do some research via that fabulous invention known as the World Wide Web when I got back to civilization.

One minute I was flipping driftwood, sending small crabs, springtails, and sow bugs scuttling in my wake, and the next I found myself face to face with a small though cantankerous young American alligator. Alligators have always had a special place in my heart. At the age of ten my dad took me on a guided boat tour of the Okefenokee Swamp in Norfolk, Georgia, where we were "guaranteed to see alligators." Of course, the boat ride was a herpetological flop. The same never-give-up spirit that so often brings me success in the field as an adult was already blossoming in my young herper's heart then. So I convinced my dad that we should picnic at a roadside stop just outside the park, where a meandering creek could be seen in the background from the road. While my family had a picnic, I made for the reeds, which I parted to find myself toes to face with eight feet of my first American alligator. There was no fear. Not even then, when I was still small enough for the gator to grab me by the ankle and take me on a one-way tour of its watery realm had it felt so inclined. No fear. Only that rapid surge of adrenaline that quickens the pulse, drums the heartbeat to a fever pitch, and at the same time sends a sense of satisfaction in knowing that a goal has again been attained. "Gator!" I yelled out with pride, and the family dropped their sandwiches and came running.

Nearly three decades and dozens of American alligators later, another one sat before me. This one looked much less formidable than that first fine specimen had, with my own body gaining well over a hundred extra pounds and

Juvenile American alligator on the beach at Sea Rim State Park

two feet in height and it being only a juvenile of twenty-four inches instead of a hulking black and green modern-day dinosaur. But you wouldn't have guessed it by its demeanor. The little reptile gave a loud, drawn-out hiss, which could have stood for "back off, or I'll snip off your fingers!" in gator language. Once again I triumphantly declared: "Gator!" This time it was Michael who came running, with camera in hand.

An American alligator is no uncommon find along the Gulf Coast, but finding one on the beach was surprising indeed. We took turns photographing the unruly little beast, which flashed his toothy grin for us even as he voiced his general displeasure at our presence. I remember making the joke that perhaps he had taken a lesson from his cousin across the high seas, the saltwater crocodile, and had decided against his mother's better judgment to set off into the world beyond the marsh to seek his fortune trying out his sea legs.

In a short time I had assembled a collection of unique photos, and we left the little black- and yellow-banded reptile, which would hopefully grow up to be a big, impressive giant of a reptile somewhere on that thin strip of sand between the salt marsh and the wide-open Gulf.

We continued combing the beach for anything of interest that the tide happened to cast at our feet. An array of broken shells, human-generated trash, and flotsam outnumbered the few whole and distinguishable items, but in spite of our limited knowledge of sea life we managed to identify the shells of moon snails, whelks, and oysters as well as the iridescent splintered fragments of what I assumed to be abalone. We kept an eye out for the venomous Portuguese man-of-war, which often washes up on Texas beaches like a bloated, translucent purple plastic bag, with long tentacles lined with stinging nematocysts. Farther up the shoreline a flock of brown pelicans joined laughing gulls and sandpipers in their extraction of the seashore's provision, the odd seine-like bills of more pelicans skimming the surface of the water several yards out into the surf. It was high tide. One minute we would be walking along the sand with our feet relatively dry, with the sea heaving in from the corner of the eye, and with the next wave a six-inch-deep broth of saline foam would surge up past our ankles. It was a wonderful sight to behold, this wild gulf in all of its untamed glory, its proud waves governed only by the lunar cycle. It felt like the point of no return here, staring out at that great body of water that engulfed all that my eye could see. It was an experience that cannot be duplicated by simulation, in many ways what it must feel like to explore space. You have to be there. That's all there is to it.

From the shoreline we headed over to the boardwalk, which under normal conditions runs a little above and a half mile out across a wide-open section of water threading through great patches of reeds. But the heavy rains had taken their toll, raising the water level up to the edge of the boards and even over the top farther out into the marsh. At the foot of the boardwalk an open parking lot looked out over the bay. A shallow pool of water had collected in this lowest spot, connecting the marsh with the sea. Here a pair of unidentified sea birds had managed to flip something of interest over and were harassing the unfortunate creature like the cartoon magpies Heckle and Jeckle. From our view we could see the mystery animal slowly squirming, spindly legs flailing as it attempted to right itself. As we walked in for a closer inspection, the birds took to the wing, and we soon thereafter found ourselves gazing down upon a large specimen of blue crab.

The blue crab is an icon of the Gulf Coast. It is harvested as an important food source, and during peak season crab fishermen can be seen posted at various points along roadways and shorelines, their telltale wood and wire trap boxes set up in likely haunts of this pretty olive-brown crustacean armed with a crown of sinister-looking spikes and a pair of impressive pincers, which are cerulean blue except for their fire-engine-red tips. The crab at our feet was every bit of eight inches wide, and it showed us no gratitude when it was righted with the toe of a wading boot, spreading its pincers wide and striking its claws menacingly together with an audible clicking sound, not unlike that of a pair of vigorously snapped scissors.

We left the blue crab behind after a few photos and braved the flooded boardwalk. The first few steps were awkward as I tested the strength of the wood cautiously, but in no time I had taken the structure's stability for

Blue crab on the flooded boardwalk at Sea Rim State Park

granted and moved my eyes from my feet to the reeds around me. It was a comical sight to see small fish and crabs darting and scuttling out of my way beneath me as I walked along. Although birds were few here in terms of diversity, the herons were out in full force. Great blues, the largest of our native species, soared by on widespread wings, uttering deep throated chortles of "grawwk!" as they scanned the water below for anything edible. Beautiful tricolored herons, their loose, looping swatch of white feathers curled up and over their heads, stalked in the shallows. And a comparatively pint-size green heron, its jade wings accentuating the reddish-brown body, lifted off from the railing as it caught sight of me. Herons are long-legged birds associated with fresh and brackish bodies of water. They are excellent predators of all things found along pond edges and shorelines, with keen eyes, long necks, and a sharply pointed bill that functions as a skewer for frogs, snakes, and fish. I wasn't exactly expecting to find any herps here on this flooded boardwalk, so I turned my attention to these well-adapted avians. Admittedly, the idea that a desperately hungry Methuselah of an alligator could come erupting from the water on either side of me like a scene from *Lake Placid*, plucking me off the boardwalk, kept my eyes scanning the dark water from side to side. Likewise, large gaps in the flapping, teetering planks, whose nails had finally rusted through due to constant saltwater exposure, provided an element of suspense and potential danger.

But this was reality, and we walked the length of the flooded boardwalk with no splitting boards or voracious man-eating alligators to contend with.

Clint versus crab!

I did, however, take on the next blue crab that we came across, which ended up being another big eight-incher. My curiosity soon outwrestled my better judgment concerning what it would feel like to be pinched by a crab, and I knelt down on my haunches and offered my arm out to the creature, which had gone on the defensive with its pincers raised in a disgruntled Nixonian stance. The crab wasted no time enlightening me as to the full potential of its capabilities, and the resulting double pinch I received from both sides of the animal's business end into the fleshy part of my forearm felt not unlike being grabbed violently and unmercifully by a pair of sharp tweezers. As I watched the tiny pinpoint blood blisters begin to form beneath my skin, I felt satisfied by the new knowledge gained from this experience, even if the process had proved a bit painful.

Anahuac National Wildlife Refuge / SMITH

I had a few sketchy but positive memories of visiting Anahuac National Wildlife Refuge a number of years ago. I had a brief opportunity to see a little of this 34,000 acres of coastal prairie shading into marshland on a day at the end of winter, when the sun was out and, in my memory, dozens of alligators lay sunning on the edges of the bayous. Although it was not really a warm day, a friend and I did see a juvenile Graham's crawfish snake crossing the gravel road.

My next chance to see Anahuac was during a trip Clint and I took to the Gulf Coast in 2016. The main entrance to the refuge takes you down a road

Marshland at Anahuac National Wildlife Refuge

through coastal grasses, sedges, and reeds stretching as far as the eye can see, with patches of open water visible here and there. The roads are built up a little as a hedge against flooding, and alongside the roads there are pools and bayous populated by wading birds, red-winged blackbirds, and scores of other species. In addition to this main tract, there is a smaller one to the east, the Skillern tract, where a short road takes you to a bayou with a raised observation deck on one side and a walkway to a marsh overlook on the other. We started our visit at the Skillern tract.

After a couple of hours of walking, I sat on a bench, nestled in a tangle of vegetation with flowers and a profusion of everything from honeysuckle to giant ragweed forming a visual barrier that allows birders to peek through and get a glimpse of the magnificent bird life on the other side. On a beautiful early May morning in the refuge, this might seem like paradise, and it might have been something like that until the mosquitoes arrived. There would be no quiet respite for writing in this shaded nook! We were not entirely unprepared: we had brought insect repellent and sprayed it on copiously, but the mosquitoes treated it as an inconvenience—a sort of bitter sauce that had to be drilled through in order to get to the main course beneath. And so when you visit the coastal marshes and prairies of Texas, bring plenty of insect repellent and seek out open areas with a breeze blowing. Herping, bird-watching, or other wildlife-viewing will sometimes lead you into leafy, secluded strongholds of the *Aedes aegypti* hordes, and all we can suggest is to stay focused on what you are searching for, slap what mosquitoes you can, and ignore the rest.

Down the walkway from the bench, the shrubs opened onto beautiful marshland with open water and patches of grasses and reeds. In the sunny

Green anoles are common in trees and on boardwalks at Anahuac National Wildlife Refuge

late-morning quiet, an American bullfrog sounded off close on the left, then another began toward the center. Two more called from the right, like a low-humming, stuttering snore. There were calls from great egrets, herons, and other species I could not identify but admired for their incredible adaptations to life, wading and swimming in the marsh.

Earlier, I saw a juvenile Gulf Coast ribbonsnake on the walkway. It looked up at me in surprise and bolted away, a ribbon of dark brown and butter yellow disappearing into the tangle of branches and vines. Meanwhile, down on the other side of the long bayou, Clint was seeing several of these agile, semi-aquatic snakes. Some were basking on mats of last year's reeds and would slide effortlessly into the water and below the latticework of dead reeds to safety. Clint also saw numerous watersnakes, sometimes a muddy brown blur of sinuous motion and at other times just a disturbance of grass pushed to the side a little as the big snake made a break for the water.

During my own wandering, there was no shortage of reptiles along the bayou. Green anoles, in varying shades of green and brown, were everywhere. One made his way along a branch above my reach, bobbing his head periodically and fanning out his dewlap in a comical display of dominance. As he approached quite closely and I focused a camera lens on him, he decided that perhaps he was not quite that dominant and retreated back into the tree.

A big splash on the other side of the bayou caught my attention. I suspected it could be an American alligator and wondered if Clint had maybe spooked it while trying to get a photo. Unable to see anything in the water, I walked on but soon returned to the area. There, in the middle of the water,

Speckled kingsnake at Anahuac National Wildlife Refuge

I saw an alligator about six feet long. The top of its head and snout as well as the first several inches of neck were above the water's surface, while the rest floated just below. An alligator's nostrils are positioned on a raised area at the tip of its snout. This is one of its many physical adaptations for life in water, allowing the animal to float with just its eyes and nostrils exposed. When submerged, the nostrils can close. The alligator also has a flap at the back of the mouth that closes when underwater, allowing it to grab prey without drowning. Over each eye, there is a clear nictitating membrane in addition to the eyelid; underwater, the membrane protects the eyes while the gator can still see. At around six feet in length, this one was at the smaller end of the average adult length. A large alligator might be around thirteen feet long or longer. Whatever its reason for splashing into the water, the one I saw was probably now taking stock of what was going on in its domain. It may not have been hunting, as American alligators tend to bask in the morning and evening and hunt during the night. At present, this one simply floated, completely still, eyes watching everything around it.

At about this same time, Clint was walking along an overgrown service roadway, built up a little like a levee. Along the edge, he caught a glint of light reflecting off smooth scales. The scales were dark, with a creamy-yellow fleck of color on each one. He had found a speckled kingsnake. It was an adult male, about three feet long, and recognizing the snake was a tribute to his years of distinguishing patterns and scale textures from the background of grasses, leaves, and rocks. As a speckled kingsnake sits entwined with grasses and twigs, its speckles do a remarkable job of imitating tiny details of light and shadow, strands of dead grasses, and dappled sunlight. The kingsnake pokes around through vegetation, under rocks or logs, and in mammal burrows. As it prowls through these places, the tips of its forked tongue pick up microscopic particles. As the tongue is withdrawn, these particles are pressed against the roof of the mouth and stimulate the Jacobson's organ there. This gives the snake an exquisitely accurate sense of what we might consider smell. When the kingsnake detects a mouse or frog or even another snake, it knows that dinner is not far off.

The bittersweet search for a Gulf saltmarsh snake / SMITH

We left the refuge and drove down toward High Island as the sun slipped toward the horizon, hoping to see a Gulf saltmarsh watersnake, which would be a first for both of us. Like birders, herpers tend to keep a life list of the reptiles and amphibians they have seen, even if the list is not written down. For the two of us, this was not a half-bored wish to find the snake, check it off, and move on. Seeing the animal in front of us, alive and functioning in its habitat, gives it a reality it could not have in a field guide. It's like saying, "I always wanted to meet you, and I'm glad I can do so now."

We drove past coastal prairie and marshes as we approached the Intracoastal Waterway. At 5:22 p.m., we passed a small snake on the shoulder of the road. When we went back to it, Clint picked it up and identified it as a Gulf saltmarsh watersnake. It was limp, and its head had been hit by a car. Sure enough, its belly was brownish red on the neck and shaded to black toward the tail, with a series of pale spots in the center in an irregular, cream-colored stripe down the belly. The top of the snake was not so easily recognized, being overall muddy brown with suggestions of wavy bands but without the stripes that would be typical for this species. Perhaps this can be explained by the report in Gibbons and Dorcas's book, *North American Watersnakes*, that the coloration of the Gulf saltmarsh watersnake is variable, probably because of hybridization with broad-banded watersnakes.[1] The belly pattern clearly established it as a Gulf saltmarsh watersnake. Somewhere in our brains, check marks appeared on the life list's check boxes, with a note of sadness.

When picked up, these snakes are said to be more easygoing than other watersnakes, and they are smaller, with most of them measuring under three feet in length. They prefer the brackish coastal marshes, where they eat fish as well as crayfish and crabs. Their range extends inland a short distance, where the Gulf saltmarsh watersnake may make do with a freshwater marsh, although it is a less-preferred habitat.

The striped belly pattern of the Gulf saltmarsh watersnake, found dead on the road

Dorsal view of the same Gulf saltmarsh watersnake

We drove other roads as sunset arrived, visited the Skillern tract of the refuge once more, and returned to the road to High Island again. At 8:04 p.m., near the spot where we found the first little watersnake, there was a bigger one. It too was dead, and it also turned out to be a second Gulf saltmarsh watersnake. It is unlikely that we missed it the first time around; apparently, sometime after we found the first snake, the second one crawled out onto the highway and met the same fate. It was exciting to think that there might be a robust population of these snakes in this area but, at the same time, disappointing that we only just missed seeing these two snakes alive.

Happy herping in the mosquito-infested salt marshes of Brazoria County / KING

It was early May several years ago, and my wife and I were hoping the recent heavy rains and flooding would trigger massive reptile and amphibian movement along the Texas coast southwest of Houston. We were in Brazoria County, in low, flat coastal marshland dotted with bayous where fresh water mixes with regular doses of salt water from the Gulf of Mexico.

As usual, it was late evening by the time we freed ourselves of the vehicular congestion that composes Houston's Mixmaster, with no clue as to where to actually start and no hot spots from fellow herpers to aid me in my search. So I did as I usually do whenever I am in unknown territory, searching the map for back roads and then evaluating whether the habitat surrounding the road is favorable. I found a one- or two-mile-long dirt track that ran along the border of the San Bernard National Wildlife Refuge. This was the lowest point of elevation possible, and it looked to be bordered by brackish salt marsh on both sides. If the road wasn't flooded out from recent storms, it looked like my best bet.

We headed in the direction of the gravel road as the sun disappeared behind us. Overhead, a thick mass of gray clouds tinted with evening orange threatened more torrential rainfall. When we got to the road, I couldn't help but smile. The landscape was unbelievably consistent with the natural habitat described in the field guides for the Gulf saltmarsh watersnake. A one-lane strip of gravel had been cut in a two-mile long L shape, extending across a brackish marsh for the first mile and then running a half mile from the seashore for an additional mile. There were no vehicles, no artificial lights, and no fences or houses—just pristine marsh grasses and ocean as far as the eye could see. The only thing left between me and snakes was sweet time.

We hadn't gone fifty yards before a thick, chunky pit viper emerged from the saltgrass jungle and made its way to the center of the road in rectilinear fashion. This was a species I was quite familiar with: the northern cot-

Northern cottonmouth in Brazoria County

tonmouth. While at home in almost any habitat that provides a permanent water source, these adaptable serpents are the predominant venomous snake on the coastline. They are opportunistic feeders and make use of a variety of habitats. I have found healthy populations of cottonmouths in swamps, creeks, river bottomland, and even lowland forest and open grassland pocked with small ponds. Wherever they occur, they tend to be quite abundant. As I was about to find out, they are able to fare quite well for themselves in a salt marsh environment as well.

When I opened the door to get out and photograph the moccasin, the previously vacant space we had been enjoying in the truck's interior was filled with mosquitoes. While I am no stranger to mosquito hordes, having somewhat successfully fought them off throughout the eastern half of Texas, I have never before or since seen anything like the mosquitoes of Brazoria County. In the amount of time it took me to exit the truck and point the camera at the snake, every inch of my exposed skin became covered in the insects. They were huge and bit with such tenacity and force I swore they were using small nail guns for proboscises. I quickly decided I had plenty of cottonmouth pics on file and need not risk sacrificing several pints of blood for this one. When I got back in the truck, my wife shot me a murderous glare behind bite-swollen eyelids as I let in another rank of the bloodthirsty soldiers to replace those she had killed. It was a frustrating night as we drove back and forth across the little road, dodging cottonmouths, western ratsnakes, and Gulf Coast ribbonsnakes at a very low rate of speed. Outside, legions of mosquitoes continued to bump angrily at the windows like zombies thirsting for blood, tormented by the smell of carbon dioxide they somehow knew we were exhaling out of their disease-ridden reach.

"They're daring you to go out there onto the warfront," my wife said as we scratched incessantly.

"They'll get their chance as soon as something other than a cottonmouth wiggles in front of my headlights," I said.

A beautiful broad-banded watersnake crossed not long after that, but it wasn't prize enough to make me stop. The next snake, however, was. It was large and robust like a cottonmouth but with the telltale narrow neck and head of a harmless natricine. While it could easily have been a plain-bellied watersnake, something struck me as different about this particular one, and I decided to chance it. I stopped casually and said, "Okay, I'm getting out. When I do, you pull the door closed behind me and we'll try to let as few of those whiney little aerial vampires in as possible."

I stepped out into the coastal night and was instantly bitten by what felt like a thousand mosquitoes. There were so many of them humming through the air that it felt like walking through a living, breathing, biting black cloud, and the sound of their wings was akin to being next to tiny generators. Still, I swiped blindly through the masses and grabbed the watersnake, then raced back to the truck, hoping the serpent's musk that now generously coated my exposed arms would prove to be a previously undiscovered insect repellant. Back in the truck, much to my delight, I identified the snake not as a plain-bellied watersnake but as a Mississippi green watersnake, a lifelister for me. While abundant throughout most of Louisiana and eastward, the Mississippi green watersnake is found only sporadically along the Texas coastline. It can be distinguished from Texas' other watersnakes by its scales between the eyes and upper labials as well as a series of cream-colored half-moon shapes on the edges of dark ventral scales.

I cracked open the door and slipped the snake back out into its home. "I hope that was worth it," my wife said. "It was," I replied. But would it be again?

It was after nine o' clock at this point, so I figured we would head back to take the Intracoastal Highway, which would take us through a series of bayous and salt marshes and hopefully away from the swarming mosquito plagues.

No sooner had we pulled onto the highway than the clouds broke and rain began to fall in sheets across the roadway. Along the coastline random storms can form out on the ocean and be blown in by winds sporadically and seemingly out of nowhere. This one however had been several hours in the making, and I was actually surprised it had taken so long to fall. This usually brings a premature end to the night's activities, at least as far as snake hunting goes, but sometimes the snakes don't seem to notice at all and continue on their road-crossing forays in spite of the downpour. As our luck would have it, tonight just happened to be one of those rare nights when the snakes come out to play like giddy schoolchildren in utter disobedience of Mother Nature.

I got out to look at an eastern copperhead that would have been soaked had it not been for the water-resistant scales that this species shares with other snake species. The rain, which soaked me to the bone in seconds flat, had done virtually nothing to beat back the waves of mosquitoes. If anything, it had worked them into a kamikaze frenzy, and they attacked me again with all the gusto of their fellow soldiers back at the wildlife refuge. The copperhead wasn't worth the pain, so half-drowned and covered in itchy bumps, I beat a hasty retreat back to the truck.

But the snakes were still out, so I wasn't about to call it quits prematurely. The most successful find of the evening came in the form of a gorgeous adult eastern gartersnake, another life-lister for me. Like the Mississippi green watersnake, the eastern garter is an abundant species throughout most of its range in the United States but an unusual find in Texas. Other kinds of gartersnakes are found in parts of Texas, but the distribution of the eastern garter is limited to the Texas coastline and inland as far as Harris and Newton Counties.

At the relatively inexpensive cost of a hundred or so more insect bites, I was able to snatch it from the roadway as it wriggled in the rain, then identify and release it. Finally, we called it a night and headed back in the direction of Brazoria, where a nice long hot bath followed by an itchy, sleepless night in a hotel bed awaited us. While we had failed to locate the Gulf saltmarsh watersnake, we had been successful in seeing a great many other snakes. And while my wife called me crazy as I gobbled antihistamine, I vowed to return to the rain-soaked, mosquito- and cottonmouth-infested salt marshes again. But next time I would learn from my previous mistakes and invest in a good insect repellant.

Mama Gator watches her babies / SMITH

Having heard Clint's stories of the great clouds of mosquitoes in Brazoria County, it was hard not to think of them as we approached Brazoria National Wildlife Refuge. A short walk along a trail through one of these thickets proved that the mosquitoes were still there and still had a taste for a little DEET with their blood meals. As a refuge staff member noted ironically, "The mosquitoes are our welcome committee."

We visited the Big Slough Recreation Area in the southern part of the refuge, where there is a boardwalk crossing the open water and dense stands

Adult American alligator, Brazoria National Wildlife Refuge

of tall reeds. It was sunny and warm as we made our way down the board-walk, looking carefully around the bases of the reeds and trying not to miss anything. What came into view was a low platform off the boardwalk and, in the water beside it, an adult American alligator, perhaps seven feet long. We stopped and crept forward, as alligators tend to be shy and slip away when people are near. However, we need not have bothered; this girl had evidently seen so many birders and naturalists go by on the boardwalk that she was not about to be spooked by us. We approached slowly and quietly and were abso-lutely delighted to see eight to ten baby alligators in the aquatic vegetation at the edge of a stand of reeds.

This introduced another reason to be still and cautious and to keep a respectful distance. Mother alligators are known to be protective of their babies and will come to the rescue if one of them grunts in distress. Mother was basking, open-mouthed, but did not show any concern about our pres-ence yet. We would watch carefully for her to hiss, which would signal that she felt that the babies were threatened. If we posed too much of a threat, she might lunge out of the water toward us, and alligators can do this with surprising speed and power. So we put on the long lenses and took photos from, well, farther away than we would have for most herp subjects. One of us watched Mama while the other concentrated on the photo, and at the slightest cue of distress from her we would have retreated.

The babies were less than a foot long, brightly marked in black with yel-lowish crossbars, and probably hatched last year. One of them had an easy

Baby alligator at Big Slough Recreation Area

time foraging for small fish that gathered in shallow water over a submerged portion of the platform. A little later, as we returned over the boardwalk, the mother was a short distance farther away. Clint moved in to take another photo or two of the babies, and Mother immediately submerged and swam back over to her previous position where she had been guarding the babies. She never hissed or lunged but was clearly a watchful, protective presence over her young.

Port Bay Ranch / SMITH

I was born in Corpus Christi, and after moving away, my family returned for a year when I was an early teen. I hung out with the handful of staff at the Corpus Christi Museum when it was a little building in the shadow of the ship channel's bridge, and we visited outlying areas where rose-bellied lizards scampered around the mesquites and Berlandier's tortoises munched prickly pear in the scrub. And so the mesquite scrub prairies around that portion of the coast felt familiar to me when Clint and I arrived just up the road at Aransas Pass in 2016, with a generous invitation from Mark Grosse to visit his Port Bay Ranch and perhaps see horned lizards, rattlesnakes, or even a Texas diamond-backed terrapin.

Port Bay Ranch is not huge, but it is over 400 acres of coastal prairie, with a slice of beachfront and marsh on the margin of Port Bay. Our first visit was at sundown, and after we got behind the gates, it was dark and quiet. From nearby ponds we heard green treefrogs and American bullfrogs, and the

distant calls added to that peaceful sense that comes from being out somewhere at night, surrounded by nothing but a dark sky and a light breeze stir-
ring the grass.

The next day was sunny and warm, and we walked through some of the
prairie and out onto the bay shore. Several nighthawks danced in the air,
white wing bars flashing on pointed wings. I was reminded of how well camouflaged they are on the ground when I spotted a grayish lump huddled on
an old railroad tie at the edge of the beach. As I tried to photograph it, the
bird launched and joined the other graceful, athletic birds that called to each
other with a short, high-pitched "peent!"

As we walked toward the bay, the open sand of the beach gave way to a
community of low plants and pools of water. A band of marsh grasses covered parts of it before reaching the open water of the shallow bay. It was here
that some researchers had found a couple of Texas diamond-backed terrapins a while back. They were investigating whether crab nets fitted with a
device to keep turtles from entering and drowning would work. Would it
save terrapins? Would it still catch crabs? It turns out that the traps designed
to exclude turtles did catch plenty of blue crabs and did not catch turtles.
However, in this particular study, only a couple of terrapins were caught—
too few to reach firm conclusions. This kind of work is important, though,
because the terrapins are a threatened species. At one time, their numbers
declined because of a market for making them into soup. More recently,
threats have come in the form of habitat loss.

These are the only turtles in the United States referred to as "terrapins," and they live in salt marshes and brackish water along the coast from
Massachusetts to Texas. All of them are relatively small turtles with con-
centric sculpted rings around each scute of the carapace, thus the name
"diamond-backed." Their heads and necks are generally some shade of gray,
sprinkled with black flecks. Living in salt water or brackish water poses a
challenge for these turtles because if the salt concentration of the water is
higher than the salt content of their bodies, they could dehydrate and die
without some way to prevent water loss. Among their strategies for living
successfully in salt marshes is to have skin that particularly resists passage of
salt or water and the ability to drink fresh water from rain even when it is in
a very thin layer on top of salt water. During rains, they are even known to
extend their heads up above the water, open-mouthed, to catch raindrops.
Snails such as periwinkles, bivalves, and crustaceans make up much of the
diamond-backed terrapin's diet. They like to eat small crabs and may nibble
off the legs of larger ones. Their habit of eating periwinkles reportedly plays
an important role in maintaining some salt marshes; according to a report

Beach near where Texas diamond-backed terrapins have been found

cited by Ernst and Lovich,[2] these snails are capable of reducing an area of cordgrass to nothing but a mud flat if left unchecked.

Back on the scrubby grassland, we found a few harvester ant mounds, which are the key to finding horned lizards, but most of the mounds were inactive. We also walked around a couple of small ponds and spooked a leopard frog or two, which leapt into the water with squawks of distress. A large mesquite shaded the bigger pond, and an old neglected cistern sat beside it. Within the circle of stonework was a pile of sticks and leaves that looked to us like a southern plains woodrat's house. On the other side of the cistern, a snake had shed its skin, which we investigated. Sometimes you can identify the snake by the shed skin because traces of pattern are still visible on the skin. You can also look at scale size, whether the scales are keeled, and so on. We were pretty sure that this one came from a sizable Great Plains ratsnake. A hole led under the empty cistern, and for all we knew this ratsnake might have been tucked away right there, waiting for nighttime.

This spot seemed to be a pretty good place to have lunch, so we sat on overturned buckets and ate. As we finished, an eastern cottontail loped out from the brushy cover and stopped a little distance away. We froze at that point, and the curious rabbit sniffed, approached to about ten feet from us, and sniffed the air again. Apparently satisfied that there was no immediate threat, it came closer, always stopping to detect potential warning signs of a nearby predator. Cottontail survival must depend on a constant high level of alertness, and yet this one had an air of relaxed watchfulness, stopping to munch some leaves from a low-hanging mesquite branch. It was no more than five feet away as we continued our motionless observation. We could have remained like statues until our muscles cramped because this is the

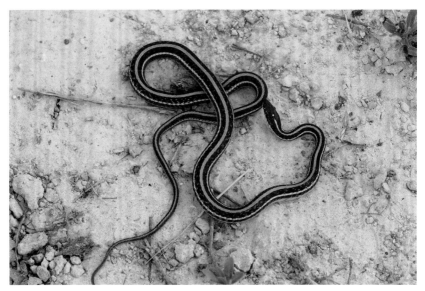
Gulf Coast ribbonsnake at Port Bay Ranch

kind of encounter that we always look forward to. For a few moments you and the animal are sharing the same world, and by watching carefully, you see a little of how it lives its life. It doesn't matter if it's a reptile, amphibian, bird, or an ordinary cottontail. When you are invited into this kind of shared moment, you accept the invitation. The moment was over soon enough, as the rabbit loped away, back to where it had come from.

A little later in the day, we looked under some boards near the pond. There was a sudden flash of striped, serpentine ribbon under one of them—a young Gulf Coast ribbonsnake. These snakes are easy to take for granted because they are common up and down the coast, but for grace, agility, and beauty they are hard to beat. In grass or vegetation the long stripes facilitate the snake's escape from a predator or potential human captor. If only part of the snake is visible, there are no blotches or spots that would shift with the serpent's movement. As it quickly slips away, the apparently stationary stripe simply becomes thinner and thinner until the snake is gone!

As the sun moved lower and the shadows grew longer, it was time for a walk in the hope that we might run across snakes starting to move. There is a short period before sunset that seems to be a great time to see many snake species, such as bullsnakes and western diamond-backed rattlesnakes. As we walked around, we checked the harvester ant mounds we had seen earlier, and they were alive with the comings and goings of ants! With controlled excitement we began to walk around each colony, finding the little trails that the ants used to bring seeds, bits of vegetation, and other good-

Texas horned lizard, foraging at sunset at Port Bay Ranch

ies back to the mound. Horned lizards do not sit directly in ant mounds, where they could be swarmed by the protective ants. Instead, they position themselves alongside the trails, where a steady supply of the little insects will come to them like little packets of food on a conveyor belt, ready to be lapped up. Within a very short time looking along these trails, we found the first of two Texas horned lizards. These stubby, prickly little reptiles sat still briefly but took off when we got close enough that they knew the camouflage was not working. Horned lizards almost seem to waddle as they make a break for it, but they can be reasonably fast and tend to stop unpredictably and start again. They have other defenses beyond blending in with their surroundings or running—sometimes they flatten and tilt their bodies toward an intruder to appear big and hard to swallow. To a small predator, it's like a spikey shield protecting the softer parts of the lizard. And of course they are a bit thorny to pick up, especially those two big sharp horns at the back of the head. And the lizard is capable of squirting a small amount of blood from the corners of the eyes toward an enemy. This sometimes occurs when a human picks up a horned lizard, but it seems most effective with canids such as dogs or coyotes, which find it quite distasteful. We don't know how it tastes to a coyote, but Jane Manaster tells about how in the late 1800s an adventurous researcher tasted the ejected blood and found it to have a "slight musky flavor."[3]

In places with reddish or sand-colored soil, the Texas horned lizard is often clothed in sandy, reddish, and brown colors. Here the horned lizards matched the shades of the soil in muted, slightly gray colors, but they were beautiful nonetheless. We interfered with them as little as possible, and no blood was squirted as we admired them and took a few photos. These lizards, remnants of what was once a common reptile over most of Texas, were the high points of a memorable day near Aransas Pass.

4 South Texas and the Rio Grande Valley

THERE ARE SEVERAL ECOREGIONS in South Texas. One is the Tamaulipan thorn scrub, referring to the generally thorny shrubs and low trees found from Del Rio eastward to below San Antonio. Further to the east are the Gulf Coast prairies and marshes that hug the shores of the Gulf of Mexico. At the bottom of Texas is the Rio Grande Valley, where priceless wildlife refuges nestle side by side with cities like Brownsville and McAllen. Much of the Rio Grande floodplain has been turned into irrigated cropland, but where there are preserves and refuges, you can find amazing subtropical habitats, including a few remnant stands of the Texas sabal palm. The patches of sabal palm woodland at the Sabal Palm Sanctuary offer an otherworldly experience that, in places, might make you think of a prehistoric jungle.

When we talk about the thorn scrub, we're referring to the thick tangle of trees, shrubs, and cacti that cover much of the land. Among the shrubs and trees found there are honey mesquite, Texas paloverde, colima, granjeño, and ebony blackbead, and all have thorns or recurved spines. Prickly pear cactus grows in clumps well above head high, and other cacti such as the barbed wire or triangle cactus can be found in the scrub.

A chain of public and private refuges provides, in many places, a conservation corridor along the river, including the Lower Rio Grande Valley National Wildlife Refuge where the river empties into the Gulf, then the Nature Conservancy's Lennox Foundation Southmost Preserve, Sabal Palm Sanctuary, and, farther westward, the Santa Ana National Wildlife Refuge, the National Butterfly Center, and Bentsen–Rio Grande Valley State Park. Almost all of these places are accessible to the public except for the Southmost Preserve.

Several Mexican herp species range northward only as far as the Rio Grande Valley or the thorn scrub, such as the cane toad, Berlandier's tortoise (previously known as the Texas tortoise), the Texas indigo snake, the speckled racer, and the regal black-striped snake. The South Texas thorn scrub and Rio Grande Valley are "must see" destinations for birders, herpers, and anyone who wants to see a unique subtropical ecosystem.

The lucky shirt / KING

I was eighteen years old when a friend and I made our first run to the Rio Grande Valley on a reptilian-focused mission; the goal was knocking two of my favorite snake species from my life list: the long-nosed snake and the Mexican milksnake. Both are tricolored beauties adorned with handsome rings of red, black, and yellow. They are both primarily nocturnal and feed mostly on smaller reptiles. I had heard South Texas would be my best bet for finding them. Thus my story unravels in the thorn scrub south of San Antonio.

It was April 1, All Fool's Day, but I had no intention of playing the fool, although some could argue that embarking on a fourteen-hour trip to find not one but two elusive target species with only one night to get it done seemed more than a bit foolish. As luck would have it, I was about to be blessed with a rabbit's foot of sorts, tipping the balance of fortune in my favor.

Even though it was only April, the midday sun was brutal, but I refused to roll my window up and was on the verge of acquiring a wicked sunburn on my left forearm. Finally, out of desperation, I pulled into a thrift store in San Antonio to pick up a long-sleeved shirt to cover my exposed skin. I was leafing through the shirt racks, looking for something in my size, when an elderly gentleman took me by surprise. He looked like he could have stepped right from the pages of the Old Testament; he was that old.

"You lookin' for a shirt, son?" he asked.

"That's right," I said.

He stepped in front of me and almost as if by magic extracted an olive-green long-sleeved button-up shirt from the rack. "Here, that looks about your size," he said, handing the shirt to me. I checked the tag and, sure enough, it was the perfect size. I held it up against my body, just to make sure, and the old man commented, "That looks mighty sharp on you, son. You never know, it could be your lucky shirt."

That sealed the deal. Now I had to buy it. The very fate of my life list could be riding on it. "Thank you," I said, and tucked the shirt under my arm and headed for the register. At some point I turned around to see if the old man was still standing there, but he was nowhere to be seen.

Back in the truck, I told my friend about my strange encounter and how the mysterious shirt had fallen into my hands.

"Hey, it could have been fate," he said. "You know, like the old country song about the guitar that sat in the pawn shop for years waiting for that one particular guy to pick it up, turning it into instant magic in his hands."

"Nonsense," I retorted. "But a little luck certainly couldn't hurt us."

We headed south from San Antonio on State Highway 16 until we reached the tiny town of Freer. Since we had no idea where to reap the highest yield of snakes, neither of us ever having been to South Texas before, we just chose a small nondescript stretch of blacktop running through Duval County as a southeastern line on the map. Donning my new lucky shirt, it didn't take long to find our first snake, a Schott's whipsnake. These long, slender diurnal lizard hunters are well adapted for the harsh environment that is the Tamaulipan thorn scrub. They are lightning fast, and the brief glimpse of this one as it streaked across the road was another life-lister for me that I hadn't expected. A few minutes later we came across a giant of a western diamond-backed rattlesnake. It was well over five feet in length, and both of us decided it was in our best interest to try not to shoo the beast from the roadway. A few minutes after that we saw a second Schott's whipsnake.

"I think it's working," my friend commented as we pulled over for a second diamondback—"it" being my shirt.

After that it was on. We cruised up and down the roadway as the sun faded over the horizon and gave way to a pitch-black, moonless spring night, my headlights illuminating the wriggling forms of dozens of snakes. It seemed we would barely climb back into the truck and get on the road again before we were pulling over for another one. There was a Great Plains ratsnake, numerous checkered gartersnakes, a few bullsnakes, Texas glossy snakes, and more diamond-backed rattlesnakes than you could shake a hook at. But still no long-nosed snake. Still no milksnake.

"Your lucky shirt sure is paying off," my friend said again, hoping for a bit more optimism on my part.

"It means nothing until I see some red, yellow, and black," I growled as I moved yet another western diamondback from the roadway.

Two minutes down the road and the telltale vivid, contrasting rings of a tricolor came into view. I put two layers of tread down on the still-warm asphalt, and a few seconds later returned to the truck with my first longnose, a giant thirty-six-inch-long female.

"Now we're talking!" I yelled with a victorious grin.

By the time we reached the end of the road I had gone from zero longnoses to three. I was having the night of my life, and I owed it all to a mysterious old man in a thrift store and a tattered hand-me-down green shirt. There was still one small problem, however—greed. The discovery of my first long-nosed snake was thirty minutes behind me now, and I was beginning to wonder what was delaying my milksnake. With only a mile left to go before we reached the highway, the outlook for my shirt's uncanny ability to enshroud

Mexican milksnake

its destined wearer with unwavering, 100 percent foolproof luck was beginning to wane. Or at least my faith in it was. Reluctantly, I gave the sleeve
a quick rub between two fingers, as if trying to conjure up some hidden
genie from within the confines of its many wrinkles. Even as I did, a snake
whipped across the road in front of us. I knew what it was, even though I had
never before laid eyes on a live one. It was *Lampropeltis annulata*, my Mexican milksnake.

As if this were not enough, we stopped at a Border Patrol station just north
of the junction, and when the agents found out we were looking for snakes,
they brought us to the side of the road to do some night-walking behind
the station. There we found eight additional checkered garters hunting Rio
Grande leopard frogs in a shallow pool of rainwater that had collected in a
low-lying area along the fence line. Back on the highway, we racked up several more western diamondbacks. It had been my best snake night ever, with
a total sighting of fifty-one snakes within the span of just five hours. I vowed
to never take the shirt off again, except of course for showers.

That was many years ago, but the lucky green thrift-store shirt is still a
vital part of each and every herping trip; when I accidentally forgot it on
one trip, I was practically skunked! It has helped me check off tons of additional life-listers. I was wearing it when I found my first Trans-Pecos ratsnake
and Baird's ratsnake in Big Bend National Park as well as my first Ruthven's
whipsnake, regal black-striped snake, Tamaulipan hook-nosed snake, Texas
indigo snake, Mexican racer, and speckled racer on subsequent trips to the

Rio Grande Valley. I was wearing it when I found every single milksnake and gray-banded kingsnake I have ever encountered in the field.

Unwelcome guests at a Texas indigo snake's dinner / SMITH

The Tamaulipan thorn scrub country of South Texas is known for many wonderful species, including one of the state's largest snakes, the Texas indigo snake. With smooth, glossy black to dark brown scales, its powerful body may reach between six and eight feet in length. Those scales, particularly on dark individuals, have a satiny, bluish sheen—the "indigo" that gives the snake its name. Snakes in this group are more at home in Mexico and Central America, and in the United States they can be found only in South Texas, with a related indigo snake found in Florida and parts of adjacent states. The Texas indigo snake is protected by the Texas Parks and Wildlife Department and may not be collected or needlessly killed. It is a powerful, active hunter that simply overpowers its prey without venom or constriction. Indigos eat rodents, other snakes, frogs, and other animals, grabbing them with strong jaws and pinning them down with a loop of their muscular bodies.

In 2009 Clint and I stopped at a roadside rest area south of Hebbronville in the sandy, mesquite- and cactus-dominated flat landscape that can be called the South Texas Plains or the Tamaulipan thorn scrub. Historically, it was described as mostly grassland, but the arrival of cattle ranching led to overgrazing, opening the way for cacti, mesquite, catclaw, and other thorny plants to take over. There were a few trees here, and we stopped during the morning hours to have a look for lizards or perhaps coachwhips or whipsnakes.

Clint heard movement in low, brushy vegetation and, peering through the branches, saw an indigo snake. And then, momentarily, he thought perhaps it was really just a rattlesnake he had glimpsed. But it soon became clear that he had discovered a big, handsome indigo snake eating a western diamond-backed rattlesnake. We both took up positions where we could watch without interfering.

In the encounter we saw that the now dead and limp rattlesnake had become entangled in low branches. The indigo pulled hard, but the rattlesnake would not come loose. Undeterred, the indigo snake continued to chew on the rattlesnake's head and to pull on the uncooperative meal. The big snake was aware of our presence and appeared to watch us with a vigilant stare while working on the rattlesnake. It urgently tugged against the stuck rattlesnake and seemed like it was trying to hurry up and get its prey loose so that it could move away from us. This presented us with a dilemma: this

Texas indigo snake eating a western diamond-backed rattlesnake

Close-up of the indigo snake swallowing the rattlesnake's head

was an incredible opportunity for us to observe one of our favorite snakes feeding, and yet we did not want to disturb the big snake to the point that it might give up and retreat.

We decided that the best thing to do was to move away to avoid stressing the snake. We thought we might give it some time to swallow more of the rattlesnake and then try to get another look, using care not to disturb the indigo. When we returned a few minutes later, the indigo snake was still intently chewing and yanking on its entangled meal. As we watched, it pulled and pulled—and the rattlesnake's head finally separated from its body, the connective tissue stretching and then breaking. The indigo now had at least a portion of its prey. Having put up with our watching for longer than it would have wished, it retreated off through the brush. In a moment we saw it behind a fence line, twenty feet away, cruising toward better shelter with the rattlesnake's head held in its jaws high off the ground.

March madness: late-winter herping in the Rio Grande Valley / KING

It had been seven years since I had had a productive trip to the lower Rio Grande Valley of Texas. Herping here comes like gambler's luck. You either win big or you totally crap out. There is little room for marginalists. The herping can be as unforgiving as the terrain that makes up this landscape. In fact, while I have made upward of a dozen trips to the state's southernmost counties in search of those rare jewels that occur only in a small area north of the Mexican border, I can recall only four times when I have struck reptilian gold. The last had been in 2009, the year I introduced Michael Smith to "the Valley," as the locals call it. In the following years two subsequent trips had yielded very little indeed. In fact, win big or go home seemed to be the running theme whenever I had pointed the Herpmobile south of San Antonio.

So when Mark Pyle, my longtime friend and field partner and the then president of the Dallas–Fort Worth Herpetological Society, sent me a seemingly innocuous text message speaking of all the wonderful treasures popping up on Facebook in Hidalgo County, those mad gears began to flake off the rust as they groaned into motion in my brain. It was early March of 2016. Would I (could I) dare to dream that the lower Rio Grande Valley could be hopping so early in the year? If the Facebook herpers were lying in all their boasting, they were doing a convincing job of it. Reports of burrowing toads (one of the strangest and most elusive amphibians in the state), Mexican milksnakes on the move, "herds" of legless lizards . . . A quick check of the radar confirmed what I would have otherwise chalked up to insanity visited upon already half-mad herpers too long pent up by the woes of winter. But, no, there it was in all the bold colors of the spectrum: The Valley was experiencing a low-pressure cell that had been circling for seven days, blown in from the West Coast across that vast open expanse that was northern Mexico. And to top that off, we were under a new moon. So, naturally, there was nothing to hinder two springtime herpers with an extended case of the winter blues except every obstacle common and possible to man. For starters, it was the middle of a workweek, and there was my job to consider, but I managed to take off from work. Second, both of our trucks were in the shop on life support, with the diagnoses uncertain at best. Getting a car would be difficult, but I had an ace up my sleeve.

The year my wife and I first met I had taken her on a trip to Freer, Texas, to find her first Texas indigo snake. Against all odds, we had tasted sweet success. So all I had to do this time around was to explain to her how neither Mark nor our own son had ever laid eyes on their first Texas indigo snake (*Drymarchon melanurus erebennus*), which many herpers consider to be a rite of passage into the Tamaulipan region, so could we please borrow her car? I promised I wouldn't put more than 3,000 miles on it.

There was no resisting such logic, and with a vehicle secure, that Saturday we fought traffic south of Austin in my wife's Pontiac, with the former Yankee turned successful Texas herper Mark Pyle riding shotgun and my son Zev sharing the back seat with an assortment of tongs, hooks, butterfly nets, and camera equipment. It was spring break weekend, and the tourists and partiers had fallen upon the region between Austin and San Antonio like swarms of booze-addled bees. But once we got south of Bexar County, the traffic thinned out as concrete gave way to the thorn scrub.

Our first stop was in Bruni, in Webb County, located northeast of Laredo by less than a hundred miles. Its nearest neighbor is Freer, a tiny, thriving community known for its annual rattlesnake roundup and trophy whitetail hunts. The region is composed mostly of thousands of acres of undisturbed ranchland and, until the oil industry fell heavily upon the area five or six years ago, was well known among herpers as a hot spot for the highly coveted local beauty, the Mexican milksnake. For me, the Freer city limits sign is like a welcome mat at the threshold of the Rio Grande Valley. Here the live oak and greenbrier association gives way to ever-encroaching dense stands of mesquite and scrubby, thorny growth as the ground flattens. This hardpan substrate is barely visible beneath the thorny carpet of cacti and hardy brush and legumes that constitute the flora of the valley. Here turkey and black vultures soar over the scene on wind currents or fight with the larger and more ferocious caracaras for position over the carcass of a deer or coyote.

Caracaras are champion scavengers, native principally to the subtropics of Mexico and Central America, but the Rio Grande Valley supports a healthy year-round population of these exotic-looking raptors as well. Sporting a handsome crest on the head, dressed in bold blacks, browns, and whites, these iconic birds of prey are among the most efficient members of nature's cleanup crew. With the rising of the sun these birds descend upon all those unfortunate victims of vehicular traffic that have accumulated during the hours of darkness, and by midmorning a small carcass is a rare sight on the roadsides south of Freer.

I knew a few reliable places in Bruni to flip tin and trash. It was a good day for it; the temperature was holding at 73 degrees thanks to a thick blanket of cloud cover, which the late-morning sunlight was only beginning to gain an advantage over. It was common knowledge among herpers that the tangled web of caliche back streets behind the high school football field hid a wide variety of cold-blooded residents at a site where rubbish had accumulated for years. I can remember unrolling a long scrap of discarded, dirty yellow carpet there and finding a different species of herp every time I exposed another layer. A flat-headed snake came first, followed by its cousin, the plains black-headed snake. Then I uncovered two western narrow-mouthed toads and at last a lively adult Texas patch-nosed snake, whose opaque eyes I accepted as a reasonable excuse for its irritable temper. I remember feeling as if I had won a wonderful herpetological package prize on *Wheel of Fortune*.

But, alas, those days had come and gone. The shingle mountains and hills of drywall and discarded roofing iron were absent. Now the thick gnarled trunks of stunted mesquites were draped in old bread wrappers and plastic grocery bags, waving in the breeze like solemn pirate flags, eyeless witnesses to the degeneration of what had once been one of the healthiest dump sites in Texas. The putrid carcasses of several goats and feral hogs, their heads and limbs removed, sat bloating in the bright sunshine, their charred hides stretched tight as banjo covers over their exposed ribs, caught in a purgatory between decomposition and mummification by the ever-shifting elements. The odd stray sheet of plywood or gypsum board lay strewn about. They were the rare surviving remnants of yesterday and, like the creatures that sought shelter beneath them, seemed doomed to an extinction in a day not too far in the future. Yet life was holding on here. We discovered western narrow-mouthed toads alongside Texas brown tarantulas, unlikely partners in a strange symbiotic relationship wherein the tiny amphibians, which are dwarfed by their hairy arachnid landlords, are allowed to live peacefully around the edges of the silk-lined burrow, where they presumably eat mites and other parasites that plague the spiders. A Mediterranean gecko, probably the single most successful introduced species of reptile in Texas, sprang from between two layers of damp drywall as I pried them apart with my snake stick.

We quickly investigated the few nice pieces of flippable material that remained and then piled into the car to try our luck on the other side of the highway. I remembered a short section of railroad track with a publicly accessible grassy border full of woodpiles and railroad ties. We hoped that it still lay unaltered. As we pulled up, it appeared that site had met the same fate as the dump. Someone had removed every tie, leaving only random triangular wedges of pitch-coated scraps behind. Others had been stacked into crooked piles, but the grass had grown up over them so intensely that they were practically wired together. To top this off, it was reaching 80 degrees now, and flipping cover is seldom productive in full sunshine at that temperature. So we bid Bruni good-bye, perhaps for a final farewell, and broke forth into the deep brush country.

Herping the irrigation canals of Hidalgo County / KING

Hidalgo County had long been another ace in the hole when it came to herping in the Valley. It is almost an hour and a half south of Freer and is where squares of sugarcane and citrus cropland fuel one of the region's chief sources of income. Scrub brush and nonnative palm trees alternate with swatches of fertile flat soil. The fields must be watered constantly, as the Valley suffers from some of the state's record high temperatures and parched summers. Inhabitants had long ago made canals to channel water from various sources to feed crops. With this near-permanent source of sustenance, legumes and dense flowering vines grow alongside introduced bamboo and Carrizo cane. This provides a flowing oasis to the local wildlife already pushed to the edge of the ever-encroaching bulldozer. One species in particular had been at the top of my list ever since coming across a dead one on the interstate highway north of Brownsville nearly fifteen years ago.

The northern cat-eyed snake is a classic example of how local wildlife utilize the irrigation canals in an effort to survive in a region whose untouched wilderness is shrinking every year. A hunter of frogs, this bug-eyed, handsomely marked serpent, banded in elongated oval blotches of russet on pumpkin yellow, is one of the few snakes in the United States found only in Texas. While a common sight south of the border, it resides to the north only in scattered locales in the handful of counties bordering the Rio Grande and the Gulf of Mexico. With the elliptical pupils of a pit viper, this rear-fanged colubrid, while mildly venomous, is virtually harmless to humans. Cat-eyed snakes are semiarboreal and are often found coiled in a tree or bush overhanging the water, where they can ambush their amphibian prey. A natural resident of the shorelines of local oxbow lakes known as resacas, these habitat specialists find both plentiful frogging and adequate shelter in the leafy brush that lines the irrigation canals.

We left the vehicle behind at the top of a particularly choice canal, and as I gazed down at the water, my eyes fell upon the striped body of a large Gulf Coast ribbonsnake draped loosely over the angled branch of a small tree. I motioned for Mark and Zev, who quickly came running, with my camera bouncing across my seven-year-old son's chest. Mark was rubbing a lucky talisman he had fashioned at home—the plastic image of a rattlesnake's head molded from the head of a dead western diamondback—and going on about

Gulf Coast ribbonsnake basking in branches over an irrigation canal

how our luck was about to change. I quickly pointed out the ribbonsnake, to which Mark flashed his good luck charm with a confirmatory nod as to its potency. After a few zoomed-in photos of the snake in situ, my competitive side, which often rears its ugly head in the field, took over and I wagered Mark that I could catch the snake if he would catch the lunch tab the next day at a local taqueria. He agreed and the hunt was on!

The canal's banks were steep, but I slid down the incline on palms and heels until I was just behind the snake. As I moved inch by inch, my eyes never left the snake's head, where a single tongue flick would detect my presence and one wrong move would send this nervous and fast species to the safety of the canal. I ignored the swarming gnats that hummed around my face and the late-afternoon sun that beat down on my neck and shoulders. There was a plate of free barbacoa tacos at Marcelo's at stake; I couldn't fail. The risk was too high. I crept up within two feet of the snake's tail. It shifted a coil nervously, and I launched myself from the elevated bankside like a runner at the sound of the shot. My fingers closed around the ribbonsnake at midbody, and I swore I could smell tacos on the breeze.

Within the span of twenty minutes all we had found was a ribbonsnake. Diamond-backed watersnakes were equally common. Mark spied a ringed kingfisher on a branch overhanging the water, waiting on its dinner to swim by. A flock of black-bellied whistling ducks winged by overhead. It was a perfect day for herping. We climbed the banks of the canal, where a family fished with large cast nets in a small lake on the opposite side. Its shoreline was lined with thick vegetation, and the heads of a snapping turtle and a Texas spiny softshell bobbed to the surface just beyond the bank. A pair of last year's baby American alligators paddled laps around an exposed log that

Texas indigo snake, Hidalgo County

was half submerged and packed stem to stern by a group of cormorants. I was pondering how many snakes must be lying just out of sight in the thick stand of cane that grew between the lakeshore and the canal and how a big black indigo would be a nice find—just as the sunlight glinted off the glossy ebony scales of one emerging slowly from the cane into my path. For a second I wondered if I had tapped into an unknown reservoir of power in my mind. After all, that strange talisman of Mark's had seemed to hold an aura of good luck. "Indigo!" was the cry, and I heard the approaching footsteps of Mark and Zev. The bold black serpent doubled back for the safety of the cane thicket, but I headed it off. It sucked in air and flattened the forebody, cocking it at an angle and hissing in low protest, but we were undeterred and encircled it with cameras flashing. Of course, this made for quite a scene, and before long the family that had been fishing nearby had dropped their nets and come running. We seized this opportunity to put in a good word for the underappreciated snake and explain the indigo's valuable role in this ecosystem. The fact that this species frequently consumes rattlesnakes was enough to win the admiration of these folks, and one young boy in particular, Jasinto Hinojosa, admitted that his interest overshadowed any initial apprehension. As I have mentioned, indigos are one of our most impressive serpents. They can reach a maximum length of almost nine feet, although most adults average between five and seven. I first met this satiny giant on the upper banks of the Rio Grande north of Matamoros, Mexico. A trip to the Valley feels incomplete without the appearance of this marvelous king of the thorn scrub, and just as memorable as the find is watching the beautiful indigo snake slither back into its native element.

At the mercury vapor light we had set up, the insect life was scarce, proving that the barometric pressure had finally stabilized. We attempted a brief road cruise, but after a couple of hours of seeing nothing we opted to turn in early for the night and get some shut-eye. After all, we were going to have to get up early if we wanted to make it to the sabal palms by sunrise.

The Sabal Palms Sanctuary—the Alamo of the subtropics / KING

The sabal palm groves in Cameron County are one of our most vulnerable natural ecosystems. Naturally occurring groves of Texas sabal palm trees have nearly been pushed out of existence by the merciless hand of human progress, but a 557-acre remnant is owned by the Audubon Society and operated by the Gorgas Science Foundation. Located just beyond the borders of Brownsville's hustle and bustle, it is as close to the tropics as one can get in the state of Texas and likewise as far south as one can get in the state without crossing into Mexico. The place is renowned for its excellent birding opportunities, where professional and amateur birders can view such localized specialties as the plain chachalaca, groove-billed ani, and green jay. It also provides nesting habitat for two of the region's rarest birds, the Lomita Carolina wren and the Brownsville common yellowthroat. The sabal palms are home to a wide variety of other organisms—from the predatory ocelot (one of our smallest native wildcats) to north-ranging Central American butterflies like the red-bordered pixie and the malachite. Whatever the interest, the sabal palms hold hidden treasures for naturalists. For herpers it stands as the final stronghold of one of the state's rarest serpents, the speckled racer.

Speckled racers are a chiefly Mexican species of snake and occur in the United States only on two tiny tracts of land in Cameron County. One is Sabal Palm Sanctuary; the other is Southmost Preserve, a section of neighboring habitat owned by the Nature Conservancy. In 2012 Michael and I ventured here under the wing of Max Pons, who manages this proclaimed "jewel of the Rio Grande Valley." While we didn't find any speckled racers, we did get a chance to wade along the edges of a natural resaca. There we found examples of the abundant ribbonsnake as well as the introduced Brahminy blindsnake, a native of Southeast Asia that most likely arrived in the potting soil of imported tropical plants and found Southmost's mild climate to its liking. Max also showed us an outdoor setup for the threatened western lesser siren, a totally aquatic species of salamander that closely resembles an eel at first glance. Locally occurring sirens are of particular interest since they live only in the Rio Grande drainage of Texas' southernmost counties.

We arrived at the Sabal Palm Sanctuary a little later than expected, but the temperature was still in the low seventies, so at least in that respect it was perfect timing. Mark had been furiously rubbing the lucky plastic rattlesnake head during the entire hour-and-a-half drive south from the hotel, promising nothing short of a speckled racer fortune. As we turned onto Southmost Road, I began to get antsy. It had been over a decade since I had visited the sanctuary, and fond memories of past experiences began to float around in my head as we neared the entrance. On my introduction to the sabal palms, I had the good fortune of coming across one of the area's local attractions, the beautifully patterned regal black-striped snake. A fossorial and secretive rear-fanged species, I was surprised to find one stretched out in the roadway at the entrance to the gates. This was only a precursor to the magnificent reptile diversity that awaited within the preserve. In the span of an hour I had found a seven-foot-long indigo snake, two Mexican racers, and a handful of ribbonsnakes. But the speckled racer, the masterpiece of the palm groves, eluded me. The following year, however, I had managed to turn one up, not in its natural state but rather poking its head and forebody from a drain pipe in the butterfly garden near the visitor center. Since 2013, the 4,000-square-foot historic Rabb Plantation house, built in 1892, has served as the visitor center for this unique preserve, but prior to that it was a quaint one-room building with a butterfly garden and bird feeders behind it.

Checking in at the visitor center, we paused to look through a binocular set up on a tripod. It pointed toward the resident great horned owl nest in a palm tree in the front yard of the Rabb house. But with over four miles of trails to explore in the old-growth sabal palm forest, we were eager to get away from the parking lot and make for the trees. As we walked down the first trail, it was like stepping into a vast prehistoric world. If it hadn't been for the occasional hiker or bird watcher crossing our path, we could have easily envisioned traveling back in time to the Carboniferous period, when giant palm trees provided a dense canopy from which emanated the weird calls of insects and amphibians.

The entire forest floor is made up of a loamy substrate kept moist by the fallen fronds in various stages of decay. Lush legumes, milkberry, and blackbrush acacia grow up between the trees, and the bright pink flowers of occasional bougainvillea provide abstract splashes of vibrance in a sea of green. Texas snakewood accentuated this with the first shy blooms of canary yellow. In the dappled light filtering in through the canopy, huge specimens of barbed-wire cactus (*Acanthocereus tetragonus*) grew. This menacingly barbed succulent was inconspicuously nestled between less formidable plants like an accident waiting to happen to any overly eager hikers who disregarded the warning signs: "Stay on Trail." My attention focused on the stacks of dried palm fronds that had fallen around the bases of the sabal palm trunks, where I knew a speckled racer might be warming up.

To my surprise, it didn't take more than ten minutes of searching before the ornate form of a black snake bespeckled in yellow and turquoise spots like rhinestones materialized on top of a pile of fronds. I froze, and Mark and Zev instinctively followed suit behind me. "There's a speckled racer," I stammered, failing miserably at sounding casual about the matter. Indeed, there it was in all of its rare glory. Luckily for us, the snake was still relatively cool, and it posed wonderfully for our cameras. This is an uncommon occurrence, as anyone with any experience in speckled racer photography can attest. The species as a rule is flighty, easily spooked, and lightning fast. It is usually seen as a greenish blur passing between layers of fronds before disappearing into the brush or the labyrinth of decaying vegetative debris on the forest floor. We all stood there for ten or twenty minutes, relishing our unlikely encounter with this magnificent creature, whose bright coloration appears to be painted on, each scale resembling a shining black pearl with its tip dipped in a mixture of turquoise and cream. The head, which is distinct from the coloration of the body, is of a soft brown hue, with a handsome dark stripe just behind the eye and fine-point black lines separating the cream-colored scales along the lips. It is an animal that truly must be seen in the flesh and in the heart of its natural environment to be fully appreciated; no elaborate concoction of words or digital photos can truly do it justice.

We couldn't believe our luck! "I told you this snake head is a lucky rabbit's foot!" Mark piped. "We were just in the right place at the right time," I responded. "If that trinket is so lucky, why did we get skunked last night?" But Mark wasn't listening. He had already returned to rubbing on that silly talisman again. Under his breath, I could barely make out his nearly unintelligible mutterings: "Two for one . . . two for one . . . this time it's Mark's turn, baby . . . speckled racer . . ."

We left the racer to its morning basking and continued down the trail toward the resaca loop. While speckled racers have been known to consume a variety of prey items—from smaller reptiles and their eggs to small mammals—the bulk of their diet consists of frogs. In fact, they are seldom found far from water, and we were betting on the resaca loop if we were to find any more. A long stretch of boardwalk extended out over the water in the resaca, and this time it was Mark's turn to claim victory. "Speckled racer!" Zev and I rushed from the trailside where we had been lagging behind, and we showed up just in time to see the green blur of the racer as it shot across the shallow

Speckled racer

Speckled racer's head

water like blue-green liquid shot from a tube. "Lucky snake's head!" Mark proclaimed behind a wide grin. "Right place and time," I assured him.

Our luck had been phenomenal. We had located not one but two examples of the speckled racer within the span of a half hour. With the main course out of the way, we leisurely observed some of the desserts. A spiny-backed orb-weaver was photographed as it spun an intricate web between a hackberry bush and the ground, its strange, spiked clown-face abdomen defying the common body shape of its more typical North Texas relatives. Some birders passed by, with the leader pointing at a rapidly departing yellow blur of feathers and shouting out the species' scientific name in a thick French accent. "Sorry, we're herpers," Mark told him. "We're unfamiliar with the . . ." But the man had already lost interest in this conversation and was

Bougainvillea and sabal palms near the butterfly gardens, Sabal Palms Sanctuary

focusing on the whereabouts of the bird. Later we learned that this was a mangrove yellow warbler (*Setophaga petechia*), a species whose wintering range extends only as far as the southern tip of Texas. We took all this with the typical nonchalance of those who get their kicks a little lower to the ground, and I laughed as I pictured this most eccentric and enthusiastic birder chancing upon one of our beloved racers with the same indifference we had bestowed upon his bird.

Green anoles were everywhere, climbing and clambering and performing their nimble acrobatic acts from the bases of palm trees. Mark snapped a particularly nice picture of a large male chewing up an insect, which it washed down with a droplet of water that had collected at the base of the leaf it had been basking on. Behind the resacas the trail opened up into a field of thick grass that grew beneath the mixed shade of honey mesquites and Mexican lead trees. Mark discovered a prairie lizard hanging head down from a fork in one of the honey mesquites, and a birding couple paused to join us in photographing this Valley local before it tired of our company and, in typical *Sceloporus* fashion, moved around to the opposite side of the branch.

We paused at the observation deck to get a glimpse of turtles and water birds as they basked and foraged in the shallows of the mighty Rio Grande. All sizes of Rio Grande cooters were stacked on a log in the full sunshine. Whistling ducks and coots dove for tidbits amid the floating vegetation. A spectacularly adorned tricolored heron stalked frogs and fish not fifteen feet away from us. Zev was more interested in the spiders, so I pointed out a handsome marbled orb-weaver that had constructed its web between a small palm trunk and the railing to the entrance of the observation deck. From there it was a short, shady walk to the butterfly gardens. Although it was too early in the year for the flowers to be in sufficient bloom to attract mass quantities of butterflies, Mark did find a red-bordered pixie butterfly as it rested on the underside of a leaf. A member of the metalmark family of butterflies, it is a vividly patterned insect with red and yellow splotches of color on a smoke-gray background.

It was past noon, and Zev was beginning to tire. After all, I had promised him a visit to Boca Chica Beach, which lies at the very southern tip of Texas where Highway 4 runs out and empties into the sandy shores of the Gulf. But first there was that matter of Marcelo's tacos to contend with, and Mark proved to be a man of his word when it came to fulfilling his obligations in regard to snaky wagers.

Boca Chica—the beach at the bottom of Texas / KING

On the highway to Boca Chica Beach we pulled over for the local flavor of whipsnake, the Ruthven's. In life, it had been a rather drab-colored example of the snake, and it was now roadkill. However, it was in good condition, and I posed it for a photograph before leaving it to the harvester ants. I had seen only one other specimen of this particular brand of snake, and it too had been run over on this same stretch of highway in some bygone year.

We reached the beachfront in short time, and my son's eyes lit up as they fell upon the inconceivable magnitude of the Gulf of Mexico. Full sensory overload hit him, and I was enthralled to see him having so much fun outdoors in a generation that is growing up with their eyes and minds glued to social media and mindless morning television. We took off our shoes and walked along the seashore, picking up shells and admiring two flocks of brown pelicans as they coasted by overhead. A vendor drove by in a van, its sides advertising all manner of both hot and frozen delights. I opted for a traditional *elote* on a stick. But Mark and I could hold out for only so long, and we took turns watching Zev while the other tried his hand at photographing the resident population of cryptically colored keeled earless lizards, whose telltale tracks made them easy to locate amid the clumps of grass in the high dunes to our west. These alert little lizards, while quick to dart down a hole or shimmy quickly into the loose sand, were easy to photograph at an approachable distance with the aid of a long lens.

That night was a repeat of the previous night in that we failed to find a single live herp on the road. Outside of Rio Grande City we stopped beside the road to check out a dead Mesoamerican cane toad, the largest toad spe-

Keeled earless lizard in the sand dunes of Boca Chica

cies in the state. This is the same bedeviled cane toad that has brought such misery on the continent of Australia, but here in the Valley they seem to do minimal damage. We also found a dead ribbonsnake and the only western diamond-backed rattlesnake of the trip, a puny little two-footer. We checked in by midnight and back out the following morning before the sun came up. The initial plan had been to herp our way back up through the Freer area with the hope that Mark could find his first Berlandier's tortoise, but a dense fog hung around until past ten o'clock, with the temperature holding at a constant 63 degrees, reminding us that we should consider ourselves fortunate to have made out like bandits so early in the year with what we had already found. And no amount of rubbing on that weird little plastic rattlesnake head was going to coax out any herps, although it didn't stop Mark from trying. It may have actually paid off in some small way, for we stopped to flip tin around an abandoned shed in Brooks County west of the town of La Gloria and were rewarded with both an adult and juvenile example of the short-lined skink. Even in such dreary conditions the skinks proved difficult photo subjects, and eventually we tired of their resistance and settled for what we had.

It was still a good eight hours from La Gloria to Granbury, where I would be dropping Mark off, and we had miles of spring break traffic to look forward to, but that was okay. After all, coffee and gasoline were still cheap, there was more spring rain in the forecast for the entire state, and the metroplex was experiencing a rapid warm-up from three days of the same storm that had previously affected the southland. We had an entire year of good herping ahead of us, and there had been no better way to kick it off than with a very successful and memorable trip to the lower Rio Grande Valley.

5 The Edwards Plateau

CENTRAL TEXAS IS HOME TO large expanses of relatively flat ranchland, and it also contains beautiful rivers that flow peacefully between high limestone walls where yuccas and cacti grow alongside ferns. A great many caves and canyons have been formed as water gradually dissolved the rock, and in places the water that extends through honeycombs of limestone emerges in beautiful, clear springs. It is a beloved part of Texas, and with good reason.

This part of Texas started out as an extensive seabed under a shallow ocean where limestone built up over the eons. Most of the rock is from the lower Cretaceous period, toward the end of the age of dinosaurs, while some of the underlying rock above and west of Austin is much older. (Those of us who know little of geology but studied dinosaurs incessantly as kids tend to overuse the age of dinosaurs—the Mesozoic—as a reference point!) It is thought that Central Texas was uplifted in more recent times, creating the Edwards Plateau, with an elevation of around 2,000 feet. Additionally, the area to the southeast sank along a fault line, leaving the southern and eastern edges of the plateau raised fairly abruptly from the surrounding land. The many rivers and creeks then began to do their work, eroding the edges of the plateau and creating canyons and hills. Thus the eastern and southeastern parts of the Edwards Plateau are known as the Hill Country.

In the canyonlands and hills of the Edwards Plateau, shallow soils and rocky slopes are often dotted with live oak and juniper (or "cedar"). In places, the juniper grows in thick stands known as "cedar breaks," in which dense stands of Ashe juniper grow out of thin soil and broken limestone. Narrow canyons may be dominated by oak trees, with cliffs that have numerous seeps and small springs fringed with maidenhair fern. The cool, clear water trickles down to shaded creeks with clear pools, so that a walk in these places is like a visit to a miniature paradise. Among the amphibians found in the Hill Country are the cliff chirping frog and the barking frog. In Texas these two species can be found only in the oak-juniper woodlands and rocky outcrops in parts of the Edwards Plateau and westward into a few areas of the Trans-Pecos. Living in the various springs and caves of the Hill Country are various kinds of lungless salamanders, some found in only one locality like Barton Springs or Georgetown.[1] Because of their dependence on specific small localities, they depend on water quality and uninterrupted spring flow in places where growing cities may place the health of those springs at risk. Among reptiles, the beautiful Baird's ratsnake is found in wooded canyons in the southern and western Hill Country and into the mountains in the Big Bend country. The Texas alligator lizard follows a somewhat similar distribution.

West of the Hill Country the plateau is dominated by grasslands and scattered woodlands on a fairly flat landscape. Eventually, with more arid conditions and little soil, the gravelly ground supports fewer trees and more succulents. Where the plateau reaches the Pecos River, the plant communities give way to those of the Chihuahuan Desert, with such plants as sotol, yucca, and creosote. Here amphibians must be able to stay sheltered underground or in burrows for long periods and be ready to take full advantage of rains when they come. Reptiles include heat-tolerant, diurnal lizards such as whiptails, earless lizards, spiny lizards, and—in places—horned lizards. Some snakes are similarly heat tolerant and active during all but the hottest parts of the day, such as the western coachwhip, the Central Texas whipsnake, and the Texas patch-nosed snake. Others make use of crevices and burrows to escape the daytime heat of the summer and emerge mostly at night. These include the western diamond-backed rattlesnake, the western ratsnake, the Great Plains ratsnake, and others.

Austin's Barton Creek Greenbelt / SMITH

The Colorado River runs through the city of Austin, and Barton Creek is one of the waterways that drains into that river. The creek meanders through a woodland with oaks and junipers and in many places flows past gray limestone cliffs and large boulders. It has been set aside by the city as a greenbelt, with hiking trails that run alongside the creek. The city loves the Barton Creek Greenbelt, and it has the joggers and bikers to prove it. In spite of all this human traffic, the greenbelt is home to a number of reptile and amphibian species, including the most beautiful gartersnake in Texas and the arboreal Texas alligator lizard. So what better place could there be for spending the first day of spring?

Clint and I sat on the hillside, looking down at the weekend joggers and bicyclists on the trail below. They were enjoying the spring sunshine just as we were, and it seemed that Austin could use eighty miles of greenbelt along Barton Creek rather than just under eight, judging by the popularity of the

Rocky slopes above Barton Creek

place. However, the herps seem to coexist with the greenbelt's joggers and cyclists pretty well.

The Texas alligator lizard manages to coexist with people by living on rocky outcrops or in the lower branches of trees, out of sight and so well camouflaged that hardly anyone sees it. This is actually one of the largest lizards in Texas, with a snout-to-vent length of nearly eight inches and a long tail that can stretch its total length to nearly twenty inches. Several years ago in this spot Clint captured and photographed an adult male whose snout touched the tip of his middle finger and whose tail tip curled around the base of his elbow. Alligator lizards are long and fairly slender, with long snouts and small legs. The scales along the back are rectangular, and the pattern is light brown or tan with scattered lighter and darker scales that can suggest bands running across the back. This species is unique among Texas lizards in that it possesses a prehensile tail. Alligator lizards are the sloths of the reptile world, extremely slow-moving and prone to spending hours on end lying in the same spot in dappled sunlight draped along a branch. When stalking the insects that make up much of their diet, they move deliberately and slowly and then capture the unsuspecting arthropod with a quick strike. Texas alligator lizards are generally found in rocky, wooded canyons along the Balcones Escarpment and in the Chisos Mountains of the Big Bend. While females of many kinds of lizards lay a clutch of eggs and go on their way, mother alligator lizards stay with their eggs until hatching (after that, apparently, the kids are on their own).

We wandered among the trees near the limestone cliffs and outcrops, trying to examine each branch for a telltale patch of scales that would give away the presence of one of these lizards. And, alternately, we scanned the ground for gartersnakes. Looking up in the trees and then down, we might have looked like birders who could not decide if they wanted to go herping instead, although the species we hoped to see in the trees was reptilian, not avian. The Ashe juniper is very common here, with its brown trunks, branches with long strips of peeling bark, and scratchy evergreen foliage. The oaks were developing leaves, but other midstory to understory shrubs had leafy branches that shaded the ground. Scores of busy bees and butterflies took advantage of the newly blossomed flowers, and small birds twittered among the sunlight-dappled branches.

Within the first half hour, scanning along a series of rocks, I spotted a familiar pattern in the leaves. Just at the edge of a sheltering rock was an eastern black-necked gartersnake poking around near a crevice that extended back into the sheltering ground. Amid the various tones of brown and yellow in the leaves and twigs, it did not stand out dramatically. In fact, it would have been surprisingly easy to walk by that fluorescent orange stripe. As is often the case on these trips, I worked on zooming in for a photo while Clint circled around to see if he could temporarily capture the snake for a more close-up view.

"I got it," I exclaimed. It was a good thing, because as soon as the shutter snapped, immortalizing the serpent, the reptile spooked and retreated back into the inaccessible confines of its labyrinth. Clint would have to wait until later to get his hands on one of these beautifully striped and spotted snakes. They are endemic to the Edwards Plateau, meaning that the subspecies is found only in that area. This gartersnake spends its days searching around seeps, rock crevices, and other spots to find the small frogs and salamanders that it feeds on. Creek corridors such as this one are ideal places to find this beautiful reptile.

Thrilled to have found one of the species that we had particularly hoped to see, we continued on, flipping choice rocks and logs and stopping every few seconds to peer into the thick network of vines and branches in hopes of seeing an alligator lizard. Clint worked the hillside while I followed the nearly dry creek bed upstream where it widened out and large boulders were jumbled amid small pools of water. Such places offer shelter at the base of the rocks and basking spots higher up, while the currents around the boulders during times of high water may scoop out deeper pools in the limestone

Juvenile eastern black-necked gartersnake, Barton Creek Greenbelt

gravel. After searching some of these areas, I climbed onto a boulder to take a couple of photos from that vantage point.

Later Clint told me about being on a nearby hillside and hearing what he described as "the familiar crack of herper-on-rock." What had happened was this: I was attempting to jump from one boulder to another, forgetting that such acrobatics are best left to younger and more daredevil herpers. I smacked into the boulder and got a nice patch of scraped, bleeding skin across one cheek, and my glasses were flattened. I only wanted to see that the camera was okay, and since it was fine, I limped on with no worries. It was a small price to pay for being in the field.

After we met up and moved on down the trail, Clint thought about poking some fun at my lack of coordination, but Mother Nature made him eat his words before he had a chance to spit them out. A pile of loose limestone gave way, and he dropped, banging his left hip against a protruding rock. We were now two beat-up herpers, trying to scan the branches and the rock crevices as if nothing had happened, making our way down the trail while showing as little limping as possible and pretending to be invincible twenty-year-olds.

We made our way back downhill, where we followed Barton Creek along its dry bed. Only a few pools bore any water to speak of, but these were being taken full advantage of by numerous Blanchard's cricket frogs and leopard frogs. We came across a large female red-striped ribbonsnake, which may be the most commonly found serpent in the area. Usually a high-strung, nervous species that is hard to catch and even harder to photograph, this specimen posed like a model as I took several pictures. She was so big and beautiful that I could not be satisfied until I had the snake in hand, but she did not sit passively while being grabbed. The heavy smell of victory hung in the cool spring air in the form of fragrant ribbonsnake musk as I looked her over, felt the strong, slender loops of her body, and then let her go.

Over the next hour we combed the vegetation at poolside as people waded and picnicked, unaware of the reptiles and amphibians just footsteps away. We found six more ribbonsnakes as well as an adult eastern yellow-bellied racer that was rendered slow enough to catch by a large meal it had recently consumed. We photographed the racer, joking that the meal in its stomach was probably our alligator lizard.

On the way back to the car, we stopped occasionally to check out a nice-looking pile of rocks or a clump of brambles that might harbor some other scaly gem. Around 4:00 p.m., this paid off handsomely. Clint spotted a small male gartersnake head poking up through the leaf litter. As we approached a little closer, he withdrew his head and was completely hidden. Clint moved in from one direction and I from another, and Clint reached into the leaves and said "got it!" We carefully extracted him, taking our time so as not to hurt him, and took a close look. The top of his head was a bluish slate gray, and the second-to-last upper labial (lip) scale was smudged in light blue, contrasting with the other white labials edged in black. Down the back was a bright orange stripe and to either side an olive background (with the keels of the scales very dark, creating an almost pinstripe texture). The side stripes were cream-colored, and starting on the neck a series of large black spots interrupted the olive ground color. Farther back, the spots became smaller and somewhat fused with each other, so that what might have been a typical garter snake checkerboard was instead a zigzag of black, gradually taking over and becoming a black ground color against which the orange and cream stripes stood out. He was a magnificent jewel of the Hill Country! A group of curious onlookers gathered behind us with the typical herp-related questions. These folks seemed genuinely interested in this snake, and no one expressed fear or suggested that we kill it, which was reassuring. Soon after this, we were forced to call it a day. Of course, there was still the matter of the elusive alligator lizard, but the lack of its presence opened up a new possibility for yet another trip to the greenbelt. After all, what better place to spend the last field trip of the fall!

The Barton Creek Greenbelt still gets a lot of loving from the people of Austin, and the trails are sometimes crowded. We suppose the herps are still managing to get by, despite the number of people walking through their living room, so to speak. Additionally, the place has a reputation for alligator lizards and black-necked gartersnakes, as described earlier, and that can lead some herpers to visit the place in order to collect. We hope that readers will use good judgment when visiting the greenbelt and other places—especially small, protected places where lots of people go.

Return to the greenbelt / KING

It was a cool, yet sunny day in October of 2012. A recent flurry of much-needed storms had passed through the area the day before, dampening the ground just enough to possibly coax out some reptiles. Lo and behold, my wife, Amber, and I were stuck in Austin traffic on Interstate 35—and on a Monday, no less.

I saw the exit for Barton Creek and that was all it took. True, it was only two hours before sundown, but the weather was perfect; Michael and I had failed to turn up a single alligator lizard the previous March, and this fact ground deep under my flesh like a bothersome splinter. Resistance to the temptation to give it another go proved futile, and a half hour later found us walking the trails that wound through the small canyons along Barton Creek.

Just off the trail in a pile of deadfall my eyes picked out a pattern that was a little too bold to be just another drought-dried stick, and I reached down and plucked up a perfect little neonate eastern hog-nosed snake. These are one of my favorite snakes, and it had been almost fifteen years since I had found a juvenile. The brazen little harmless showboat, barely six inches long, instantly fanned out its neck like a miniature cobra in my fingers, and when that trick didn't work in its favor, it rolled over "dead" in my palm. Snapping photos, I placed the snake on the ground and tried to right it with my finger, but no matter how many times I rolled it over, it would flip back onto its back, the tiny black tongue hanging limply from the corner of its mouth. Eventually I had to play the waiting game for a photograph of the snake turned right side up, but in all truth the antics of these comical little snakes always bring out the kid in me, and I have yet to come across a single specimen that I could resist pestering enough to get it to put on a rerun of the same great show.

I left the little beauty to resume its search for toads and headed back down the trail a much happier herper. We found a little brown skink and a couple of Gulf Coast toads, no doubt hiding from the hungry hognoses beneath chunks of loose limestone, and then my eyes fell upon a small Texas spiny lizard that was basking on a fallen log in a patch of dappled sunlight. Moving in for a closer shot with my camera in hand, I crouched down as close as the lizard would allow, and as I did, something once again caught the corner of my eye that seemed slightly out of place on the forest floor. On the same log,

Texas alligator lizard, Barton Creek Greenbelt

tucked neatly beneath a tangle of broken branches, the cream-colored zig-zag pattern of a Texas alligator lizard materialized. I turned slowly, ever so cautiously, so as to not disturb the lizard, and snapped a single photograph. But there was a twig in the field of the lens that obstructed the reptile's head. When I tried to push it to the side, the alligator lizard spooked and dove into the tangled maze of brush, out of sight and out of reach.

I scanned the underbrush and surrounding rock outcrops for the better part of an hour in an effort to find a second alligator lizard, but came up with only a few more Texas spiny lizards. Then, just when I had almost reached the trail's end, a particular pile of brush shone like some divine golden hope in a sun-bathed glen to my right. I stepped from the trail and braved my way through the ranks of relentless greenbrier until I stood in front of the pile in the clearing. A large fallen juniper tree was sandwiched in the midst of the brush, and on a snag of broken branch from this tree sat an enormous Texas alligator lizard, basking silently in the final glowing rays of dusk. My heart shot up into my throat like an elevator gone haywire.

The lizard must have fancied itself well camouflaged, for it sat still for the better part of ten minutes as I got shot after incredible shot. "I hope you're happy now," I heard Amber say as we watched the beautiful prehensile-tailed lacertilian creep back down into the deadfall. "You got your precious alligator lizard, even if it did take a year to do it."

A day at Colorado Bend State Park / KING

It is better to see something once than to hear about it a thousand times.
—*from a trailside bench at Gorman Falls*

The day was balmy and overcast as we turned off the highway following the state park signs that led to Colorado Bend, but I was bound and determined not to let the morning's dreary frown dampen my explorer's spirit. Amber and I had home-brewed our own mini Hill Country vacation package several nights earlier and had declared the third Friday in April ours, come rain or shine. We were going to celebrate it Texas-style, with some afternoon hiking and herping followed by a good dose of Texas barbecue and a Willie Nelson concert that evening on the banks of the Guadalupe River in New Braunfels. The front door of the Texas Hill Country is located about three hours south and slightly west of my house, where scenic US Highway 281 sprouts from Interstate 20 west of the Brazos River. This slower-paced winding byway is the sensible and leisurely alternative to the construction-crippled nightmare that is Interstate 35. We packed last-minute and light (camera, sunscreen, and bug repellent seemed sufficient) and were out the door by eight.

Colorado Bend State Park opened to the public in 1987 and provides a hearty welcome to the splendor of the Hill Country experience from the moment you arrive. Below the park's 5,328 acres is a karst formation, a geological wonder made up of an underground network of caves, sinkholes, and subterranean springs. The porous rock contains fragile ecosystems and the myriad organisms that call these places home. On the surface the sluggish Colorado River etches a gentle course through high-walled canyons adorned in live oak and Ashe juniper. The river feeds Lake Buchanan ten miles to the south and provides some of the state's most renowned white bass fishing during the season. Spelunkers travel here on their own annual pilgrimage to explore the mysterious caves on guided tours, and birders flock to the park with their eyes to the skies in hopes of spotting a black-capped vireo or, if they're exceptionally lucky, a golden-cheeked warbler.

But we were after reptilian payout, and while the place was new to both of us, I had ferreted out a few good spots from my friend Ryan Blankenship, who did his internship here. I was particularly eager to turn up an example of the park's resident eastern black-tailed rattlesnake population. Although these snakes are a more common find in the mountain ranges of the Trans-Pecos, I was delighted to learn that they occupy space here at the eastern end of the Edwards Plateau as well.

By the time we had driven the six miles of park road to the pay station, the intense spring sun managed to bore its way through the thick cloud cover, and the wild things were responding accordingly. An assortment of brush-footed butterflies mingled along the muddy edges of rainwater collected on the trail to Spicewood Springs, their long thin tongues unfurled, probing for moisture. Eastern black and pipevine swallowtails hovered among the flowers like small iridescent kites at low wind.

I had never seen such a congregation of buckeyes, painted ladies, red admirals, and sleepy orange sulphurs. They flitted everywhere, bursting out of the wake of our invasive hiking boots, erupting from blossoms of paintbrushes in brief clouds of abstract, vibrant color. Mockingbirds began to tune up with the emerging warmth, playing a diverse medley of the local birdsong in an erratic, fast-paced chain. To our left the river whispered, its banks masked by a virtual field of six-foot-high ragweed, their flowering tops pungent in the humid air. Up the hill to our right two white-tailed deer grazed on with all the indifference of wild animals that live in close proximity to man, seeming to know they were protected here. We hiked a mile or so down the Spicewood Springs Trail to the springs, where clear groundwater bubbled up to the surface to flow over white rocks and collect in transparent pools tainted green with algae. Just beneath the surface, the algae waved in thick strands that seemed to float hypnotically like the hair of some witch confined to a watery grave of unspeakable beauty.

Amber was the first to spy a herp, a six-lined racerunner. These skittish little lizards seem to suffer from hyperactivity, constantly poking here and scratching there, their sharp eyes darting in a never-ending race with their flicking tongues. Luckily it was still cool enough for the lizard to be unusually calm, or at least enough so that I was able to get a few good pictures. While I was busying myself with the yet unmastered art of racerunner photography, Amber turned up a second herp, a Blanchard's cricket frog. Agile little amphibians that seem to make use of every inch of permanent and semipermanent water in the eastern two-thirds of the state, this particular individual seemed by chance to have inherited prime real estate at Spicewood Springs.

Never to be outdone, I holstered the camera and began to conduct my own search for something scaly as a pair of hikers shed their footwear beside us in preparation for a cold dip in the springs. It didn't take long to turn up a small assembly of native lizards that had gathered around the base of a couple of live oaks. A pair of Texas spiny lizards showed their territorial dominance over a single ornate tree lizard that hugged the tree trunk just below them. In the fine carpet of last fall's crisp, elongated tan leaves a little brown skink made a brief appearance as its snakelike bronze form passed amid the detritus.

Texas spiny lizard

As the sunlight began to break the clouds into disorganized, fleeing huddles, we backtracked our way from the springs in favor of a two-mile loop carved out along the borders of a great grove of Ashe juniper on the park's eastern edge. The Cedar Chopper Loop trail starts out in a relatively flat, rock-studded meadow dotted with a generous mixture of evergreen, live oak, and mesquite. Here, by gently turning the rocks, I quickly uncovered several variable groundsnakes as well as the freshly cast skin of an adult Great Plains ratsnake, a large *Scolopendra* centipede, and some of the biggest and baddest examples of bark scorpion I have ever seen. Plains bristlegrass overlooked smaller patches of yellow star grass, the familiar canary-colored petals of the latter unfurled and attracting skippers as well as the more plentiful buckeyes. An unusual purple bloom close to the ground caught my eye, and I was delighted to find it attached to a horse crippler cactus. The scene got even better upon closer inspection, and I photographed a bee assassin bug dining on a buprestid beetle inside the flower. Assassin bugs are efficient predators of flower-visiting insects. Armed with a hollow proboscis that serves as both a puncture wound delivery system and vacuum, these well-camouflaged flower residents are the epitome of ambush predation.

The trail narrowed, winding its way into the thick cedar breaks that grow uphill from the river. Here broken jumbles of immovable gray rock lay in cracked piles. Hopelessly tangled stacks of fallen dried juniper branches lay here and there, and as the afternoon sunlight fell in random scattered patches over the needle- and leaf-strewn ground, I found it easy to believe a black-tailed rattler could call this habitat home. I kept my eyes peeled for the telltale cream-colored diagonal barring of a basking alligator lizard as well, as they are quite fond of both cool days and dried juniper piles, but both species would prove too elusive.

Unfortunately, our time was running short. Looking for these two well-camouflaged species demands careful scrutiny of the habitat, and this had whittled the afternoon away all too quickly. We decided to spend what time we had left at the park exploring the popular Gorman Falls Trail.

Gorman Falls is one of Texas' largest and best-known waterfalls. Here spring water carries a great deal of dissolved limestone from the bedrock. This water is very rich in calcite, and it provides the necessary ingredients to support a variety of aquatic plant life. Calcium carbonate deposits form a soft rock called travertine, which is easily crushed underfoot. This makes for a very fragile ecosystem, and thus the sixty-five-foot falls are blocked off from human access via posted signs and trail ropes.

As we rounded the bend, we bypassed a group of middle-aged hikers like ourselves taking a rest on a shaded rocky outcrop at trailside. Why did they look so weary? The trail was only a little more than a mile long. We should have known something was up when the trail map described this trail as "Challenging, 3 hours." As the trail gradually dropped through the scattered oaks and junipers on rocky ridges, I began to notice the ever-rising cliff wall to my right. Then the path literally broke away beneath our feet in a series of large, jumbled rocks. The trail dropped the last thirty feet to the pristine, fern-laced pool that briefly contained the spill from the falls at the bottom. So this was what they meant by "challenging." The final steps! We descended the tricky natural staircase of shelf rock, its surface worn dangerously smooth by years of calcium-rich moisture and foot traffic. My ears began to pick up a faint trickle, and Amber began tugging at my shirtsleeve. I followed her gaze fixed toward the source of the sound. The magnificence of the waterfall materialized in my field of vision where just a second ago it had been hidden behind a palette of greenery. My eyes required a moment of readjustment before I could take in this scene in its entirety. Age-old hardwoods stood tall in front of jutting, dark gray rocks stroked artfully with the subtle lime-green tones of moss. Over this flowed an oddly quiet whisper of fast-paced spring water that turned to droplets so fine just above its surface that a mystical fog seemed to hang over the falls even as the water plummeted some twenty yards to the pool below. Cascades of clear water seemed to shoot from the moss itself, giving the illusion of a hundred tiny falls within one large one.

Gorman Falls, Colorado Bend State Park

This fantastical scene was so enchanting that for a moment I felt as if I were staring into some still-life painting that had suddenly come to life. Amber summed it up in two words: "It's beautiful." I could only nod my head in agreement. I could understand why the park was so adamant about preserving it, a true oasis of tranquility and natural perfection.

After admiring Gorman Falls for an unknown span of time that could have been minutes or hours, I began walking a primitive trail that ran parallel to the banks of the Colorado River. Insects hummed, buzzed, and trundled over tree trunks and fallen logs in the thick riparian vegetation. I am easily intrigued by these tiny organisms that constitute the most populous group on our planet. I admired bluet damselflies, shield bugs, and a tiny caterpillar suspended from a silken strand that resembled an elaborate thorny sculpture. But my attention quickly shifted to a Texas map turtle sunning itself on a rock in the middle of the river. Map turtles are fond of basking on sun-exposed rocks or logs. Somewhat more oval in body shape than the more familiar sliders and cooters they share their habitat with, they are easily startled animals, ready to scuttle from the rock and drop into the current seconds after being discovered. Map turtles are so named for the markings on the carapace of younger and lighter-colored individuals, which with a bit of imagination can resemble contour lines on a map. As a rule, adults are smaller than most sliders and cooters, and there is at least a slight ridge or series of knobs running down the center of the carapace.

Texas map turtle

This specimen was lying in full sun with legs and neck extended, its beaked head masked in pleasant stripes of vivid yellow on a background of greenish black. Its eyes were closed, and I could have sworn it wore a look of reptilian bliss on its face. I snapped several voucher shots from bankside just in case the turtle bolted, as I was sure it would. A series of flat, watermelon-size boulders formed a natural set of stepping stones out to where the turtle basked. I eased along with great caution, gaining ground two feet at a time. With no small amount of stretching I balanced precariously on the last rock, mere feet from the turtle. It had finally opened its eyes and was wearing a befuddled look not unlike the one I've been known to get after being abruptly awakened from an afternoon nap. In disbelief I ducked down and got several good closeup shots before the creature seemed to suddenly recollect the proper flight response when approached by large bipedal mammals. In a blur of green legs it shot across the rock and plunged into the river. I sat there for a while on the riverbank, watching a small plain-bellied watersnake as it sat still as an exposed root in the shallows, waiting for a mosquitofish or cricket frog to chance by. For a brief moment in time I became lost in the essence of the river—the rocks and birdsong and vigorous green spring energy, bulging at the very seams with countless organisms eager for the arrival of summer.

My wife's voice broke through my surreal daydream, and I knew it was time to go. The day had come full circle, climaxed, and now there was only the long dreaded drive home with a head full of fresh memories whose high would be slow to dissipate. Oh, wait! We still had an evening of the soulful

Western ratsnake, glaring defensively from up in the branches

serenading that is Willie Nelson to enjoy! As I turned the truck southbound from the park road, a western ratsnake almost five feet in length slipped from the road into the grama grass like a mirage. I parked to watch it ascend a small tree with amazing speed and agility, each belly scute seeming to grip low limbs and branches as if by memory. And thus a gorgeous spring day in the Hill Country began to wind down as we headed south down 281 through Lampasas and Marble Falls, with the wind blowing our hair and the fields of bluebonnets and paintbrushes that are the signature of this land seeming to sway back and forth in a trancelike ballet. I tried to hold on to the moment, but it began to fade as the sun set over the hills to the west. I found myself thinking of how great it felt to live in the state of Texas. It is a state I love; the place I am proud to call home, a land borne and formed and established on the same spirit of diversity that its ecoregions echo. I thought of a million worlds at my doorstep.

An untimely and undignified end for an ornate box turtle / SMITH

In 2002 I participated in the Dallas–Fort Worth Herpetological Society's first field trip to the Trans-Pecos. I drove there with Steve Campbell, and our route took us through the western part of the Edwards Plateau. Somewhere north of San Angelo, we came across an ornate box turtle that had been run over on the highway. We stopped and examined this unfortunate turtle.

Sometimes we take road-killed specimens so they can be preserved and added to a university's scientific collection; much can be learned about animals in this way. If you look at a map showing university records of where specimens have been taken, high densities of dots (representing many specimens) suggest more abundant populations, although to some extent it can show where people have been looking most often. Fewer dots suggest that the species is found there, but it may be less common. Preferred habitats can be suggested by such records. Have they mostly been collected from areas where there is woodland? Desert? Near water? Collection records can be very useful, and taking a road-killed specimen makes an animal's death less of a waste. Perhaps collecting "dead on road" (DOR) specimens means that there is less need for taking live specimens out of the population.

We were naively optimistic, scooping this smashed turtle into a plastic bag at the beginning of several days in the field. Keeping roadkill from decomposing is not the ideal use for an ice chest, and if it is used in this way, some method has to be devised to keep the specimens separate from the snacks. But nevertheless we bagged the turtle.

We certainly needed more information about how box turtles were doing in the wild. Because they reproduce slowly and in small numbers, box turtle populations depend on the individual adults living for a long time. These turtles lay a limited number of eggs each year, and predators dig up many of their nests. Once hatched, box turtles are easy prey for crows, skunks, some snakes, and many other animals. Their mortality is very high (one researcher who was working on repopulating box turtles in east Texas remarked in frustration that releasing baby turtles was little more than "feeding the crows"). Only after several years does the box turtle's size and shell hardness offer much protection. Sexual maturity may depend on size as much as age, but they are generally not reproductive until they are more than five or six years old. Only by living to a very old age can these turtles produce enough clutches of eggs to keep the population going.[2]

Living to an old age is more and more problematic for box turtles. They wander onto roads where they are likely to get hit by cars, like the one we found. New roads increasingly fragment habitat, which increases the likelihood that resident box turtles will be hit. They used to be collected in large numbers for the pet market, although in recent years the Texas Parks and Wildlife Department's nongame regulations prohibit the commercial trade in wild box turtles in Texas. The extent to which pesticides and other pollutants impact these turtles is not clear. It is likely that periodic drought and climate change could harm them in parts of their range. Not only might they lose habitat or die of dehydration during droughts; their sex ratios might become skewed with higher average temperatures. The sex of a baby turtle is generally not determined by chromosomes; rather, the incubation temperature triggers development as male or female. For many of our North American turtles, higher incubation temperatures mean more females. If populations experience shortages of males, less reproduction might occur.

A common observation by Texas naturalists and people who live in more rural areas is that box turtles are becoming less common. I remember that driving in the country after a spring rain used to mean dozens of observations of box turtles, but that was about forty years ago. In more recent years, seeing even one or two box turtles on a trip seems remarkable, at least in many parts of Texas. Their apparent decline should be mourned, as these are inoffensive, often beautiful, fascinating turtles that eat many insects and all kinds of other material, including carrion. Ornate box turtles tend to dig through cattle dung to find grubs and insects. In captivity, they are visually attentive creatures that will recognize their keeper and quickly approach him or her to be fed.

The unfortunate turtle that we salvaged from the road was put in the ice chest but did not stay there. The next day at sunset we drove a considerable distance, looking for herps. At some point during our drive, I noticed an unpleasant smell but had no idea what it might be. Steve said nothing. A few more miles down the road, and there it was again, but still Steve said nothing when I asked about it. I began to wonder if there might be some problem with Steve's hygiene. I rolled the window down for a bit, and it would help temporarily, but then I would catch another unwholesome whiff. Steve continued to be clueless. Finally, after we had stopped for some animal, it occurred to me to look under the seat. There in that plastic bag was our poor box turtle, now seriously decomposing. While Steve placed high value on contributing to science, he also placed a high value on a good prank.

The Central Texas whipsnake that almost got away / KING

I was in Mason County, in the western part of the Edwards Plateau, with some members of the Horned Lizard Conservation Society and the Dallas–Fort Worth Herpetological Society as well as staff from the Texas Parks and Wildlife Department. Since the previous evening, we had been on the Blue Mountain Peak Ranch, coping with late August's unbearably hot daytime temperatures and trying to find horned lizards and any other reptiles and amphibians that came our way. This was rocky country, with rolling hills composed of limestone and thin soils. Mesquite and prickly pear were common, along with small stands of live oak in places.

As we cut across a savannah where patches of bluestem grasses grew amid clusters of mesquite trees, I had noticed a rock wall off to our right. On sunny, mild mornings snakes often frequent rock piles, where they lie on the sun-warmed rocks to thermoregulate in close proximity to easily accessible shelter. Here they find the added benefit of plentiful prey. I abandoned the vehicle and walked over to the rock wall, my eyes scanning the ground and rocks.

The satiny black pattern of a Central Texas whipsnake materialized as a blur in the heat-withered yellow grass that surrounded the rock wall. I had been wanting to get pictures of this lightning-fast, diurnal predator of mice and lizards for many years, and while I had found my fair share of them, getting my hands on a live one had been a different matter. I saw my chance here and now though, as the four-foot-long colubrid made for the safety of the rock wall and did the trademark whipsnake disappearing act on me. I called out to Ryan Blankenship, my partner in crime, in the traditional form and dialect: "Snake!"

Ryan sprang into action, and we began making short work of a sizable section of the rock wall. In no time we had reduced it to a disarrayed pile of limestone rubble. Only a single flat slab lay at the bottom. "Okay, it has to be under this one!" I announced the obvious. With team effort we overturned the final stone, which was massive, and I prepared to make the split-second crucial grab. A state of confusion fell over me as the rock was flipped, only to discover nothing beneath it but a few harvestmen scurrying from the sudden flood of sunlight. A grass-lined mouse nest lay at the center of this mandala, and comprehension fell on me. The whipsnake had escaped once again. As I dug through the mouse nest, I heard Ryan behind me yell, "There it is!" Spinning on my heels, I followed his extended finger to a patch of dried hackberry leaves, where the large-eyed, almost avian head of the whipsnake protruded with what looked like a proud smile on its face.

I made the grab and was successful. Apparently the mouse burrow had an escape exit, because we had to pull the serpent out six inches at a time as it forced its body against the tight inner walls of the hole. Finally it came free, and the thrashing creature was extracted from the hole and secured at mid-body with my free hand.

The Central Texas whipsnake is a common denizen of the western two-thirds of Texas, but it is most often seen in the hill country south of Austin. Its close cousin, the Schott's whipsnake, occurs from San Antonio south to the Rio Grande Valley, where it is replaced by the Ruthven's whipsnake as the thorn scrub gives way to what remains of the subtropical sabal palm habitat around Brownsville. All are diurnal, heat-tolerant reptiles whose high metabolism and rope-thin, wiry bodies demand that they chase down plenty of rodents, lizards, and smaller snakes to eat in order to survive. Usually the closest encounter that naturalists get is a blur of striped dark and light contrasting scales as the snake seems to disappear before their very eyes. But this one was interrupted midway through its disappearing act, and as a result we were able to take pictures of this amazingly athletic, slender serpent. We then released it back near the stone wall to nurse its injured pride.

6 The Cross Timbers

ACROSS MUCH OF NORTH TEXAS, as you travel from west to east, the scenery changes from flat or rolling open plains to an area with belts of trees and open patches of grassland south and east of the town of Bowie. Essentially this part of Texas was a series of geological ripples running north to south, with sandy or gravelly soils supporting oak woodland and black soils supporting prairie. The trees are dominated by post oak and blackjack oak, rather small to medium-size trees that often have crooked branches and large-lobed, rounded leaves. They are able to thrive in the reddish, sandy soils and relatively dry climate of the area. Farther east, around Fort Worth, the trees largely give way to prairie, or at least that was true before this part of Texas became so developed. A large part of the Grand Prairie has become a series of cities, highways, some pastureland, and more cities and towns, although patches of the original landscape remain, mostly north and west of the Dallas–Fort Worth area. As we head still farther eastward, near Dallas, we begin to enter another area that was once oak woodlands and open fields. There are remnants and preserved pieces of what is called the western and eastern Cross Timbers. Some of these places are tucked away behind fences as private ranchland, but there are a few publicly accessible places.

Both of us grew up in the Cross Timbers, and our stories and experiences tend to focus on the areas around the western Cross Timbers and the prairies just southeast of there. This chapter is concerned with the oak woodlands and prairies that stretch from Montague County southwest through Wise County and parts of Jack and Parker Counties, and on toward the southwest to Erath and Brown Counties.

Three nights on the LBJ National Grasslands / KING

The Lyndon B. Johnson National Grasslands comprises more than 20,250 acres of mixed grasslands and woodland, with several intermittent streams and small ponds as well as four larger impoundments of 30 acres or less.[1] It is a patchwork of units scattered among private horse pastures and homesteads,

LBJ National Grasslands

but there are places where a hiker can walk considerable distances without crossing roads or seeing houses. The soil is sandy and easily eroded, and in some places steep arroyos trace across the savannah like tiny canyons. While post oak may be a signature tree of the Cross Timbers, there are junipers, bois d'arc, and scattered thickets of sumac and little plum trees. Among the oaks, thick patches of greenbrier often grow, ready to trip unwary hikers and scratch their arms and legs.

Night one

I watched through the window of my truck as an immense gray mass of storm clouds began to pile up in the evening sky to the northwest. The barometric pressure was dropping slowly and steadily, and I was counting on this for a successful night of road-cruising through the grasslands. It was mid-May of 2006, and the oncoming storm signaled an end to a four-month-long drought that North Texas had been suffering. If my calculations were right, the storm would pass to the north by fifteen to twenty miles, and the area I planned on cruising would see no rain, only an increase in humidity and a drop in temperature.

I turned off on one of the many gravel Forest Service roads that weave through the center of the grasslands like the chaotic web of a black widow spider. I cruised along at a slow pace, eyes scanning ahead of me for any sign of movement. A few dead snakes that had been recently crushed by vehicular traffic were proof of the fact that the local drought-starved herpetofauna was at last on the move. The first was a huge adult western ratsnake that was being pulled to roadside postmortem by a hungry black crow. The lyrics of Ray Wylie Hubbard instantly came to mind: "Even crows act like eagles when they find a dying snake." With feathers ruffled and eyes outgrowing its stomach, the bird looked like quite the braggart as it pulled the five feet of dead ratsnake with confidence, pausing occasionally to back up and take a quick look around, as if to declare, "That's right, I slew the dragon," to any observer who might be watching. Meanwhile, the storm was showing definite signs of passing over to the north without giving a single drop of precipitation, so my hopes began to rise with the sinking of the sun.

As darkness approached, I drove down into a sandy hollow spot around Cottonwood Lake, a huge, shining black drop of fresh water bordered along its shores by wild, dense bands of greenbrier, grapevine, and poison ivy. No sooner had the sun disappeared than I spied a snake stretched out in rectilinear fashion in the middle of the dirt track. I pulled over and found it to be a young northern cottonmouth, out and about on an evening hunt in search of frogs. Unlike older, more mature examples of the species, young cottonmouths are adorned with an ornate pattern of wide, chestnut-brown and orange-tan broken bands that make them more closely resemble dark-colored copperheads than their own species. A dark diagonal stripe that extends behind the eye toward the chin helps to distinguish them from their upland cousins. This one looked up at me with its triangular head held high, tongue testing the air for any sign of danger. In me it would find none. Since the road was a seldom-traveled track, I left the snake to its own priorities and resumed my own search for snakes and frogs.

Minutes later the frogs and toads made themselves known, starting with the calls of Blanchard's cricket frogs, the most common amphibian denizens of Cottonwood Lake. Woodhouse's toads emerged onto the road to plop themselves comfortably in the sand like plump brown wads of dough, while frantic southern leopard frogs fled my penetrating headlights in long, gangly leaps. These, along with the cricket frogs, were typical of almost any night's drive in the area, even in periods of drought. In the past I had occasionally found more elusive frogs and toads. One of my favorites was the Hurter's spadefoot, a strange toad that spends over half of its life underground. I had found them only on three or four occasions. Each time, they had appeared in great numbers on cool nights after heavy thunderstorms had flooded out the fields on either side of the road. Tonight was too warm and dry, I feared.

In the midst of this sudden flurry of amphibian activity my eyes picked out yet another snake. I braked and jumped out, and the creature sensed the vibration of my feet on the sand and sped up toward the shelter of the grass. But I headed it off, and it paused and began vibrating its tail. The tiny rattles on the end were invisible as it buzzed a silent warning for me to take heed. This was the beautiful, rarely seen western pygmy rattlesnake, our smallest

Western pygmy rattlesnake

native rattler. At just over a foot in length, it was already an adult. I marveled at the luck of chancing upon this magnificent little serpent. It was a stunning specimen, freshly shed, with ebony rings and blotches bedecking the back and sides of its lavender-gray body, the face masked with the telltale black striping of its kind. After taking a few quick photographs, I stood at a distance and watched it crawl away at a leisurely pace, disappearing into the night.

I will never forget the first western pygmy rattlesnake I found. After years of unsuccessful attempts to find one, I used museum records and Werler and Dixon's field guide, *Texas Snakes*, to narrow my search to a few small spots. In 2007 I drove down a narrow strip of sandy road, eventually coming to a natural low-lying area bordered on the left by thick oak trees and on the right by open bluestem prairie. The temperature dropped with the elevation, and in a sharp bend in the road my headlights fell upon a large pond bordered by a thick wall of greenbrier. The habitat was prime, as the species requires loose, sandy soil with adequate permanent sources of moisture as well as dense undergrowth where it can bask, hide, and hunt the small frogs and lizards that make up the bulk of its diet. My wife and I found two pygmy rattlers, but both were dead, killed by passing cars or trucks. The next night I was back again, eager to end the hunt that had long ago turned into an unhealthy obsession. It took us only ten minutes. With the evening sun still peeking over the western horizon, I declared victory at last as I stopped for a western pygmy rattlesnake, and this one was alive. The snake sprang into a defensive coil, its tiny head twitching in tight spasms, a mysterious behavioral trait common to all members of the genus *Sistrurus* (pygmy and massasauga rattlesnakes). Its tiny rattle, barely audible or distinguishable from the taper of a nonvenomous snake's tail, whirred an almost comical warning for me not to tread on it because a rattlesnake is a rattlesnake, no matter how small. After taking some photos, the pygmy took off into the brush, its rattle still vibrating faintly as it angrily departed into the roadside grass.

Night two—following the river's tributaries

I turned onto a dirt road cutting through another familiar piece of territory that led to the far northwestern end of the grasslands. A growing storm was crowding out the unimaginably vibrant orange sunset. I was hoping that the grasslands and agricultural fields that would soon be converted into temporary floodplains would bring out the spadefoot toads.

The road dipped down into a low spot, the light drizzle of rain still falling just steadily enough to make windshield wipers necessary, adding to the obstructed visibility. But I still saw the snake. The cryptic pattern, which would have rendered it all but invisible among a pile of dead leaves and oak branches on the forest floor, made it stand out like bold print against the evening glare on the wet asphalt. I slammed the truck to a stop. It was another uncommon rattlesnake native to the grasslands, a timber rattlesnake (sometimes called a canebrake rattlesnake). It was a subadult around two feet long, with a pastel gray ground color broken by a line of ink-black chevrons that ran the length of the back. This pattern was split down the center by a thick, sepia-colored vertebral stripe. I followed the beautiful little crotalid as it slowly made its way to the fence line, taking photos from various angles. For a brief moment I paused, resting on my haunches, and watched the last inch of its tail disappear into the long green grass at the side of the tilled field. It was an encounter to remember, and I was ecstatic. With the little snake safe from the road, I climbed back into my truck just as a brisk wind began to pick up.

Five minutes later I came across the second timber rattlesnake. I couldn't believe this. Like the first, it was a subadult around two feet in length. Also, like the first, it was lying stretched to its full length in the roadway. I pulled over again, eager to get pictures of this surprise second specimen. When I got within a few feet, I could see that it was dead, though, and my heart sank. Although there were no abrasions or blood on the serpent, it had clearly

Adult timber rattlesnake

been hit. The black forked tongue hung from the corner of the mouth at an odd, lifeless angle, and a small troupe of straw-colored ants had congregated around the head. While this is the last scenario in which I want to encounter any herp, I took a single shot with the camera, still feeling like a winner for having found not one but two uncommon rattlesnake species over the course of two days.

The storms moved in not long after that, sending the temperature plummeting down to the sixties and subsequently driving the crepuscular snakes back to their shelters. This brought about an opposite response with the amphibians, however, and within a half hour, I could hear frogs vocalizing, their distinct calls mingling as the winds carried the sounds over the rain-soaked open fields. I rolled down the windows in spite of the downpour in an effort to single out each species' unique call. There was the sheep-like bleating of Woodhouse's toads, the bird-like chirps of gray treefrogs, and the shrill buzz of western narrow-mouthed toads, all blended together like some great amphibian symphony. I could almost envision Kermit himself conducting, his green Muppet arms flailing with the rise and fall of the music. But, alas, I heard no spadefoot toads. Eventually the calls reached the eardrums of their intended female audience, and they came hopping to the roadside. I began to pull over for each and every one, giving it a brief shine with the light from window side for identification. But each toad bore the telltale pale vertebral stripe of the abundant Woodhouse's toad. There were a few more interesting finds throughout the rest of the drive, although none were reptilian. Raccoons, armadillos, cottontail rabbits, and even a gray fox all came out to get a drink from the puddles of rainwater that had accumulated in the roadside ditches after the storm passed sometime after 9:00 p.m. By this point I was backtracking away from the grasslands, the herping over, at least until the next day.

Night three—Black Creek Lake

It was my last day on the LBJ National Grasslands, so I arrived as early as I could, a little after 4:30 p.m. The sky was balmy and overcast, with just enough sunshine peeking through the clouds to offer the false hope of the sky clearing up and drying everything out. I was hoping that the sunshine would also coax out some herps. I was planning on hitting a flooded field or two to see if any Hurter's spadefoot toads might be calling.

When I arrived at my first stop, I was pleased to see that the entire forty or so acres of grass that skirts the nearby mixed forest were under several inches of water. I left my vehicle in a parking space and walked back down into the field, following a deep ravine that I knew eventually made its way to a natural pond. The ravine was full of dead mesquite brush and overgrown with prickly pear cactus and dewberry brambles, and the recent rains had filled the first few inches of it with dark brown water, creating an excellent herp spot.

Sure enough, it didn't take long to spy the first snake. A small eastern yellow-bellied racer was lying motionless atop an exposed mesquite branch. Still bearing its juvenile pattern, white-bordered brown blotches and a scattering of dark freckles along the anterior portion of its body, the racer blended in perfectly in the brush pile. This common diurnal hunter of mice, lizards, and invertebrates is more often seen zipping across one of the grassland's network of gravel back roads, and I relished the opportunity to photograph one in this more natural setting. But in true racer fashion the wary little serpent detected my presence and slipped down into the brush maze, out of sight and out of reach.

A short time later I reached the pond, swelled beyond its banks up over the cattails and willows that it fed. I picked my way through these, my shoes soaked through, spooking several red-eared sliders and a yellow mud turtle and making them drop from their perches on floating logs. Scores of immature American bullfrogs made splashing leaps from bankside, each screaming their distress with a high-pitched "cheep!" A small plain-bellied watersnake that had no doubt been busy pursuing the little frogs darted underwater with a ripple, and minutes later a tiny diamond-backed watersnake slipped down the bank with a wriggle of mud-colored scales, stopping briefly in the embedded hoofprint of a deer before it shot into the pond.

I circled the pond all the way around while picking ripe black dewberries and tart wild plums and munching on these and scanning the lower willow branches for more snakes. Seeing nothing more, I headed back up the other side of the ravine. In a short while I happened upon a pair of discarded sheets of siding that had been washed down into the ditch from the roadside uphill, and I wasted no time flipping them over. The first uncovered a large Wood-house's toad that had dug itself a snug little bowl-shaped burrow in the moist soil beneath. The second revealed a huge western ribbonsnake, the biggest one I had ever seen. It was a full three feet in length and as big around as my thumb. I grabbed for it and was able to snap off a few photographs of this yellow- and orange-striped frog-hunting species; in the process I was rewarded with a hefty dose of musk, which superficially resembles the odor of a dirty sock stuffed with overripe fruit. That was okay, though, for it was the smell of victory!

In the flooded fields the second movement of the Great Grasslands Anu-ran Symphony resumed from where it had left off the previous night, with western narrow-mouthed and Woodhouse's toads and Blanchard's cricket frogs, all buzzing, bleating, and clacking. But there were no Hurter's spade-foots in the group, or at least none that I could hear. A half hour before dusk I made it back to the truck, muddy, wet, stinking of snake musk, and happy beyond all measure.

Although I failed to find a single spadefoot, it ended up being another memorable night on the grasslands. I found three more timber rattlesnakes—two dead on the road and a tiny juvenile less than a foot in length that was very much alive and willing to be scooted to the side of the road to safety. But eventually my time ran out, and I was forced to leave my beloved grasslands in the rearview mirror. As I turned the truck back onto FM 730, reluctantly headed south toward the city, I couldn't help but find myself longing for just one more day and night out there in the vast, peaceful sea of little bluestem grass, the storm clouds overhead mingling with a warm, gentle May sun.

Timber rattlesnakes on the LBJ National Grasslands / KING

Many Texas field herpers are aware that timber rattlesnakes live in the Piney Woods of East Texas, but few herpers think of the woodlands and savannahs in the north-central part of the state as prime habitat also. Yet they are there if you only know where to look for them. Timber rattlers are habitat specialists, and a typical excursion to the Cross Timbers will almost

Timber rattlesnake, Wise County

certainly fail to produce one unless the field herper takes the time to go habitat-hunting.

As a young boy I had the good fortune of growing up on the fringe of the grasslands, and it was equally fortunate that I encountered this state-protected crotalid at the age of twelve. The snake was a tiny neonate, under a foot in length, swallowing a road-killed mouse beside a bridge overlooking the Trinity River on a miserably wet, humid day in late August. I was taken aback at its presence here, where I had somehow overlooked its occurrence in my field guides. And yet there it was. Over the next sixteen years I learned the art of finding them and as a result found many additional specimens.

Whenever I wanted to find timber rattlesnakes, the first rule was to follow the Trinity, as the species seems confined to within a mile or two of its banks in North Texas. I eventually learned to pinpoint localities well enough so that I could usually turn one up without too much effort, provided the weather conditions were right. First and foremost, I learned that timber rattlesnakes require a fairly dense canopy as well as dense undergrowth to provide the dappled sunlight they prefer when basking. Likewise, the area must have plenty of toppled logs and stumps, as individual serpents are known to frequent the same logs like clockwork. Once I became aware of this, it was sometimes possible to find the same snake day after day by revisiting its log of choice.

The next rule was that North Texas timber rattlesnakes are very picky as to temperature and cloud cover. While they are fairly cold-tolerant, having shown up as late as mid-November on warm days, they are quick to retreat to underground burrows when the weather becomes too hot and dry. They are active primarily early and late in the day. In the early-morning hours between sunrise and noon, they coil patiently in sunlight filtered down through the greenbrier, their color pattern rendering them all but invisible on the leaf-littered forest floor. During the heat of the day they retire, emerging again a few hours before dusk to their evening ambush sites, which are usually different spots than their morning ones. It is during these two brief windows that they are most often observed abroad, crossing roadways on little-traveled back roads that bisect the river. Apparently the timber rattlesnake will sometimes abandon its nocturnal post and venture out into the open, though it is rare to find them crawling after nine-thirty or ten o'clock at night. By keeping good field notes with details of each and every timber I found, I summarized their observed activities and all but foolproofed my ability to locate one.

While not a species for the novice to interact with due to its highly potent venom, the timber rattlesnake is, in my experience, a mild-mannered and generally laid-back rattlesnake, especially when compared with its often irascible and much more common cousin, the western diamond-backed rattlesnake. Nevertheless, this complacence varies among individual snakes, and I have been rattled at, snapped at, and met with twisty and squirmy specimens that were at best downright uncooperative. Their large size and long fangs are reason enough to appreciate the species from a distance, and it deserves mention that it is unlawful to catch, attempt to catch, or possess timbers in the state of Texas.

In a bygone memory that will certainly outlast all of the photographs and field notes I have acquired over the years, I am reminded of perhaps my most treasured encounter with a timber rattlesnake in North Texas. It was a warm, promising spring day, and I was walking uphill along a steep bank of the Trinity River and soon encountered a northern cottonmouth. The snake detected my presence and turned for the water some twenty feet below. As it did, it slipped into a hollow oak log, where I followed with my snake hook, trying to coax it out. Something made me look down at my feet, and right there, mere inches from my boots, lay the biggest timber rattler I had ever seen. It was coiled perfectly, its jet-black tail possessing a long string of battered rattle segments draped lazily over the top of its head. The snake was as big around as my bicep and formed a coil the diameter of a steering wheel. Slowly I backed up, forgetting all about the cottonmouth. When I had achieved a safe distance from the snake, I knelt down on my haunches and observed it. Meanwhile, its highly sensitive heat pits detected the presence of a large warm-blooded animal, and the snake raised its head slightly, tongue flicking. For twenty minutes it allowed me to share its domain, tolerating my presence provided I was willing to sit still and show a little respect. But my muscles began to tire, and when I could stand the discomfort no longer, I raised up to stretch. This unnerved the big old timber, and it uncoiled and slid silently through the dried leaf litter alongside the log, stretching out to full length, which was well over five feet. I stood there and watched the rattler go until it disappeared in the interior of the log with the cottonmouth. When the final inch of tail tip was out of sight, I turned and resumed my snake hunt, feeling lucky to have been there at that exact moment in time. Although I hadn't brought a camera along, there was no regret. It was a once-in-a-lifetime moment, one of my most treasured encounters in the field. And with any luck the North Texas timber population will continue to thrive and produce another generation of snakes for my son and other future generations to enjoy, admire, and learn to respect and leave unharmed in the place where they belong.

Snake encounters on the prairies / SMITH

The Fort Worth Prairie is an area of gently rolling grasslands between the western and eastern Cross Timbers. This prairie has supported a wealth of reptiles and amphibians, from box turtles to massasauga rattlesnakes to small-mouthed salamanders to chorus frogs and many other species. Located in a busy and growing part of Texas, the Fort Worth Prairie has mostly been developed and plowed, but there are still some viable remnants. One such area, near Benbrook Lake, may be lost in the coming years as Fort Worth continues to expand. Another remnant, just west of Fort Worth, is being sold to developers. There are still high-quality patches of prairie north of Fort Worth and near Denton and Decatur, most of it privately owned ranchland.

I remember the sounds at sunset at a time when there were fewer nearby highways and less traffic. In the soft light of sunset you heard doves cooing, and if you stood in the quiet for a bit, you might hear the whistling tones of a chuck-will's-widow, one of the birds called "nightjars" that may sit unnoticed near the side of the road or be flushed by the approach of the car and fly up and out of the way in a flash of gray or brown wings in the headlights. In the spring I listened for the long trills of toads calling, and the shorter wirrrt-wirrrt-wirrrt of the spotted chorus frog, like running one's thumb over the teeth of a comb. A related anuran, Strecker's chorus frog, might also chime in with its call like a squeaky wheel that needs lubrication.

Prairie remnant near Bear Creek Road, Parker County

The prairies and fields west of Fort Worth have been, for me, the quintessential places for snake hunting. Not that these places are better than numerous other places in Texas. But they have been etched into my experience over a period of fifty years during which I have walked or (more often) driven across them, and the first few years were the most magical. During those years in the 1960s I was learning about Texas snakes and getting some of my first experiences with bullsnakes, prairie kingsnakes, and particularly the western massasauga. Parker County was legendary for its population of these small rattlesnakes during that time, as large numbers of them would emerge at sunset, and under the right conditions you could see several massasaugas on just about any evening. Back then, my parents did the driving. One evening, around sunset, we drove along the little farm road that ran from Benbrook out west to Aledo. Easing along the road in our old Ford Galaxy must have been a sight to see, a great iron and sheet metal battleship creaking along at twenty miles per hour (we didn't want to miss *anything*!). Up ahead I spotted a box turtle making its way across the road, so the big road-hunting machine squeaked to a stop and I piled out to pick up this turtle. On the way back to the car, my mother said, "Don't you want to look at that snake?" It was very embarrassing; in my preoccupation with the turtle I had totally overlooked a young bullsnake stretched out on the road a few feet away!

But the western massasauga was the number one attraction. These little rattlesnakes seldom grow longer than two feet, and they differ from their larger rattlesnake cousins in their coloration and scale patterns. For example, massasaugas have several large scales covering the top of the head, while others such as the diamond-backed rattlesnake have a larger scale over each eye

Western massasauga

but mostly small scales across the crown of the head. Their venom should be taken seriously, but only a small dose is delivered through short fangs. In a 1965 article that examined massasaugas, including those from the Fort Worth Prairie, Harry Greene and George Oliver found that the snake's diet includes mice, lizards, small snakes, and the occasional frog.[2]

Greene and Oliver also noted that the western massasauga was often seen at night stretched out on the road but when approached it usually coiled, rattled, and struck. I moved a great many massasaugas off the road and into the surrounding bunchgrass and wildflowers in those days, and most of them remained motionless until touched with a snake hook, whereupon they moved off in a flurry of frantic, sinuous curves. Some of them pulled into a defensive coil and might strike out in short jabs against my intrusion on their evening movement.

One other observation of a massasauga's behavior helps explain why people may claim that one or another venomous snake chased them. On a spring night out on the road near Weatherford, Steve Campbell and I came up on an adult massasauga. It was Steve's first encounter with this species, so we got out and lingered over it for a couple of minutes, admiring it. The snake remained motionless on the caliche road under our lights, and we talked about the intricacies of its pattern. At some point I wanted to see it in a different position, and I nudged it with my snake hook. It exploded into movement, heading straight toward where Steve had crouched to look at it. He, of course, also exploded into movement, and in my memory it is always something close to a back flip that I witnessed, although I doubt he was that acrobatic. In any case, as he moved out of the way, the snake continued past him and toward whatever spot it had selected for shelter. There was no chase and no attack—the snake was simply racing for cover, with no thought of who might be in the way.

Over the years, there have been dry periods and wet periods, but hardly anything as miserable as the 2011 drought. That summer I saw the prairies withering in the merciless record heat. Not that I did much wandering and looking for wildlife during the worst of it because everything still alive had disappeared into burrows and crevices, seeking cooler temperatures and moisture. In late September I drove out along Bear Creek, in Parker County, and the foliage had the dead, dry look of winter. At a creek crossing, the channel was mostly dry and dusty, except for a small patch of mud where several honeybees kept landing, trying to obtain some moisture. It was hard to imagine when we would get enough rain to refill the creeks and bring life back to the grasses and trees. We had to wait until December, but some rain did come, and in the first few months of 2012 life returned early and quickly. By late March it was time to see how those prairies and fields were doing.

Out at Bear Creek Road, the water flowed over the roadway a little at the first crossing, and a turtle made his way across the road in the shallow water. A shy red-eared slider, he hurried the last foot or so and dropped into the pool. What a difference from the dry, baked limestone creek bed I had seen six months before. After tracking the creek for a few miles, the road pulls out into the open, and here the fields were becoming green with new growth. Patches of bluebonnets were scattered here and there.

At around 8:00 p.m. a dark, uneven line stretched across the pale caliche road ahead of me, and I knew this was a fairly large snake. Getting closer, it proved to be a bullsnake with a dark pattern and a glowering eye. These snakes often put on a loud, dramatic defense, puffing up and hissing with their mouths open and tongues hanging out, ultimately striking at the object of their wrath with a sharp hissing exhalation. Should the snake actually bite, nothing worse than some scratches will result; the snake has no venom and no real ability to inflict much injury on a human. However, a big one that is fully enraged can make even an experienced herper pause. The hissing is amplified by a flap of tissue just in front of the windpipe in the floor of the mouth. The banded tail may nervously vibrate like that of a rattlesnake (though it is not held off the ground as would be the case with a rattler). But to "deflate" this act just a little, the last time Clint and I encountered one, we picked it up to rescue it off the road, and it did not bite. Sometimes it's just a big bluff.

This particular bullsnake flattened its neck and eyed me cautiously as it began to move. I walked around in front of it, and it pulled back a bit and stopped. I noticed on the side of this one's face there was a big scar, perhaps the result of a run-in with a predator brave enough to try to make a meal of it. We looked at each other, and the snake was content to watch and wait. I slipped my hand under its midsection to check its weight and tone, and it felt strong but light, as if it had not yet had many meals since the cold months of winter. The snake began to move again, but without hissing or striking. I watched it move into the wildflowers, gliding in no particular hurry and looking up above the vegetation here and there to decide which way to go. It felt great to have had this encounter, checking out this handsome snake without particularly disturbing it, and then going our separate ways.

Rippling water and sun-warmed limestone / SMITH

In the mid-1960s, soon after moving back to Texas and settling in Fort Worth, I was introduced to Mary's Creek. Winding in from the west on its way to join up with the Trinity River, this prairie stream provided a thirty- to sixty-yard-wide corridor of heaven for a preteen who was becoming serious about field herping. There were stream riffles and pools, perfect for wading, as well as a band of trees and understory plants along either side, perfect for exploring. I soon discovered that the pools were thickly populated with cricket frogs, ribbonsnakes, watersnakes, and the occasional red-eared slider turtle, softshell turtle, or snapping turtle.

The creek cuts through the Fort Worth Prairie, and over the years the water had eroded the thin soil down to a layer of whitish-gray limestone, over which the stream flows and gathers in pools up to about four feet deep. Because the creek bed is limestone, with a little shale, the water is quite clear in most places—enough to see the sunfish, bass, and occasional turtle swimming through it. A typical pool might be partly shaded by pecans, sycamore, or other trees, with sunfish visible in deeper areas hovering over gravel nests. At the shallow margins, out in full sun, water pennywort or other plants might grow in the water between broken chunks of white limestone, and cricket frogs congregate to feed on tiny invertebrates at the water's edge.

Blanchard's cricket frogs may be small and short-lived, but they are amazing frogs. They are so well camouflaged that they can barely be seen until you step among them and trigger them to jump; the scattering of a group of three or four makes it very hard to focus on just one. When you do isolate one, it typically jumps and then may do one of three things. It may freeze, its

Mary's Creek, western Tarrant County

Blanchard's cricket frog

little gray body blending in with the limestone and mud and the occasional small splotch of green or orange on its back mimicking tiny bits of vegetation or gravel. Thus, the frog may simply "disappear." Second, it may immediately leap in a completely different direction, making it very hard to follow. Third, the frog may jump about a foot out into the water, whereupon it often doubles back a few inches and digs in among moss and stones in a different place than where you just saw it enter the water.

All these ingenious tricks for avoiding detection are very much needed, as cricket frogs are part of the diet of wading birds, snakes, and many other crea-

Plain-bellied watersnake

tures. In particular, they are hunted by the western ribbonsnake, a fast and agile little serpent that patrols the vegetation along the water's edge. These striped and slender relatives of the gartersnake thread their way through sedges and reeds and react instantly to movement in their field of vision. A ribbonsnake will chase a cricket frog, and if the frog stops and freezes, so does the snake, awaiting the frog's next move. The pursuit often ends with the frog being grabbed and quickly swallowed whole.

In many wetland environments in the Cross Timbers, cricket frogs make up a sizable portion of the diets of many animals. For a population to survive despite being eaten in such numbers, it must constantly replenish itself, and cricket frogs are prolific breeders. A walk down the creek on a late-spring afternoon usually takes you past large gatherings of calling males trying to attract females for breeding. One bold frog may start the chorus with its repeating "grick-grick-grick," like two stones being clicked together. This triggers a second and then a third, and soon the whole creek bank is resonating with hundreds of overlapping calls. At night the chorus continues and seems even louder and more "present" in the ear. These frogs may also chorus in the mornings, too. Later into the summer, they may call during the day or night. There is hardly any time of the year, except in the winter, when ponds and creeks remain silent, with no breeding activity from cricket frogs.

The same watersnake, swimming away

Spring has always been one of the best times to walk the creek, after early spring rains have replenished the flow of water and the warm sun has coaxed the new growth of green leaves on trees and shrubs. Careful watching may pay off, and the observer may get to see things that are on the one hand simple and at the same time beautiful. Once I stood in shallow water while a plain-bellied watersnake swam along the bottom nearby, unaware of my presence. It poked its snout into any available crevice where a frog or fish might be hiding, as its body undulated easily and effortlessly through the clear water. Its big round eyes were set high on the head so that it could easily spot potential danger from above as well as movement of prey at eye level. However, the watersnake's vision is programmed more to react to movement than to recognize the outlines of big objects like a man standing motionless in the creek. And since I remained motionless, the snake came to the surface for a breath of air less than a foot from my shoe, then pulled back down and resumed the hunt. After a little more of this graceful watersnake ballet, I shifted slightly. The snake instantly froze to size up the situation. Then it suddenly shot away from me, like an arrow pulled tight against the bowstring and released to fly through the water to safety. I was grateful that it had shared a few minutes of its hunt with me.

Spotted whiptail, Fort Worth Nature Center and Refuge

Whiptails and skinks at the Fort Worth
Nature Center and Refuge / SMITH

We spend a lot of time at the Fort Worth Nature Center and Refuge. With an area exceeding 3,600 acres, it is one of the biggest city-owned nature centers in the country, and it encompasses an area where several habitats meet: Cross Timbers forest, prairie, bottomland forest, marsh, and some of the Lake Worth shoreline. Many species of herps are found there, and for me it is a sort of home away from home. On one of those visits, in 2012, Clint and I looked for as many species of lizards as we could find.

One of our first finds was nine inches of pure nervous energy that darted away on the rocky ground, stopped, and looked back at me from under a fallen branch. The lizard jerked ahead in short movements, as if barely restraining itself from sprinting through the leaf litter and underbrush. Eight thin greenish-yellow lines ran down its body from the back of the head to the hips. From there, a long tapering tail extended back, longer than the lizard's body. Between the stripes, far down on the sides were a few suggestions of light spots. This was a Texas spotted whiptail, a species often seen in the hot sunlight nervously poking through leaf litter for small insects. This one continued to make its way through branches and leaves, warily tolerating my presence about five feet away. Several other encounters with whiptails on this day at the nature center consisted of a glance before the lizard disappeared under vegetation.

Prairie racerunner

A closely related lizard, the six-lined racerunner, can also be found in the Cross Timbers; it can be distinguished by a lack of spots between the stripes and by a green wash of color over its back on the forward part of its body. The number of stripes is problematic—there may be six clear stripes with a central seventh one in the middle, this one less well defined than the others.

The Texas spotted whiptail has traditionally been found through most of Texas except for the western Trans-Pecos, parts of the Panhandle, and most of southeast Texas. Open, rocky habitats, prairies, savannahs, and grasslands are preferred habitats, where it may seek refuge in rock crevices or dig burrows in sandy soil. I am delighted that this lizard continues to do well at the nature center, but it seems unable to persist within the city as it once did. In the 1960s the species skittered along sidewalks and in gardens, darting down into burrows when chased. I no longer see them in parks or yards, and I hope they do not become even more uncommon.

I was not tempted to try to catch this particular whiptail, as I might have been when I was a kid. Teenage herpers are like cats in that any reptilian movement elicits an uncontrollable urge to chase and capture. Additionally, teenage herpers are among the only humans with enough agility and energy to have a shot at catching one. It is even trickier to catch one without breaking off that long tail—grabbing or restraining the tail causes it to break off, and the tail twists around and distracts the predator while the lizard gets away. The tail will regrow, though the texture of scales and the length will not be like the original one.

Female broad-headed skink

These lizards are quite active when temperatures reach 95 to 100 degrees, though they will shuttle between shade and sun to keep from overheating and may not be active during the midday heat in summer. Their legendary energy and speed depends on being quite warm, and on sunny days they are continuously on the move to find the grasshoppers, beetles, spiders, and other invertebrates that make up their diet. They may dig burrows for refuges or take advantage of abandoned mouse burrows or other tunnels.

Some related whiptail lizards are parthenogenetic; that is, they exist in all-female populations that lay unfertilized eggs that develop into female lizards that are genetically just like the mothers. However, the Texas spotted whiptail is a species with males and females. Sexually mature males have distinctly different coloration on the underside. The throat and chin may be pink or orange, and the large scales of the chest and belly may be blue with mottled blue-black patches, especially on the chest. Females lay several eggs—usually fewer than eight—that hatch in late summer into little one-inch-long babies with bright patterns.

After walking the prairie and oak motte trails in search of whiptails, Clint and I took a walk through the bottomland forest near the marsh. The old cottonwoods, burr oaks, and other trees there are an excellent place to see the broad-headed skink, another common lizard at the nature center. Actually, without a very close look, it is hard to tell if a large skink in the eastern third of Texas is a broad-headed skink or the related common five-lined skink. Both lizards are smooth and shiny and reach a head-body length of at least three inches. The broad-headed skink gets a little larger, around five and a half inches in head-body length, and with a complete tail may extend to about a foot in length. The broad-headed skink has five small labial scales on the upper lip in front of the eye; the five-lined skink has only four. Both are sexually dimorphic, meaning that females remain somewhat striped while males lose most evidence of stripes to become fairly plain brown, and may have considerable orange color around the head. Babies hatch with a strongly striped pattern and bright, electric-blue tails.

Catching the lizard is not recommended, largely because this is another lizard species that easily loses its tail. Once again, this appears to be an evolutionary adaptation that makes it more likely to escape from the numerous birds, snakes, and other animals that look at these lizards and see lunch. Many lizards have tails that can easily break, with weak fracture planes in the tail vertebrae and muscle attachment that allows separation with limited trauma. Not that the lizard would regard tail loss as "no big deal." Tails can store fat (energy), and regrowing a tail takes energy as well. Some lizards will even return to a shed tail and consume it, once the danger has passed, to reclaim the energy in the tail. One additional note about tail-shedding: the bright blue tails of baby skinks is apparently a lure to distract a predator away from the parts of the body that cannot be sacrificed.

The long-overdue sighting of a Graham's crawfish snake / KING

I had been searching for Graham's crawfish snake for going on seven years with no luck. My yearning to find and photograph this elusive semiaquatic species had led me on more gas- and money-consuming wild goose chases than I cared to recollect. I had carefully pored over old museum collections of specimens and information on where they were collected, over many books, stared at range maps until my eyes were red, and talked with dozens of herpers who had already had the privilege of encountering one in the field. I had searched ponds, lakes, and rivers in almost every county of the snake's range, had dug up crayfish burrows, and had driven back roads that cut through the middle of East Texas swamps after warm spring rains that are known to trigger the snake's breeding season. I had flipped countless rocks on steep hillsides of lakes and peered through binoculars at exposed snags in the heart of the Graham's territory. And yet still, for seven long years, the species had evaded me. So it came as a surprise when I finally learned where I could find one with relative certainty: a locality that happened to be a mere eleven miles from my house.

Graham's crawfish snake is a denizen of swamps, bogs, lakes and ponds, rivers and streams, or just about any other permanent or semipermanent body of water in the eastern half of the state. They range as far south as the coastline and as far west as the northern Texas plains, where they are found only in a few small pockets. At first glance they are a drab brown, run-of-the-mill-looking, semiaquatic species under thirty-six inches in length. What makes the crawfish snake so different lies more in its specific habits than in its physical description. Crawfish snakes are so named because they are exclusively predators of crayfish. There is little evidence of their consumption of any other prey, according to published reports of examinations of stomach contents. As if that were not specific enough, the crayfish has a hard, spiny exoskeleton that is tough on the snake's digestion, so they are usually consumed only during their molting stage in the brief lapse of time between when the crayfish's old exoskeleton is shed and before the new one has hardened. Thus, finding the snake becomes linked to finding crayfish burrows and "chimneys," so that one has to study the range and habitat of not only the snake but its prey as well.

Another interesting note on the biology of these creatures is that their mating rituals consist of a single female emerging from her winter hibernaculum, emitting a pheromone to attract the males, and then waiting patiently while sometimes dozens of male crawfish snakes entwine themselves over the female in a sort of "mating ball."[3] This behavior is only rarely observed among herpers, since it usually occurs at night.

I was volunteering at an educational event when Tim Sellers brought in a large female Graham's crawfish snake. I was dumbfounded. I knew they were native to the area but had come to the conclusion that they were so elusive or rare that my chances of finding one locally were virtually nil. But here one was right in front of my eyes, and not only a beautiful specimen but a gravid female.

Of course, the immediate question that followed was: Where had he come across the snake? When he told me, I was both ecstatic and beyond surprised. It was on a fishing pond on the Tarrant County College campus across from a reservoir. This place was a twenty-minute drive from my front door. Tim confirmed that not only had he found this particular one there, but that he found these snakes there on a regular basis.

It should go without saying where I ended up the next day. Just over ten miles from my house, at 8:00 a.m. and on a bright sunny day at the end of May, I was ankle-deep in muddy water in a small fishing pond on the property of a college campus. It was a tiny, unremarkable place, a far cry from the previous textbook-perfect habitats I had previously searched. The pond was some 300 feet long and half as wide. It was flat and bare on three sides, where several dozen weekend fishermen and their children sat with coolers at their sides and lines in the water. My only hope of turning up a Graham's would be on the quiet north end of the pond. This tiny, 100-square-foot section was the only favorable habitat that the snake could possibly be occupying.

A thick tangle of impenetrable brush covered this end of the pond. Water-logged stumps protruded from the shallows like old broken teeth. Farther upland, on the bank, this combination of vegetation continued for some fifty feet, where the sunlight filtered through the thicket and created a dappled effect, perfect for basking semiaquatic reptiles. Even farther up, a thin rivulet of stream water masked by a tall jungle of green cattails wound 100 feet up to a culvert, which had been dug beneath a section of roadway. I took all this in at once and immediately knew why my friend had been so successful here. It was a perfect microhabitat for the species, condensed down into an area so small that the population had been forced together.

I began my walk around the perimeter of the shoreline, keeping my eyes open for anything scaly that might be basking in the warm spring sunshine on an exposed branch. I made my way up to the trickle of water running down from the culvert, where I predicted I would find my prized snake. I stepped off into the shoulder-high cattails, my eyes scanning the water-saturated ground that flowed around my bare feet for a blur of something serpentine. After half an hour or so of careful observation, I began to wonder where all of the snakes were. This had to be the spot; it was too perfect. It was then that my foot got caught on something under the water, and a bolt of pain raced up my leg and solved the seven-year-long puzzle for me. I looked down and saw that I unknowingly had slid my foot up under a pile of dead cattails, where a loose sharp stick had lodged up under my toenail. Maybe this was where the crawfish snakes could be found. After all, they could slither their way up into the pile of dead cattails, keeping themselves both hidden from predators, and still benefit from the warmth of the sun. My suspicions were confirmed as I began rooting up these piles of cattails, where previously hidden crayfish burrows and chimneys emerged from the shallow water.

Two piles of dead cattails later and I struck gold. I flipped up a small, rather insignificant-looking mass, and there it sat, coiled, looking like a photo out of a field guide. I shot my hand down and grabbed the snake before it could attempt an escape. The Graham's crawfish snake in my hands was a stunning example of the species. It was about twenty inches long, light brown on top and butter-cream-colored on the bottom, with the telltale thin, radiating black lines extending from the sides and on down the belly, which distinguishes crawfish snakes from their watersnake cousins. How long I had waited for this day! As I held my prize aloft, staring closely at it and marveling at finally holding it in my hands, the snake crawled between my fingers, gently flicking its tongue in and out as it perhaps wondered just what in the world was happening to it and why it was not being attacked.

I walked out from the mud and back onto the bank, where I found a clearing in which to photograph it. When I finished, I took the snake back to the pile of grass where I had found it and watched as it slid silently back into the debris, none the worse for wear. I left feeling ecstatic, shaking my head at the irony that all those years I had been searching for the Graham's crawfish snake in supposedly prime localities hundreds of miles from my house, and they had been in this little pond just around the corner from home all along.

Sadly, two years later someone decided that this ugly little stain of thicket and cattails at the north end of an otherwise popular fishing spot needed to come down to make more room for the bankside fishermen, and the last little section of crawfish snake habitat was bulldozed. I visited the area several more times, but the habitat was gone, and thus the snakes themselves appeared to have been eliminated from the area. This is one reason why it is important to conserve our few remaining wild places for snakes and other wildlife, especially those species that can still be found within their ranges in tiny pockets of favorable microhabitat such as this one. While the crawfish snakes of the college pond are gone, I will always treasure the memory of spending some time with one on that special spring morning in late May.

Sid Richardson Scout Ranch / KING

The Sid Richardson Scout Ranch is located just west of Lake Bridgeport near the border of Wise and Jack Counties. Twenty-five years ago, it was a hot spot for finding reptiles and amphibians. Some time ago corporate bigwigs bought it, sectioned the land off into sublots for wealthy people wishing to live close to Runaway Bay, which makes up its eastern edge. However, at one time it was crawling with snakes, lizards, frogs, and turtles. I first heard about the place through my older brother, who had a trucking job hauling gravel there for a brief period in the late nineties. He told me about seeing copperheads and rattlesnakes on the roads in the late evenings. As soon as I got my first vehicle, it was the first place I went one early September evening.

The Scout Ranch was a summer camp for Boy Scouts for years, and hundreds of trails blazed by eager naturalists crisscrossed the land. It was a rocky grassland, thick with mesquites and junipers, rising in elevation as you drove along it and topping out at a large hill. Sandstone and limestone outcrops formed out of the hills, replete with rockslides and huge boulders the size of small cars. It was dotted here and there with stock tanks and small creeks that flowed into the lake, and prickly pear and bull nettle grew so abundantly that one would be a fool to traverse the land in mere sandals or low-

Sid Richardson Scout Ranch at sunset

top sneakers. From the first night there I fell in love with the Scout Ranch, as it was easily accessible private land that cost nothing to get into and no one seemed to be bothered by me herping on it.

I hit the roads, creeks, meadows, and hilltops with a vengeance, and one by one the herps came to me. Western ribbonsnakes and watersnakes patrolled the shallow creek beds by the dozens. At times, it wasn't uncommon to see ten or more in a single morning's stroll. Some of the ribbonsnakes were of the blue phase, wherein the normally yellow stripes down the snake's back and sides are instead a turquoise blue. Likewise, broad-banded copperheads lay beneath logs and rocks near the banks. One particular fall morning I sat and watched a large northern cottonmouth lazily ride the flowing current down to the lake. DeKay's brownsnakes were equally common in the fallen leaf litter when the creek was dry, and Texas spiny lizards and their smaller cousin, the prairie lizard, hung out on cottonwood trees, clinging to the bark, head downward, in patches of sunlight.

Farther up on the creek there was a deep depression in the earth, and when spring rains came, it turned into a temporary floodplain. On warm spring nights the sound of multiple frog species calling simultaneously would be nothing short of deafening. Narrow-mouthed toads, Woodhouse's toads, two species of spadefoots, gray treefrogs, American bullfrogs, leopard frogs, cricket frogs, chorus frogs, and eastern Chihuahuan green toads as well as red-spotted toads could all be heard on these nights. The last two were uncommon, especially the green toad, and finding one was always a real treat. On several occasions I turned them up under a pile of old shingles that someone had discarded at the roadside, although I soon learned to watch for

Western diamond-backed rattlesnake

scorpions and rusty nails, which were much more common in the pile than toads. A couple of stings and pokes and I learned to use the hook for flipping. The green toad is one of the smallest toad species in the area. Delightful lime-green creatures with an array of black spots and squiggles on their backs, they are highly adaptable to the dry summers that occur where they live, and they spend most of each year tucked underground in cracks in the earth.

Farther north from the floodplain stood an immense rock-strewn hillside. The dirt was deep red and crumbly, making the flat rocks that lined its surface easy to overturn. It was here that I took joy in catching eastern collared lizards, the largest lizard native to the area. They are territorial, and in the breeding season males are a vivid blue-green, with fluorescent yellow bars, flecked with white spots. When alarmed, they will take off with a sudden burst of speed, then stand up on their hind legs with their tails raised, like a tiny dinosaur. They are fast, and I rarely got one in hand, but when I did, I usually suffered the wrath of their powerful jaws, as they are not shy about biting.

I had to be careful when walking the hillside because western diamond-backed rattlesnakes were by far the most common species. In the fall the newly born babies would take shelter under flat rocks and on certain days would outnumber the variable groundsnakes two to one. Large adult western diamondbacks were found less frequently, but I would occasionally jump from one large boulder to the next and startle one that was basking, whereupon it would slither away in a blur of scales, rattles whirring a warning and letting me know it was annoyed by my presence. I recall one evening when I came across a small diamondback whose pattern lacked diamonds. Such unusual specimens actually possess genetic deformities that are the reason for their atypical markings. This one wore a series of black squiggles and dashes, and it took me a minute to realize I was actually looking at a diamondback and not some new species. On a nearby hill on another evening I came across a beautiful kingsnake that was wrapped around a yellow-bellied racer that it was constricting and preparing to eat.

A communal western diamondback den was located on the south end of a road where a rocky outcrop ran parallel with the road. It didn't take me long to figure out that I would see many snakes traveling to their winter hibernaculum if I drove along this outcrop on early October evenings. This was the best time to spot the biggest rattlesnakes, and on any given night before the first freeze it was not surprising to see up to a dozen of them headed uphill from the lowlands. It was on such a night that I encountered my first Texas nightsnake on this same road. Nightsnakes are mildly venomous nocturnal reptiles that are harmless to people because of the low potency of their venom, their small size, and their enlarged teeth in the back (not the front) of their jaws. Their elliptical, catlike pupils differentiate them from similar-looking species. This find was a real rarity to the area and ended up being a record for Jack County.

Unfortunately, the Sid Richardson Scout Ranch seems to have gone the way of the buffalo. While not exactly gone (the hills and valleys and creeks and ponds are all undoubtedly still there), people slowly but surely moved in over the years, pressuring the owners of the ranch to sell it to developers. When the construction hammer came down, the snakes seemed to have packed up and said "adios." Oil tanker trucks and a procession of lake tourists now line the roads on summer weekends, and one would be lucky to turn up a single copperhead or western ratsnake after a day or night of searching. But such is all too often the case with our wild places, and the best I can do is reminisce back to the good old days when the Scout Ranch was teeming with snakes, frogs, and lizards, all just sitting in wait to make my acquaintance.

7 The Blackland Prairie and Post Oak Savannah

EAST OF THE CROSS TIMBERS, at least historically, the oak forests gave way to open expanses of tallgrass prairie. These prairies include little bluestem, Indiangrass, and other grasses that can sometimes grow as tall as a person. A healthy prairie contains a great many plant species including wildflowers and other forbs along with the tall grasses. Prairies are kept healthy by a number of influences, especially by periodic fires and grazing. The Blackland Prairie exists in small remnants, but much of it has been plowed, has grown into woody thickets, or been developed.

As we go from the Blackland Prairie into East Texas, the land transitions from prairie to an area of grasslands and open woodland, known as the Post Oak Savannah. A savannah is an ecoregion with grassland and trees where the tree canopy does not close overhead. The trees may be scattered in clumps or may simply be separated enough that plants growing on the ground get plenty of sunlight. The transition from Blackland Prairie to the Post Oak Savannah on the surface of the land corresponds to a geological transition underneath the surface. Millions of years ago, when North America and South America pulled apart and the Gulf of Mexico opened, the southern shore of North America would have run through Texas. Over the millennia river systems dumped massive amounts of sand and clay into the Gulf, extending the land mass and forming East Texas. Thus, the geologic foundations of Texas shift from limestone to layers of sediment estimated in places to be 40,000 feet deep.[1] The limestone and shallow black soil work very well for prairie, and the deep sand and clay and greater rainfall are what is needed for the forests and Piney Woods of East Texas.

The Post Oak Savannah stretches from the northeast corner of the state all the way to an area just below San Antonio, depending on whose map you are looking at. Like the prairies, the savannah was formed and maintained by the regular occurrence of fire and the grazing of bison.[2] These forces tended to keep the land from being taken over by woody plants and shrubs and to encourage the growth of bunchgrasses. Historically, it was used as farmland

and then for cattle ranching. Today much of the area has been plowed, and pastures are often planted with nonnative grasses. Among the places where you can see relatively undisturbed Post Oak Savannah habitat is at wildlife management areas or parks in the region.

An afternoon at Parkhill Prairie / SMITH

Walking around a big pond at Parkhill Prairie in Collin County, Clint and I held out a little hope that we might see a Texas gartersnake in the wet grasses near the pond's edge. Approaching the water's edge, near a clump of willows, what I saw was not a gartersnake but a chocolate-brown reptilian head suddenly sink below the water. We froze and closely watched the water by the willows. The snake's head came back up, watching the shore, no doubt with the same concentrated attention as Clint and I. Below the water I could make out a curve of the body, dark on the top but transitioning to yellow where the belly scales made a zigzag edge along the body. The eyes were two round circles, visible just above the waterline. This was a plain-bellied watersnake, until recently known as the blotched watersnake because it has a series of rounded blotches down its back that may nearly disappear as the snake gets older.

The plain-bellied watersnake is commonly found throughout most of Texas in ponds, cattle tanks, creeks, lake shores, and almost any other wetland. And while they live in or near wetlands, they are known to wander farther from water than do some of the other watersnake species. My approach to them has changed with age and maturity. As a child in the 1960s, I responded to each and every plain-bellied watersnake by pursuing it, diving in the water if necessary, until I had it in hand. Without fail, each and every one would repeatedly bite my hands and arms and sling copious amounts of musk from its cloaca as it frantically thrashed and tried to escape. Dripping a little blood from the scratch marks left by the teeth and stinking of the vaguely skunk-like musk, I'm sure I had a foolish grin of victory as I examined my prize.

In appearance, the species teaches us to appreciate subtlety; it might at first be described as being ugly as mud, but the belly is a pretty yellow color, often shading to orange toward the tail. The scales down the back may be gray-brown but sometimes have more chocolate tones. Plain-bellied watersnakes are excellent swimmers, and while their diet includes small fish, they are voracious frog-eaters and consume more amphibians than most other watersnake species.

In the shaded water of the pond at Parkhill Prairie, this particular plain-bellied watersnake pulled back under the water's surface the moment we

Parkhill Prairie, Collin County

moved closer, and we did not see it again. While we were delighted to have seen this snake, I lost my desire to be splattered with watersnake musk some years ago and did not jump in after it. Clint and I circled around to the other side, and near another group of willows Clint saw a striped snake dash into the tangle of branches and grasses at the water's edge and disappear. This was, no doubt, a western ribbonsnake, a slightly more streamlined and aquatic version of a gartersnake with three light stripes on a dark background. Ribbonsnakes are a different species from gartersnakes, but within the same genus, and specialize in cruising along the edges of ponds and creeks looking for cricket frogs and other prey. When ribbonsnakes disappear into a tangle of vegetation, as this one had, they are unlikely to be found without investing a lot of effort in tearing up a little patch of microhabitat that is better left alone. We bade good-bye to the ribbonsnake and finished our walk around the pond.

The two main trails at Parkhill Prairie both provide good walks over the gently rolling landscape, ending in a circular patch bordered by a low semi-circle of stonework that suggests a magical spot for stargazing or listening to summer frog calls. However, Parkhill is open only from sunrise to sundown, so don't pack the flashlights and camp chairs expecting a nighttime visit. During the day it is a beautiful remnant of prairie grassland of the sort that is almost gone now. The tallgrass prairie of Texas history consisted of native grasses such as little bluestem, big bluestem, switchgrass, Indiangrass, and many other plants such as Indian paintbrush, winecup, snow-on-the-prairie, Maximilian's sunflower, and what almost seems like a million other species. You can look at a small patch of ground in one of these prairies and get lost in the complex visual array of different shapes, heights, and colors.

On this particular day in mid-April, many of the taller dried stems of last year's grasses still stood tall while new green growth emerged beneath them. Patches of Indian paintbrush added bright red color in places, with patches of yellow in other spots. On one of the gentle hillsides blackberry vines were interwoven with the grasses and forbs, adding their white flowers to the mix.

And as we walked among all this complex growth, a patch of scales caught Clint's eye, and he called out, "Prairie kingsnake!" Seeing this snake moving around at about 3:00 p.m. was remarkable for a couple of reasons. First, we would have expected the snake to be threading its way among the plants at ground level and, as such, mostly covered by the thick growth of grasses and forbs. It was a stroke of luck that Clint happened to see a section of its skin, as well as a tribute to his many years of spotting snakes in the field. Second, through much of the year, prairie kingsnakes appear to spend most daytime hours underground, in mammal burrows or in crevices in the ground. Only in spring and fall, when daytime temperatures are very mild, are there greater chances that the snake will be above ground in the afternoon. This snake was a male, roughly thirty inches long, on the small side of average for a prairie kingsnake. In typical fashion it squirmed to get away but did not bite, despite our attempts to pose it for photos. It had a relatively small head, scarcely wider than its neck, and the top of its head was tan with darker brown markings edged in black. As with others of its kind, the darker markings included a vaguely spear-point shape, pointing backward, and two dark brown elongated blotches running from the back of the head down the neck for an inch or so. After that, a series of dark saddles ran down the back, in places dividing into a double row of dark spots. Its species name, *calligaster*, means "beautiful belly," and the broad ventral scales are white with sections of dark, grayish-to-charcoal irregular rectangles that may have a reddish tinge—pretty but not spectacular.

One more thing that sets it apart, in a good way, is its musk. Snakes generally are able to exude substances from glands at the base of the tail and are especially likely to do this when frightened or attacked. As described above, watersnakes smear copious amounts of unpleasant-smelling viscous musk when captured. The scent is different for different species, but it often could be described in terms like "burnt," "old socks," "skunk," and so on. It is my experience with a great many prairie kingsnakes that their musk has a somewhat pleasant and almost floral scent. I am really not putting you on—go ahead, find one, and see if you agree!

After taking a few photos, we set the kingsnake free to resume its wanderings, perhaps in search of the mice, voles, and other small mammals that make up the bulk of its diet. In an instant it was gone, threading its way

Prairie kingsnake

beneath the thatch of prairie grasses and flowers. We resumed our walk up and over the low hillside and down the other side. In the annual succession of prairie plant growth, different species have their own season. Last August some areas were heavily dotted with the beautiful snow-on-the-prairie, with its thin, white-edged leaves and little clusters of white flowers. In other places sunflowers grew high in the summer sunlight. Now, in the spring awakening of the prairie, those species were nowhere to be seen.

On the walk back we picked our way along a thin thread of drainage, too small for a creek but wet enough during parts of the year to sustain a small grove of small trees like hackberry. Halfway along the grove, Clint said, "Stop—you'll never believe this." He had discovered mid-step that his foot was on a rough greensnake. I reached down and picked up the snake from where it had been restrained under Clint's boot, and we marveled at the animated vine with the light green dorsum and creamy yellow belly. Rough greensnakes can be abundant in some places but hard to see because they camouflage so perfectly. In foliage with new green growth or among vines, such as greenbrier, with stems the same color and nearly the same size as the little serpent, a rough greensnake is nearly invisible. When moving from one branch to another, it slowly extends its head and neck, then nearly half of its body, gently swaying back and forth like a vine in the breeze. This camouflage is virtually its only defense, as it is nonvenomous and almost never bites. However, the rough greensnake is a formidable predator of the caterpillars, spiders, and insects living among the leaves.

This afternoon on the Blackland Prairie was our chance to explore in an endangered ecosystem. The native prairie ecosystem still hangs on in small

Clint photographing a rough greensnake

preserves and a few patches of farmland where the land may have been mowed but never plowed. But only about 1 percent of the native tallgrass prairie remains, according to the Native Prairies Association of Texas,[3] and the little patches of prairie could easily wink out of existence if we do not actively work to preserve it. Put a visit to the tallgrass prairie on your bucket list and do what you can to conserve it!

Salamanders at the Sabine, 2011 / SMITH

After the months of withering drought, it was good to see bands of rain go through East Texas. At least a little relief rained down from the clouds, providing some hope of better days. And in the winter the best way for herpers to take advantage of this is to head east to search for salamanders. The two of us set a course for the bottomland forests of the Sabine River as it passes north of Tyler, an area of tall elm, oak, and ash trees growing in clay soils covered with a wintertime carpet of leaves. Creeks and depressions fill with water after good rains, so the area near the river is wet and dotted with ephemeral pools. Here and there the fan-shaped leaves of palmettos grow close to the ground.

Right away, we had a chance to poke around some discarded items lying in the leaf litter, and as I lifted a wooden box, a familiar figure slithered away. A little brown skink—the lizard formerly known as a "ground skink"—

Flooded bottomland, Old Sabine Bottom Wildlife Management Area

seemed to swim through the curled brown leaves and avoided being caught for a photograph. Like other skinks, these little creatures have relatively long bodies and small legs, so their bodies and tails undulate as they move along the ground. The lizard's sides are a dark brown, but a broad band of coppery brown runs from the head down the back and onto the tail. After only enough of a glimpse to positively identify it, this little brown skink was gone.

Farther down the road we began seeing pools scattered out among the trees, so it was time to get wet! With all the leaves off the trees, the sun shone brightly on the forest floor, and the water was shallow and clear. In many places green sedges grew from the wet ground and up through the leaves, looking like clumps of green winter grass.

In short order, Clint was out of the car and hard at work lifting logs, of which there was no shortage. Invertebrates were everywhere, hidden away in the pithy centers of the rain-swollen wood. Two-inch-long centipedes, social bess beetles, and the ever-present tenebrionids crawled through the mulch of each and every branch, log, and stump. Larvae of the eyed click beetle, which resemble giant mealworms, wriggled in and out of the detritus, and Clint managed to pin and pick up a giant fishing spider, a distant relative of the wolf spider that grows so large as to include minnows in its preferred diet. But we were looking for something a bit slimier.

A dozen or so logs down and Clint got lucky. Beneath an oak branch not unlike a million others in the woods he flipped up a large, typical example of the small-mouthed salamander.

"Success!" he cried as he scooped it up and dashed back through the green-brier that covered the forest floor like a carpet of floral barbed wire wrapping doggedly around his calves and ankles as his tennis shoes filled with water. The two of us looked at this little prize, with its glistening dark skin mottled with a silver-gray pattern like the lichen growing on some of the logs.

Salamanders are fascinating animals, and ones that many herpers seldom see and seldom look for. Wintertime and very early spring, after rains, are great times to look for a number of species that breed during that time of year. The small-mouthed salamander is one of those species, and they are described as "explosive" breeders. What this means is that, when conditions are right, large numbers of them breed at the same time in temporary ponds and roadside ditches.

These amphibians do not breed by external fertilization like frogs, with the male fertilizing the eggs as they are laid. Neither do salamanders reproduce by the usual internal fertilization, with a male copulating with a female. Instead, during courtship, the male deposits a spermatophore (a sort of package containing sperm) externally and then will typically nudge or maneuver the female over the spermatophore so that she picks it up into her cloaca. There the sperm is stored until egg-laying.

While some salamanders have very slimy skin, making it extremely hard to hold on to them, the small-mouthed salamander's skin feels like that of some frogs, only moderately slippery. The skin secretions work in several ways to keep the salamander healthy. A salamander that is slippery is harder for a predator to grasp and eat. Furthermore, the secretions are toxic, making a predator regret eating the salamander. In fact, some amphibians concentrate toxins from the things they eat and have dangerously toxic secretions, like some newts and the poison dart frogs. Others, like our small-mouthed salamander, manufacture their own mild toxins that are not dangerous to humans. In addition, skin toxins protect the salamander from many bacteria. When you think about the delicate and semipermeable skin of salamanders and frogs, it makes sense that they would need some sort of defense against the many microorganisms in their environment.

On the other hand, one advantage of having permeable skin is that amphibians can exchange water and gases easily. No need to drink when you have osmosis working for you! Since water tends to cross membranes in this way, a salamander can take up water without drinking a drop. And, of course, if your surroundings get dry, you can lose water. The mucus secretions of some amphibians help prevent drying. The costal grooves along the sides of some salamanders are another helpful adaptation for keeping the animal from drying out too much. A small-mouthed salamander exposed to the air

Small-mouthed salamander

but sitting on wet substrate can stay moist because these costal grooves will wick the water up over the sides by capillary action.

What about exchange of gases through the skin? In their book on amphibian natural history, Stebbins and Cohen note that some mole salamanders (a genus that includes the small-mouthed salamander) release up to 80 percent of their carbon dioxide through their skin.[4] They also reported that in some salamanders most gas exchange of oxygen and carbon dioxide occurred through the skin.

Small-mouthed salamanders eat small insects, other invertebrates such as spiders, and earthworms. These salamanders spend much of their lives in dark, moist places, working their way through leaf litter, under or inside logs, or inside the burrows of other animals. Their eggs are laid in the water, and their larvae are aquatic and have external gills. Once they metamorphose into adults, they live on land.

The species name is *texanum*, but this salamander is not found solely in Texas. Its range extends through the eastern half of Texas and northward to Iowa and then east to Ohio.[5] Along the Gulf Coast it ranges as far east as Alabama. The salamanders do well in bottomland forests or prairies that receive enough rain to create plenty of ephemeral pools. Carl Franklin reported that a bottomland area near Joe Pool Lake, in North Texas, used to contain a healthy population of these salamanders before the area was inundated by the lake.[6] Small-mouthed salamanders are in trouble for similar reasons in many locations as habitats are altered or destroyed by humans.

Another hour and a thousand or so more logs flipped, and I began to wonder if we had somehow managed to get ourselves lost. "Nonsense," Clint assured me. "A herper is never lost as long as he is still finding herps."

"But we're not," I reminded him. This was inarguably true. The problem was that neither of us could remember exactly what direction we had come from. Every rain-filled pool, leafless tree, and herpless log looked just like so many countless others. The bottomlands stretched on and on, and we began to make a few references to *The Blair Witch Project* (the 1999 movie about three filmmakers who wander in circles for days while researching the story of a malevolent witch). Of course, we could search for the road and talk about using the angle of the sun to find our way while still searching the pools and turning logs, and that is exactly what we did. As luck would have it, there were no egg masses or amphibian larvae in the water and no herps under the logs. That first salamander had just been a tease to lure us into the woods and get us lost!

But the sun was still up and the day was beautiful in that way that bright winter days can be, and we proved our woodsman's skill (barely) by figuring out that the sun needed to be at our backs and to the right, and found our road. The problem was, this dirt road forked into two smaller trails. A snippet of a Robert Frost poem came to mind, although both roads appeared equally less traveled.

We rolled the dice and headed due west, where we soon ran into another common sight in East Texas. In the midst of all the peaceful woodland serenity there sprang up a towering totem of man's latest weapon of mass destruction against the state's flora and fauna: the gas drilling rig. Clint half expected Hexxus from *Fern Gully* to come slipping from some open pipe in the pumping and groaning oil-belching machinery like some vile grinning pollution phantom. While nothing does as good a job of drowning out the birdsong and harmony of Mother Nature as a drilling site, we did take advantage of the situation by asking a huddle of oilfield workers just where in the hell we were. We had walked almost two miles from our car through the woods.

Back at the car and safe now from all the thorns and stings and back-breaking, water-laden logs, Clint flipped up a second small-mouthed salamander in the middle of a pile of loose bark that was so spongy it crumbled as he ran his fingers through it. The salamander's dark gray body, splotched along the ribs with a patchwork of lichen-like markings, made the creature resemble just another wet, decomposing leaf at first glance, but it seemed to magically materialize into its true form in front of Clint's eyes.

Although we tried our hand along the bank of the Sabine, hoping to spot some sunning turtles or flip up a northern cottonmouth, our efforts yielded nothing. As we turned back up the dirt track that acts as the main road of the Old Sabine Bottom Wildlife Management Area, we couldn't help but be reminded that this was the last herping excursion of 2011. And while both our bodies seemed possessed by the burn that is the kiss of greenbriers and fire ants, coupled by throbbing soreness from the flipping of what had to have been a thousand logs, we found ourselves thanking the lowly salamander for one more chance to appreciate nature in its herpetofaunal form before the real cold set in.

Searching for salamanders in winter woodlands, 2013 / SMITH

It was the sort of day that does not make many herpers think of getting outdoors: gray and overcast, with temperatures in the upper forties. Rain was expected later in the day. And yet the two of us jumped into the car early with high hopes of good herping. After all, searching in quiet, damp refuges within bottomland forests on winter days like this may reveal salamanders. Two years earlier, we had found small-mouthed salamanders in the bottomlands of the Sabine River; this year we were headed farther east, where we hoped to find such species as the spotted salamander or the marbled salamander.

The Texas range of the marbled salamander extends along part of the Red River and down the eastern counties to around Houston and Galveston, according to *Texas Amphibians*.[7] It is part of the mole salamander group, which also includes the small-mouthed and the tiger. Marbled salamanders grow to about five inches in length and are black with irregular bars of silver-gray color across the back. Spotted salamanders, also part of the mole salamander group, have yellow spots on a very dark background that shades to gray on the salamander's sides. This species ranges into East Texas in a narrow band running from the Red River to about the Big Thicket National Preserve area.

Adults of these salamander species do not live in water but rely on nearby sources of water and cannot live in dry conditions. They stay burrowed down and under cover during warmer months but emerge during or after fall or winter rains to breed in shallow ponds or pools. In winter they are sometimes found in damp leaf litter and under rotting logs. These amphibians have lungs and breathe air, and yet a fair amount of respiration takes place across their moist and rather delicate skin. Areas that may support these salamanders include low areas near creeks or rivers that flood or collect rainwater. Bottomland forests, where deep layers of leaves may accumulate under the trees, are often great places for them.

So we headed for the northeast corner of Texas, around Titus and Morris Counties, near the Sulphur River. The first location we investigated was a broad, flat, forested area with little rivulets of water slowly making their way through leaf litter and green sedges. Here and there a palmetto grew. The temperature was struggling up toward 50 degrees, but with light jackets we were comfortable. Dense, moisture-filled clouds loomed overhead as our feet crackled ankle-deep through the thick carpet of dead oak leaves that made up the forest floor. The hardy, ever-present greenbrier etched stinging tattoos across our legs, and a murder of invisible crows alerted the forest of our presence.

There were plenty of branches and logs for us to check under, and I soon found a young little brown skink, which managed to slip through the mix of damp, decaying leaves, wood, and soil and disappear. Clint awakened a sleepy green anole, cold and dark brown, which tolerated our taking a few photographs as it slowly warmed and then attempted to escape. We put the lizard back under cover and wished it well.

There was a bit of standing water, and across a small, overgrown levee there was a pond. Underneath the surface of the leaves was a nice damp mixture, dark and with the earthy smell of organic material being broken down and returned to soil. But we were not finding salamanders or frogs. Could it be that the salamanders were absent because the nearby pond was loaded with predatory fish, therefore rendering it useless as a breeding pool? We could not be sure, but this did not appear to be our lucky spot. And so we moved on to another area.

At the next promising spot, Clint remembered to don his lucky green shirt. After all, a bit of luck would probably be required to turn up some herps during our eleventh hour on a cold, overcast February day.

We followed a vague trail through trees and woody growth that no doubt forms a nearly impenetrable thicket in the spring and summer. Around two pools of dark water we sifted through leaf litter and peered beneath logs. Again the ground was covered with a spongy, moist layer of what would seem to be great amphibian habitat, but none were to be found. Skirting the sides of the shallow water pools and raking back the detritus uncovered dozens of crayfish burrows, some of them undoubtedly occupied by all manner of brumating creatures, from insects to snakes, frogs, and of course the crayfish themselves. We checked another location around a larger shallow pool that flooded a stand of trees. At this location there was evidence that feral hogs had been rooting through the soil. In varying degrees, the ground seemed to have been plowed, with the leaf litter turned under and bare soil exposed. Hogs will eat nearly anything, including amphibians, but it was hard to blame our bad luck completely on the hogs.

We looked for a new location. The afternoon was winding down, and darkness falls early in February. A couple more hours and we would be driving home with nothing but memories of a pleasant road trip and time spent searching under logs and finding centipedes, beetle larvae, and a few lizards. In fact, there's nothing at all wrong with walking through the forest, seeing a few lizards, feeling and smelling the leaves and earth beneath our fingers, and wondering about what makes the ideal microhabitat for salamanders. Like all of nature, there is beauty in the winter forest and the dark, shallow pools under the trees. The leaf litter is a mosaic of different leaf shapes, textures, and hues of brown—some of it a warm dark tan, others deep reddish brown or almost black. Peering into water that has collected in a decaying tree stump can produce interesting little discoveries. And of course navigating around the tough curving strands of greenbrier is like getting through an obstacle course. This woody vine, like tangled barbed wire, makes each false move a quick lesson in the geometry of making a path through the forest. This challenge, along with the challenge of finding your way back through the forest to the car, becomes just part of the fun.

But we still wanted to fill our cameras with images of salamanders, not just portraits of their habitat. As we arrived at the place that would give us our last chance for success, drops of rain began to sprinkle on the windshield. The temperature had managed to climb to 50 degrees and would soon start to fall again. Thunder rumbled through the forest, and the sky was a little darker. We wound down a little path to another small, dark pool and investigated the area around it. Continuing further into the forest, the thunder was closer, and what I thought was a flash from Clint's camera was actually lightning. We dared to hope that the onset of rain might improve our chances, but time was running out.

The minutes ticked away, and then the thunder cracked, Clint turned a log, and he exclaimed, "Marbled salamander!" Finally we had found the object of our search. Of course, what followed was a long series of photos being taken while the salamander was reasonably cooperative, sitting still in several poses. Of course, following this exciting find, we were too pumped up to declare victory and return to the car. As the rain continued to sprinkle and show signs of strengthening, we continued checking under as much deadfall as we could. Soon Clint called out "snake!" and held up a DeKay's brownsnake. This was not a surprising find, since these inoffensive little relatives of gartersnakes are common residents of the forest leaf litter. Next it was

Marbled salamander

my turn to lift a fallen branch and, in the pocket of earth beneath, discover a black and silver salamander treasure. We looked at this second marbled salamander for a brief time, returned it to its shelter beneath the branch, and headed for the car as the sprinkles turned into light rain and the thunder rolled.

It had been a great day! We got to explore some wonderful riparian woodlands, review what we knew about the natural history of salamanders as we searched for better locations, and think about how we get enjoyment from nature even when we are not finding many herps. And then finally, as the woods darkened and the rain fell, we found our salamanders.

Peach Creek and the search for Slowinski's cornsnake, 2003 / KING

Brazos County, home of Texas A&M University, is found within the southern part of the Post Oak Savannah. Over a decade ago, I drove on Peach Creek Road, a five-mile-long stretch of herper's paradise that was mostly kept a secret outside of those closely associated with the biology department of Texas A&M. Ironically, it was research based out of this biology department that instigated my initial expedition into the area. In the late nineties herpetologists Vaughan, Dixon, and Thomas conducted a comprehensive study of the genetics and physical characteristics of ratsnakes and cornsnakes and confirmed that the Great Plains ratsnakes of East Texas were actually cornsnakes.[8] This snake was described as a subspecies of the cornsnake *Elaphe* (now *Pantherophis*) *guttata slowinskii*, named after the late herpetologist Joseph Slowinski. In the years to follow, the subspecies would be abandoned and the snake was thought to be a western population of the red cornsnake, *Pantherophis guttatus*. More recently it has been given the name Slowinski's cornsnake (*Pantherophis slowinskii*), showing how rapidly herpetological names can change.

Peach Creek Road still lies just off of State Highway 6 north of College Station, although the scenery has changed for the worse. While a drive down it today would showcase rows of two- and three-story mansions lined up single file like dominoes, nestled in uniform beds of San Augustine grass watered by synchronized irrigation systems and separated in half-acre plots, this was not the case ten years ago. Back then, acres of post oak and live oak forests replete with natural bottomland were broken by the occasional section of abandoned farmland or patch of shortgrass prairie. This sandy-soiled river bottom ecosystem, located roughly between Austin's greenbelt and Houston's coastal swamps, was where the oaks met the pines. It supported late-springtime population explosions of native anurans, which congregated in the shallow, tannin-rich breeding pools along the roadsides. This, in turn, coaxed out the snakes that fed on them.

Peach Creek was made up of just the type of river bottom floodplain that can conjure up phenomenal numbers of herps on a perfect night, or at least that was the case a decade ago before the landowners sold out to commercialization. When I turned onto Peach Creek Road, I was soon greeted by the scores of eastern copperheads that had crawled up onto the warm, rain-wet tarmac to gulp down road-killed frogs. I found almost fifty snakes that night. Over thirty of them were copperheads. At several stops I observed male copperheads trying to mate with females that had been killed by passing vehicles. From that night on, it was Peach Creek or bust whenever I found myself in the area around College Station. Twice each year, in May and September, I would return to the locale in my attempt to find and photograph the "East Texas cornsnake," making the four-hour drive southeast from the Dallas–Fort Worth area after large amounts of rain had fallen in the area. Each trip was sure to provide plenty of opportunities for photographing copperheads, western ratsnakes, and a healthy mixture of semiaquatic snakes, but Slowinski's cornsnake eluded me each and every time. Then, on a single night early in May during a full moon after recent thunderstorms had swelled the nearby Navasota River beyond its banks, I chanced upon the single greatest concentration of snakes I have ever witnessed in the state. The original itinerary hadn't even included a trip to College Station. Amber and I were on our way to hit the Texas coastline, the target species of the trip being the saline-tolerant Gulf saltmarsh snake. Slowinski's cornsnakes were a side thought, but when we passed the exit for Bryan the urge to lay over for the night in College Station and hit Peach Creek was unbearable. Needless to say, I made the exit and threw our baggage into a hotel room in town.

My wife and I were on the road by sunset. Less than a minute later I slammed on the brakes to retrieve a large eastern milksnake that was winding its way across the blacktop like a kinetic liquid candy cane. This remarkable little reptile would soon prove to be only the cherry on top of the proverbial cupcake of herps that we would feast our eyes upon as the sun disappeared over the tops of the oak trees and darkness took over the landscape. The same recent floods that had raised the river had likewise filled the ditches on both sides of the road. Watersnakes and ribbonsnakes made their appearance by the dozens. At any point we could stop in the road at random and roll down the windows, and the raucous combination of frogs and toads calling together in different notes and trills would drown out all other sounds until the cacophony was almost maddening. For the life of me I cannot figure out how the frogs located members of their own species by sound alone. There may have been a fair amount of hybridization going on at this point. We pulled over and got out to try to identify some of them with the aid of a flashlight. Walking along either roadside for sixty yards or so produced quite a list in a short time. Leopard frogs and Gulf Coast toads chorused alongside each other, with the deep baritone of male bullfrogs resonating behind them. In the foreground hundreds of gray and green treefrogs further complicated the noise, while in the distance the banjo-like plunking call of green frogs seemed to answer the random cicada-like buzz of narrow-mouthed toads. In the midst of this amphibian orgy swam dozens of watersnakes, the majority of which were already so stuffed with frogs that they floated more than swam. Plain-bellied watersnakes, by far the most common species present, were everywhere. Diamond-backed watersnakes were also common as well as the beautiful broad-banded watersnakes that I had become acquainted with on my first trip to the area.

Back on the road, we drove along slowly, stopping every thirty seconds, it seemed, to move another snake to the roadside. We found western ratsnakes, DeKay's brownsnakes, and ribbonsnakes as well as more eastern copperheads than we cared to keep a tally of. Copperheads were peeling dead frogs that been mired to the road by passing traffic, and one could literally stop for any random snake and see copperheads crawling just ahead in the area lit by the headlights.

The night wore on as my brakes wore down to nubs. Snakes kept crossing in droves. Most interesting were the Graham's crawfish snakes, which showed up in the form of three tiny juveniles barely six inches in length. Like

Clint holding two Slowinski's cornsnakes

perfect miniature replicas of their parents, these semiaquatic crayfish specialists bore the same cream-and-chocolate stripes down their backs. We found another eastern milksnake, this one unfortunately run over, and then a huge western ratsnake that my wife snapped a photo of as it bowed up in front of my face while I held it out at midbody. Two minutes later I straddled another large snake in the roadway. As I hit the brakes yet again, I remember thinking, "That was a huge Great Plains ratsnake." This thought had barely finished processing when the snake's true identity dawned on me. It was a *slowinskii*!

Sure enough, the snake in the road was none other than Slowinski's cornsnake itself! While similar to the Great Plains ratsnake in color and pattern, Slowinski's cornsnake is a much larger and more robust serpent than its western relative. In all honesty, it looks just like a cornsnake from the eastern seaboard, minus the bright orange or rust-red coloration.

"Was it the snake you've been looking for all these years?" Amber asked as I returned to the truck with my prize. "Oh yeah," I replied. "Snap a quick pic of us together if you don't mind." I held the snake, which was twined around my right hand, close to my face as she snapped a shot, and when the camera flashed I felt a sudden light blow to my right cheek. My wife was laughing as she took a second photo. This one showed a herper with a sheepish look spread across his face, which dripped blood from a perfect U-shaped pattern on his right cheek. The sweet kiss of victory!

To sweeten the deal further, after stopping for several more copperheads on the way back to the hotel, a second *slowinskii* came into view. This one was a monster! It was so big that it looked like a cornsnake skin stretched over a western ratsnake's body. It was lying parallel with the white line, and by the time I got the truck stopped I had put about fifty yards of ground between us. Nevertheless, I jumped out with flashlight in hand and ran back to the approximate spot where I thought I had seen the snake. But I could find no trace of it. Finally, after ten or more minutes of exhaustive searching, I picked out the pattern from the roadside grass, where the snake was lying perfectly motionless. It was a beautiful female, over five feet long and as big around as a baby bottle. Later, as we pulled back into the hotel parking lot, I found myself thankful that I had decided to delay my trip to the coast in favor of a night on Peach Creek. It had definitely paid off.

Unfortunately, as reported above, Peach Creek's heyday has come and gone. The soggy, useless bottomland (at least as it must have been seen through a developer's eyes) has been pushed beneath the sandy soil. The groves of mixed pine and deciduous hardwood have been felled and converted into upscale housing locked within gated communities. And the roadside ditches that filled with rainwater twice a year and supported untold thousands of amphibians and the predators that relied on them for food have long been filled in. In fact, the only thing here that remains the same is the road's name. I just consider myself fortunate to have chanced upon this long-gone paradise in the final moments before its demise. It must have really been something in the days of my ancestors.

8 The Plains Grasslands and Palo Duro Canyon

THE NORTHWEST CORNER OF THE STATE is in the southern "tail" of the Great Plains, the ocean of grasslands in the country's midsection was once prairie and now is mostly agricultural land. The Panhandle of Texas, that big rectangle in the northernmost part of the state, is famous for flat, relatively featureless grasslands from Dalhart to Amarillo to Levelland, a small town a little west of Lubbock. From the air, much of this part of West Texas is a series of circles where farmers have set up huge irrigation sprinklers, each forming a radius of the circle as it moves around, irrigating cotton or wheat. The climate of the Panhandle is arid, and farmers are able to grow crops by tapping into the Ogallala Aquifer, an expansive reservoir running under the plains from Texas to South Dakota. Unfortunately, the rate of use exceeds the rate at which the aquifer is recharged, so the water table is being depleted.

The western part of the Panhandle, the Llano Estacado, or "staked plain," is indeed flat. Geologists tell us that this all started about ten million years ago after the Rocky Mountain uplift created lots of sand and rock that could be carried by rivers downstream to the east.[1] As the rivers slowed, they deposited sediment that gradually built up the area that includes the Llano Estacado. Wind-blown sediment added to what was washed down from the mountains. As the area became more arid, a layer of caliche formed as water evaporated and left calcium carbonate to mix with gravel and silt to make a cement-like layer beneath the soil. It is referred to as "caprock" because it caps the more erosive rocks below it. A layer of reddish, sandy topsoil covers the Caprock, and this is where endless miles of open grassland grew and supported bison, pronghorn, and nomadic Native Americans.

East of Lubbock and Amarillo, the Caprock gives way to the Rolling Plains, less flat and windy but still dominated by grasslands along with mesquite, shrubs, and scrubby trees. Prickly pear cactus is common and in some places (especially where livestock have overgrazed the land) nearly fills a pasture or hillside. In the western parts of the Rolling Plains, the soil contains much red dolomite and shale, and these areas are referred to as the "red beds." The

Red River gets its name from these soils and sometimes runs nearly as red as tomato soup from the sediments that it carries from west to east. Hills and bluffs in this region may have rocky outcrops and partly buried slabs of limestone that provide great shelters for reptiles and amphibians as well as other wildlife.

Knox County, March 2013 / SMITH

Every spring, a day comes when it seems like the herp season gets started. Often it's one of those days when the sun is so bright and warm that it is easy to imagine what summer will be like. It is almost impossible to predict when this day will arrive, but in 2013 Clint and I guessed well. On a cold, cloudy day in late March, Clint started talking about returning to a couple of locations near Abilene. He said the weather forecasts predicted sunny days and temperatures of at least mid-sixties out there. He had access to private property where we could do some tin-flipping, and in the context of a sunny morning with temperatures reaching for the sixties, that sounded pretty good. And, as Saturday approached, those forecasts shifted to higher temperatures and maybe scattered showers. We were convinced that this would be a good day.

On March 30 we headed for the Rolling Plains with high hopes of seeing lots of species. As we got west of Graham, the landscape alternated between cultivated fields and mesquite scrub, and we wondered why we find some herp species in areas with high cultivation. We noted that sometimes diamond-backed rattlesnakes or bullsnakes live around cultivated fields, no doubt eating the rodents that may be found there. However, there is little in the way of shelter to be found in cultivated fields. We concluded that these snakes must shelter in small pockets of better habitat and come to the big fields to forage for food or simply cross through cultivated fields on their way to better places.

Our first destination was one of those small places that offer shelter, an island surrounded by cultivated fields. On a farm road in Knox County, in a little corner that did not fit the geometry of the tractor and plow, there was a grove of trees surrounding a broken-down rock house. Scattered around were some sheets of tin, daring us to see what was beneath. The sunshine was warm as we began exploring. The usual tin-flipping involves corrugated sheets lying on the ground or perhaps stacked in layers. These tin sheets were half buried, so considerable prying and pulling was required, and of course we needed to be mindful that we were in a prime area for western diamond-backed rattlesnakes. It would not do to simply grab an edge and pull without knowing what might be tucked away a few inches from our fingers.

Under one sheet Clint found a female checkered gartersnake and carefully

Male and female checkered gartersnakes

extracted her from her hiding place. She was a fine specimen with a narrow, straw-colored, almost pinstripe line extending from the back of the head to the tip of the tail. In typical checkered gartersnake fashion, she thrashed around briefly but made no attempt to bite. Here at the end of March in this part of Texas, she was probably just beginning to be active and had likely spent the winter in a pocket where the tin reached at least a couple of feet underground. Wedging the sheet of tin farther back, Clint exposed a second gartersnake, this one a male. He was a beauty, with a wider, pale straw-colored vertebral stripe and a background color that was a lighter shade of olive than the female. Each of the snakes had an alternating series of black spots in a checkerboard pattern between the top stripe and the thin, pale side stripe, but his stood out more boldly than hers on account of the light background. Undoubtedly these snakes had mated or were going to mate, and after snapping a few photos we let them slip back under the tin. Hopefully, a new bunch of baby gartersnakes would be the result.

Few gartersnakes are as tolerant of dry conditions as the checkered gartersnake, which is found throughout West Texas and South Texas as well as the Hill Country. In the grasslands of West Texas and the Panhandle, it may be found near creeks and ponds, though not necessarily at the water's edge. These gartersnakes will take advantage of a wide variety of animals in their diet, chiefly frogs and small toads, but also earthworms, lizards, and occasionally small rodents. Most adult checkered gartersnakes measure from about eighteen inches to two feet in length, with females generally reach-

Western diamond-backed rattlesnake

ing much bigger sizes than males. This is a pretty species, sporting shades of olive and cream along with a black checkerboard pattern. The irises of their eyes are a coppery color, a final touch that adds to their beauty.

Nearby, under more tin, we found a small western diamond-backed rattlesnake that politely tolerated our snapping pictures, even when we had to block it from disappearing down a rodent burrow. Not twenty feet away, while photographing a prairie lizard, we discovered another rattlesnake a few steps away from where I stood. With rattle buzzing, it disappeared under the blocks of concrete from a collapsed structure. Meanwhile, we found two prairie lizards, both males with bright metallic blue patches on their bellies. These guys were clearly posting their availability on whatever dating service lizards may use.

Shackelford County, 2012 / KING

The Morris Ranch contains 1,500 acres of rugged, arid, rocky landscape, replete with limestone hills. Dense thickets of mesquite and honey locust provide dappled shade over impenetrable stands of prickly pear cactus. The stony ground yields little to offer for all but the toughest flora, such as horse crippler, pincushion, and pencil cacti. Small stands of the resilient scrub oak are the only real providers of shade, and even these are scarce, choked out by the countless mesquites.

The ranch had been handed down to my cousin's husband, Rob Morris, by his grandfather, who had purchased it because of the large hill that made up the property's northwest corner. It is a place of rare and true seclusion,

A hillside on the Morris Ranch

located on a dirt county road some thirty miles from the interstate.

Gaining access to private land is a field herper's dream. Your presence there is uninterrupted and unbound. There is no sharing of space with other visitors or abiding by rules other than those given by the state and the landowner. There are no gates that lock at sunset. It is an all-around splendid isolation, surrounded by habitat just waiting to be trekked. Amber and I were the first people to explore it aside from a handful of family friends, who have been hunting deer on it for three decades. In other words, no stone had ever been turned, or at least not in search of anything reptilian, and I felt like some early American herping pioneer on the forefront of discovery.

We visited in late May, several days after the area had received a series of light thunderstorms. We arrived around six in the evening, and the ambient air temperature was in the low nineties. It was a mile drive down a primitive dirt path to the back of the property, which ended at the foot of the hill. The path narrowed as it made a sharp rise in elevation and soon became impassable except by foot or perhaps an all-terrain-vehicle. Being without an ATV, we parked the truck and began hoofing it up the incline toward the hilltop, where there was a good vantage point to view the property as a whole. Our plans were to scope out the lay of the land for a suitable place to camp, then find a way to get the truck there and pitch a tent. Of course, being an amateur herpetologist and entomologist, even something as simple as a hike up a hill becomes complicated, and I was soon encumbered with an aerial net, jars, a camera, and my trusty snake hook.

Once we reached the summit with a jar full of rainbow grasshoppers, which are a stunning, tricolored, arid land species, we pushed our way through the dense carpet of dried grass that covered the hilltop like a wild crop of straw-colored hair. The prickly pear grew higher here than on the lowland and in certain places was well above our heads. But in a short time we found a break in the brush and gazed down on the property in awe. To my surprise, there were four ponds, and I knew these scarce water sources would be perfect places to find an array of thirsty fauna. There were also several deer stands and feral hog traps set up near these ponds, and I had brought along a .20 gauge shotgun to help whittle away at the nuisance hogs that have been devastating the land all across the state.

The best place to set up camp appeared to be a large, open area of sandy ground along the eastern edge of one of the smaller ponds, as it appeared to be devoid of mesquite and cacti and, with luck, would provide us with the opportunity to see some nocturnal animals near the tent. So we hiked back downhill and returned to the truck, then drove to the site. There was still an hour or so of daylight left, and the inquisitive child in me triumphed over my adult reasoning, and I suggested a little nature-exploring around the pond prior to throwing the tent up. Amber, long accustomed to this type of behavior, only nodded in reluctant agreement and without saying a word handed my snake hook to me.

Immediately I began finding herps, in spite of the heat that was beating down upon us like God's very own private incandescent lamp. A pair of Texas spotted whiptails broke up their courtship ritual and headed for a stand of greenbrier, with the male in hot pursuit behind the female. Down at the pond's edge, newly metamorphosed Blanchard's cricket frogs and spotted chorus frogs exploded from the mud to the safety of the water like tiny kernels of popping corn. Plains leopard frogs and American bullfrogs also hit the water with loud "ker-plops," some of them crying out in alarm with high-pitched squeals.

Before too long the sun began its inevitable descent over the western horizon, and Amber suggested we pitch the tent soon unless we wished to do it by flashlight. On the way back to the campsite we came across the first snake. An adult western diamond-backed rattlesnake came cruising across the trail in front of us at a leisurely pace. Amber spotted it first, and the proverbial cry of "Snake!" rang out in the air. Our thundering footsteps caused ground vibrations along the rocky path, and the creature, sensing our movement, picked up the pace from rectilinear movement to the faster S curves of serpentine motion. By the time I had the camera ready, it had crossed the trail and disappeared into a dense crop of six-foot-tall prickly pear.

Not long after this, another exciting find added to our good fortune, this one of the invertebrate kind. It was a tarantula hawk, the largest predatory wasp in the United States. These bold insects are solitary hunters, the females seeking out tarantulas and fearlessly overpowering them with a paralyzing sting before poking them down a preexcavated burrow and inserting an egg into the body. The still-living, immobile spider then serves as a host for the larval wasp. It takes a lot of wasp to subdue a fully grown tarantula, and this one was two inches in length, with a wingspan of over three inches. It flew in from the mesquite thicket like a miniature Cessna, hovering on rusty-orange wings for a second before landing on the ground in front of us, its metallic blue-black body scampering along the ground in a manner that could have passed as the thrill of the hunt or eager blood lust.

Once we set up the tent, I stretched a white sheet between two forked branches of a honey locust tree and turned on my portable blacklight in order to attract nocturnal flying insects, which are drawn in by the ultraviolet light. Amber commented that I was the only camper she had ever known who purposefully attracted bugs to a campsite. I pointed out that perhaps she had been camping with the wrong types of people all these years.

No sooner had we set everything up than I was ready to get in the truck and do some night cruising on the dirt trail in search of snakes. The headlights pierced the darkness, illuminating the dirt track ahead, and it wasn't long before they revealed a second western diamondback, caught in the middle of a nocturnal foray. This one stood its ground boldly in defiance of my intrusion, and I snapped a quick picture of it in its typical defensive posture before moving on.

Next we came across an adult western massasauga stretched across the trail in the process of swallowing a Great Plains skink. Only the robust, smooth-scaled tail of the hapless lizard could be seen protruding from the voracious serpent's mouth.

The remainder of the night revealed two common kingsnakes that, in this part of the state, are hybrid forms between the speckled and desert kingsnakes. We also found a nice adult western ratsnake as well as a huge centipede of the genus *Scolopendra*. By eleven o'clock the activity seemed to have shut down, so we retired to the tent in an attempt to get some rest for the day ahead.

We awoke bright and early at sunup (Amber is a trooper) and elected to hit the hill for some rock-flipping before it got too hot. We traipsed along at a slow, steady pace, Amber scanning the ground for arrowheads (her principal interest) as I tried to look for insects and lizards at the same time. The insect fauna was magnificently diverse. I found flightless tiger beetles, ornately patterned orange and black checkered beetles, and a katydid in the genus *Neobarrettia* with a pair of jaws that looked like serrated tree loppers. When provoked further, the three-inch-long beastie leapt to the ground from its perch on a bush, raised its spiked front legs above its head, and did a strange, tribal-looking dance with its brightly spotted turquoise and yellow under-wings exposed.

We investigated around a small pond where a large yellow mud turtle climbed onto a raised mudbank and proceeded to bask in the rays of the quickly rising sun. From there, we traveled uphill, me flipping rocks like mad and Amber claiming victory at last as she discovered an arrowhead unearthed from the recent rains after several hundred years of burial. On a steep butte under a boulder that was almost too heavy to lift, I scared up a male eastern collared lizard, his stocky jade green body taking off like a reptilian rocket across the ground, putting as much distance as he could between himself and the intruding human. He was so fast I didn't get to see where he went, let alone get a picture.

All this rock-flipping was quite a workout. The term "flipping" sounds like casually tossing rocks around. The reality is, you are carefully lifting large, heavy, flat rocks, looking beneath, and then lowering the rock back just where it was. If you just drop the rock, or worse, leave it flipped over, the tiny microhabitat under the rock will be destroyed. The ideal conditions that made this just the right rock to turn over will be lost, forcing invertebrates, reptiles, and amphibians to seek some other refuge. It's more work to do it the right way, but in our opinion it's the only way to do it.

West Texas rock-flipping is one of the best methods for finding those liz-ards with smooth, glossy scales and diminutive little legs, collectively known as skinks. Once, in another Shackelford County location, I found an enor-mous Great Plains skink beneath a large hatchet-shaped rock midway up a hill. The Great Plains skink is the largest skink in North America, and this particular specimen was about as big as they get. These are my favorite skinks, although I have learned the hard way that grabbing them without restraining the business end can be a bit of a mistake. Like miniature croco-diles, these robust, strong-jawed lizards have a "bite-and-spin" strategy that works wonders for regaining them their freedom, and several times I have sacrificed a sizable chunk of flesh from one of my fingers in exchange for a skink in the hand.

We herped the hillside for another two hours. Amber turned up a handful of beads and flint chips, and I discovered a prairie ring-necked snake, which posed in typical ringneck fashion, flipping over and forming its body into a

Western massasauga eating a Great Plains skink

A katydid confronts its perceived attacker.

series of yellow kinks, the vivid scarlet tail curled into a tight corkscrew. I also flipped up another collared lizard, this one a comparatively drab female, but she got up on her hind legs and sprinted uphill for a good ten yards like a tiny dinosaur; yet again I was unable to get a picture. The presence of this second individual suggested that the species was doing well in the area.

I remembered another day of West Texas rock-flipping that took place on a cool spring day. We had been northeast of Abilene. A recent cool front that had passed through the night before still lingered in the wind, but the sun was shining brightly without a cloud in the sky. It had been a perfect day for flipping. The combined conditions were ideal for reptiles, amphibians, and other ectotherms to come to the surface to lie with their backs pressed against the underside of flat rocks to thermoregulate. Early morning and dusk are usually the only times when rock-flipping is productive enough to be worth a herper's while. Once the sun is at its zenith, the rocks become too hot and the reptiles retreat back into cooler places below ground. But on cool, sunny days the rock-flipping can be exquisite. On this day, we flipped variable groundsnakes, a flat-headed snake, and several other species. Almost all of the larger rocks had mouse and rat nests beneath them, and many of these were abandoned, with the telltale shed skins of the evictor wrapped inside the balls of dried grass. At the top of the hill beneath a particularly large rock I had caught a large adult Great Plains ratsnake red-handed in a recently emptied mouse nest. The former residents of the nest had been reduced to slight bulges in the snake's trunk, even though its eyes were opaque and its skin had turned dark and muted in preparation of an upcoming shed.

The sun of today's late-May visit was now high and hot, and I had flipped enough rocks to turn my hands into a raw mess of tender, scraped flesh. So we abandoned the hill and headed back in the direction of the tent. But the herping wasn't over yet. At the foot of the hill in a bush I found a huge western coachwhip, its stomach bulging with a large, tube-shaped meal that could easily have been a collared lizard. Weighed down by its breakfast and unable to flee, the wiry diurnal snake bunched its body up into a tight series of loops and faced the human. Impressed by its nerve in the face of danger, I snapped a couple of quick shots and then left the coachwhip alone to digest its prize.

By this time it was one o'clock in the afternoon, so we went for a drive to survey the surrounding countryside and take advantage of some much-needed water and air conditioning. Driving along the county road, we crossed a creek where three different species of turtles were basking on a fallen mesquite log. Two were common sights, a red-eared slider and Texas cooter. But the one in the middle was an unexpected find indeed. It was a

Prairie ring-necked snake, dorsal view

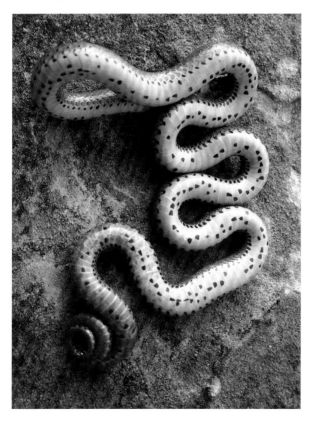

Belly of the ring-necked snake, showing yellow shading into orange and red

midland smooth softshell, a species I did not know occurred here. I had the ill luck of having left the backpack containing the camera in the bed of the truck, and although I tried my best to sneak out and retrieve it, the opening of the truck door spooked one of the turtles, which sounded the alarm for the whole lot to abandon ship. They dropped into the rain-swollen, muddy creek en masse, and yet another great shot was lost.

Time was running out, and the sun was high in the sky now, beating down on us relentlessly as we broke down the tent and set up the grill for some hot dogs. We ate at pondside and afterward netted dragonflies and damselflies and threw bits of hot dog to the turtles, which devoured them with gusto. Yellow mud turtles and red-eared sliders came to our feet as if they were on a feeding schedule, but a giant snapping turtle kept its distance, opting instead to float on top of the water, its massive knobby shell breaking the pond's surface as it watched its smaller kin chowing down on the hot dog bits.

We tried our hand at fishing, and on the first cast I caught a young small-mouth bass. But eventually that old thief time caught up with us, and the hour of our departure drew nigh. It had been a wonderful Memorial Day weekend, full of adventure, excitement, and plenty of memories from the field. And if the weekend's success was any indication of what summer would be like, we would be in for one memorable year.

Return to the Morris Ranch / SMITH

Having heard the stories of Clint and Amber's trip to the Morris Ranch in 2012, I looked forward to visiting the place with Clint at the end of March 2013. The day was sunny and warming nicely when we got there. Primitive roads wound through mesquite scrub and past a couple of small ponds (one of them completely dried up) to a rocky hillside. We started up the hillside, flipping rocks and carefully returning them to their original position. Just about every rock had one or more bark scorpions beneath. Among the rocks were various cacti, and not just the usual prickly pear. One cactus species, commonly known as the horse crippler, looks like a dull green dome, with vertical folds or ribs, and crowned with an array of stiff thorns. Our cactus-expert friend John Chmielewski said it is found from north-central Texas westward to New Mexico and south into the northern states of Mexico. John also noted that they flower in early spring and, after pollination, produce bright red fruits that contain large black seeds.

Overall, the rocks that we turned did not provide a wealth of herps, but more species turned up as the day progressed. One real prize was an eastern collared lizard that Clint saw briefly before it disappeared under a larger rock. Together with his observations from the previous year, this further suggests that collared lizards are common on the ranch. They are strong predators that can eat other lizards, even small horned lizards.

Another rock sheltered a variable groundsnake that was likely getting fat on the scorpions we had been seeing, though they reportedly favor spiders over scorpions. It seems amazing that these inoffensive little snakes can eat centipedes and scorpions. In their book on Texas snakes John Werler and James Dixon cite a description of groundsnakes seizing scorpions by the telson—the final segment of the tail—thus avoiding being stung.[2] Groundsnakes occur in a variety of colors, and this one was a plain light brown snake about ten inches long. Clint recalled another spring day in a nearby location when he had found several variable groundsnakes. One had been dove-gray, with a series of black cross bands starting behind the nape and going all the way to its tail tip. Nearby he had found a second, this one in the more typical solid-gray phase. This tiny creature was a juvenile, barely over three inches in length. Groundsnakes are the grab-bag prizes of the reptile world. You never know what you're going to get when you uncover one, and in areas of prime habitat within their range they can be the predominant snake species in the spring. A single hillside can often produce a dozen or more of these diminutive serpents in a day's search.

On our journey around the property we had seen several active harvester ant mounds. When you're in West Texas and you see big red harvester ants, if you're a naturalist, you think of horned lizards. We stopped at one more location, open flatland with mesquite trees, and Clint saw a big male Texas horned lizard—the first of the day. He had a big, bold white stripe running from his neck down the middle of his back and onto the tail and a sandy brown ground color with a double row of yellow-edged brown spots. At the center of each spot was a big spine. And of course there were the horns on the head, arranged in a frill that wrapped around his skull with two longer spikes at the back. This lizard froze in a clump of dried vegetation, counting on camouflage for safety, while we photographed him. As we continued to buzz around him like big clumsy bees, he decided that moving away would be a good idea, so we wished him well and walked off.

How long had it been since I had seen a horned lizard in Fort Worth where I grew up? It was probably sometime in the 1970s, and even that sticks out in my memory because I was so delighted to find one of these disappearing critters. They had not been common there since the mid-1960s when harvester ant mounds dotted the suburban west-side backyards and fire ants were nowhere to be seen. Since then, a number of factors have led to the eradication of the Texas horned lizard from most or all of the eastern part of the state.[3] Much blame has been placed on the fire ant, which may kill the

Variable groundsnake with plain brown color

Variable groundsnake with more color and pattern

lizards and their eggs but, more importantly, has greatly reduced the harvester ants that horned lizards feed on. Horned lizards do not feed on fire ants. Additional issues include habitat loss, as the native bunchgrass prairies have been plowed and planted with crops like wheat or livestock forage like coastal bermuda. Such grasses grow more like a carpet and not in bunches that leave room for animals like horned lizards to maneuver in. Habitat is also degraded as more roads cut through the land and fragment it into smaller patches. And of course habitat is lost due to urban sprawl and development.

West Texas remains something of a refuge for Texas horned lizards,

Texas horned lizard

though it is not clear that they are doing as well as they did in the past. Nevertheless, it helps that the land is less fragmented out there, and at least in places less of it has been plowed. The drier conditions are not so good for fire ants, and harvester ants are still found in many places. We hope that the "horny toad," or *el torito de la Virgen* ("the Virgin's little bull," as it is sometimes called in Mexico) continues to grace the landscape of West Texas.

Battle of the badlands / KING

Brick red whorls of dust rose up, skirting around my tires as I crept along at a box turtle's pace down the road south of Aspermont. This was a familiar track, a little-traveled red dirt road winding several miles through a wide section of mesquite savannah separated by small plots of wheat and cotton. It was late evening, that magical time of ecstatic anticipation tempered with some frustration as the eyes struggle to pick up fine details while adjusting to the dusky colors of a sky gearing down for twilight. I had been doing well as far as herps went. I had already seen several Texas horned lizards, a checkered gartersnake, and an irate western diamondback.

When the long, rope-like form of a large snake emerged from the high grass at roadside some twenty yards in front of me, I slid to a cautious stop. The snake was a western coachwhip and a sizable example of its species, around six feet in length. Coachwhips are probably the single most common diurnal serpent on the Rolling Plains, and the sight of one passing in front of the vehicle like a disappearing mirage is a usual part of any daytime road cruise in the area. But this one was busy, its head raised nearly a foot off the ground, the pointed birdlike snout angled sharply downward as it appeared to be studying something closely in front of it—something invisible to my faltering eyesight. Intrigued, I screwed the telephoto lens onto my camera and proceeded to slip out of the car with as much stealth and silence as I could muster.

While coachwhips are highly alert visual predators, quick to pick up on the first sign of movement, this one was so preoccupied with whatever scent had captured its fancy that it was oblivious to its surroundings. Thus I was able to approach to within ten feet and sit down cross-legged in front of my car and observe whatever little piece of its life I had the good fortune of sharing.

The snake's black tongue flicked rapidly in and out, the twin tips delivering scent particles to the Jacobson's organ, where they could be identified. Its head began to jerk in excitement some seconds later. Its neck was crooked, craning down until it almost touched the surface of the road. Then there was an explosion of sand right under the coachwhip's nose as a blurry conglomeration of tan and black scales erupted like Vesuvius, carrying a thick, robust tail on short, stubby legs. The coachwhip darted forward and plucked this bundle of rapidly departing energy from the sand with no effort. The prey item was then hoisted from the ground thrashing and twisting. It was an enormous Great Plains skink, nearly a foot long. Any herper who has spent any amount of time flipping rocks in the plains is more than likely familiar with this great fossorial reptile, as they are one of the most abundant lizards in this ecoregion. They are seldom seen above ground, opting to spend the majority of their lives in concave depressions that they excavate beneath flat surface objects or, if these are lacking, directly beneath the surface of the loose red terrain, as this one had. But the coachwhip's keen sense of smell had ferreted it out even as the skink lay hidden just below the surface. No sooner had the snake locked its jaws around the skink's back than the lizard reached its head up and clamped its jaws down on a fold of skin on the snake's neck.

The coachwhip seemed made of tougher stuff, though. It appeared not to notice the ripping, rolling jaws locked down just behind its head. It held the fighting skink aloft while slithering across the sand, then swung its head over in a wide arc, slamming its prey to the ground. It repeated this process several times over, until the lizard's jaws released, then dropped it to the ground and backed up as if it were observing its condition.

Great Plains skinks are covered from head to tail tip in large, tightly compact glossy scales that are hard to penetrate and hold onto. Although this one was bleeding, it was far from bested. Addled, it shuffled drunkenly in

Western coachwhip grabbing a skink

The coachwhip pins the skink and considers its next move.

sideways motions, the tiny claws kicking up spurts of sand as it made for the high grass. The coachwhip seized it again, and again the lizard countered this attack by biting. Once more it was slammed to the dirt several times over before being released and observed.

This time the lizard was obviously mortally wounded. It was bleeding profusely from a series of shallow slits, its body twisted and contorted by what was likely a broken vertebra. Still, it made a feeble attempt at escape. The big snake allowed it to crawl several feet, as if testing the severity of the wounds it had inflicted. Then it grabbed the skink at midbody, struck it against the sand twice more, perhaps for good measure, then worked its jaws up to the head, where it engulfed the now motionless skink up to the front legs in a series of rapid wiggles of its head.

All the while my camera had been snapping still shots of this dramatic battle of the badlands. I raised up on tired legs deprived of proper circulation and made my way slowly back to the car, doing my best not to disturb the coachwhip as it enjoyed the fruits of its labor. What a wonderful, unexpected moment I had been privileged to witness. These are the moments naturalists live for, when the private worlds of the subjects we find ourselves so fascinated with collide with our own, and they share with us the secrets of their survival.

I left the coachwhip behind, my car again raising up red dust as the sun slipped away behind those low, rolling hills bathed in the shades of late evening, bidding both snake and man farewell.

The Panhandle
The Panhandle of Texas is an area where herpers think of bullsnakes, rattlesnakes, Texas horned lizards, and, in places during spring rains, the barred tiger salamander. For some time we had wanted to visit the area, and we hoped to do so after some relief from the drought. However, the rains stayed scarce, and so in 2014 we decided to visit the Caprock and Palo Duro Canyon even if the dry conditions limited what we might see.

Even when there is no drought, the Panhandle is arid land, getting less than twenty-three inches of rainfall in a typical year. Early explorers described it as vast and desolate, a treeless grassland that seemed to go on forever. Two rivers dominate this area—the Red and the Canadian. As these rivers and wind eroded the rocks, canyons gradually formed. Chief among these is Palo Duro Canyon, where the Red River has eroded about 600 to 800 feet from the Caprock to the canyon floor. According to the Texas Parks and Wildlife Department, which manages Palo Duro Canyon State Park, the canyon winds across the land for about 120 miles. It is the second-largest canyon system in the United States. Hiking Palo Duro had been a goal of ours for some time.

Our first stop, however, was Lake Meredith, a large lake that sprawls across Potter, Moore, and Hutchinson Counties north of Amarillo. Our first day, we had just enough time to check out the lake, which had been recommended as a prime herping area in the Panhandle. As we drove north, raindrops began to spatter across the windshield. It was late afternoon, and the temperature hung at an unyielding 50 degrees. To make matters worse, a dust storm had blown in from the northwest, blotting out even the faintest hint of light along the western horizon. Tumbleweeds raced across the highway, driven by blowing wind and rain. For a moment, we questioned the wisdom of visiting the Panhandle in early April.

Lake Meredith / KING

We turned off FM 1913 and were soon greeted by a large sign that read "Boat Ramp Closed." This, in fact, turned out to be an understatement. There was hardly enough water in the lake to float a child's toy boat, let alone a real one. While the drought had been an ongoing statewide problem for years, the situation here was beyond adverse. It was downright dire. Vast tracts of agricultural land and oilfields that looked as if they had been mowed all the way down to the dirt gave way to more natural shortgrass prairie, where the withered yellow strands of dried grasses waved in the winds below scrub-like mesquite. The stubbornly hardy mesquite tree has multiplied and changed the landscape of the western two-thirds of Texas. Equipped with a tough bark and sharp thorns, mesquites are capable of surviving in almost any dry terrain and are a common sight from the Panhandle to the Rio Grande. There was a notable difference in the size of the trees here, though. Largely dependent upon available moisture, the girth and height of mesquite trees are in direct proportion to the availability of either groundwater or annual rainfall. In the Rio Grande Valley, where late-summer monsoons bring in large amounts of Gulf moisture, areas that have been overtaken by mesquite are full of relatively tall trees up to twenty-five feet in height and with trunks the diameter of manhole covers. But here, in the comparatively dry Panhandle, the mesquites were short, stubby, and more akin to desert shrubs than actual trees. Even the tallest were slightly over head high, with the girth of a man's thigh. Interspersed with the scraggly mesquites were tree cholla, creosote, and pencil cactus. This was reminiscent of the upper Chihuahuan Desert, which lay several hundred miles to our south, separated in geography by miles of Rolling Plains mostly devoid of this flora.

As we traversed a secondary road on the way to the Lake Meredith National Recreation Area, the remains of what was once a boat ramp came into view. The asphalt descended to a dry lake bed—it did not look like anyone could have launched a boat here for years. The lake basin had been dry long enough to support groves of young poplar trees as well as all manner of various succulents and prairie grasses. So much for the lake as a source of water that could support populations of reptiles and amphibians!

In these previously submerged foothills, flint, quartz, limestone, and sandstone composed the bulk of the geography. I was particularly amazed at the size and quantity of the flint in this area. Back in my more familiar

Mesquite grasslands around Lake Meredith

stomping grounds of the North Texas Cross Timbers, I had learned to asso-ciate the presence of flint on the ground with historical Native American activity. It would seem this would hold true in the Panhandle as well, for it is not uncommon to stumble across dart points (commonly referred to as arrowheads), knife points, scrapers, and other primitive tools made from flint, usually in hilly regions or along the banks of rivers and their tributar-ies and springs. It turns out that near Lake Meredith is a well-known source of very high quality flint, the Alibates Flint Quarries. The place was used by Native Americans for thousands of years and has been designated a national monument.

Flint was everywhere as we made our way from the roadside into the field. It crunched beneath our feet and also occurred in large, ragged chunks of up to twenty pounds. The two of us made our way up the hillside, flipping the occasional loose, flat slab of limestone in the hope that the space beneath it harbored some reptilian life form in spite of the chilly early-spring tempera-ture. Within a relatively short time this paid off in the form of a New Mex-ico threadsnake (until recently, threadsnakes were known as blindsnakes). Threadsnakes, while diminutive enough to be commonly mistaken for earthworms by the layman, have nevertheless always intrigued me. They are unlike any other snake on earth in several ways. While considered to be among the most primitive of types, they are highly specialized and adapted completely to a subterranean lifestyle. This suits them well, for they spend almost their entire lives below ground. The threadsnake's eyes have been

New Mexico threadsnake

reduced to vestigial pinpoints, and, unlike other snakes, their ventral scales are not enlarged to stretch across their belly. This gives them a completely cylindrical body that can wedge itself into the tiniest cracks and crevices in the earth, which is ideal for a snake that spends the majority of its life crawling through ant and termite tunnels, where it feeds almost exclusively on the insects' larvae. This highly specialized diet must come with a defense mechanism of some sort, as ants and termites possess formidable jaws and protect their mounds en masse. And so the threadsnake is equipped with a chemical secretion that coats its body and serves as a natural insect repellant. This thin fluid is best observed when holding a threadsnake in the hands and its thin, pinkish trunk suddenly takes on a shiny, silvery appearance. These snakes fulfill almost all of their biological functions underground, including feeding, breeding, and egg-laying, and females have even been known to congregate in communal nesting sites. Three species occur in Texas: the Texas threadsnake and the New Mexico threadsnake in the northern and central parts and the Trans-Pecos threadsnake across the southwestern desert. The different types can be identified only by their location or by minute differences in scalation. At Lake Meredith the only form that occurs is the New Mexico threadsnake, which made identification easy for us.

Sometime later, up a steep draw, I overturned some loose, flat sandstone and exposed a pair of variable groundsnakes. Their variability could be seen between these two examples. Both were around seven inches in length, a typical adult size, but one was adorned with dark half-moon-shaped markings down the back on a tan ground color, and the other possessed a single scarlet vertebral stripe from nape to tail. The first specimen immediately bolted back into a deep fissure in the dried earth, but I was able to grab the other snake before it disappeared.

In spite of our best efforts, no additional herps were found at Lake Meredith that first day. The overall temperatures were much too cold, so we decided to make for the hotel and start over the next day when temperatures were expected to warm as the week wore on.

Palo Duro Canyon State Park / SMITH

We arrived the next morning at Palo Duro Canyon under sunny skies but with temperatures still on the cool side. We decided to try the Rock Garden Trail, despite the park staff's description of it as a difficult hike. Near the bottom of the rock garden, with the sun shining brightly and boulders sheltering us from the wind, it was warm and pleasant. Huge boulders that appear to be chunks of the Caprock are stuck in the red sand and clay, turned every which way as if they just rolled down the canyon last week. The trail winds around them, climbing steadily but not so rapidly as to immediately wear you out. There is a long-term plan for that, and it involves getting you high up on the sides of the canyon, thrilling you with grand vistas, and luring you behind the next bend in the trail. By the time the trail is ascending in relentlessly steep grades, it is too late; you are hooked in, and turning around is out of the question. The faint smell of the junipers is pleasant, and you just go on to the next scenic view, and you begin to think that you must be near the end of the trail. By the time you turn back, your water bottle is getting low and the muscles in your legs feel like lactic acid is bleeding through the pores of your skin. And you have a two-mile return hike in front of you. Thankfully, it is mostly downhill.

Clint began checking the temperature on rock surfaces to get some idea of when conditions would be right for lizards. As the rocks began to warm, we started to see a few of them. The first to make an appearance, a little before 1:00 p.m., was the common side-blotched lizard, a four- to five-inch lizard with speckles across the back and a large black spot on the side behind the armpit. One pretty male with a scattering of blue spots across the back sat still on a rock and looked at us as we snapped photos. He was near the base of a small juniper amid a series of broken rocks along a precipice.

At some point the trail veered off along the side of the canyon through a juniper woodland. These small evergreens growing low to the ground gave the air an aromatic freshness as we walked along a narrow, twisting, red dirt trail.

We emerged at the edge of a rocky ledge that dropped off to a jumble of

View from the Rock Garden Trail, Palo Duro Canyon State Park

Common side-blotched lizard

rocks and trees far below. A bird flew past the ledge, plunged twenty or thirty feet downward and soared on as we got a look at its flight from above. It was as if we were perched at the edge of flight and could join that bird as it flew past the multicolored layers of geologic time written on the canyon walls in red sandstone, iron, yellow clay, and gray caliche. The view of the canyon from a long distance is impressive and beautiful, but looking across a few hundred yards, from the vantage point of a high cliff, is more breathtaking.

And the fact that this ledge was separating from the rest of the shelf of rock and preparing (at its own geologic pace, which might involve substantial time) for its turn to slide down the walls of the canyon gave our perch

Palo Duro Canyon

an especially gripping quality. A few feet back from the edge a good-size fissure had opened, and we could look down into the cracks that one day would allow these rocks to tumble down and add their signature to the rock garden.

The temperatures warmed nicely, so we resolved to explore around the boulders of the lower twists and turns of the Rock Garden Trail, where we believed the prospects for seeing collared lizards might be best. Farther up the trail, Clint quietly exclaimed, "There!" Up above us, looking out over the edge of a boulder, was a male collared lizard. He calmly basked in the sunlight, surveying his domain. No doubt he took note of us, but he showed no concern. Clint climbed around the rock, taking a few steps as quietly as possible, and then stopped to assess whether our subject was getting alarmed. He gradually moved in and got a few photos.

We went different ways in search of more lizards, and we covered considerable ground without seeing any. In places, hikers had built small cairns, stacking stones in little towers or making arches of rocks. I moved around clumps of prickly pear cactus with extremely long thorns and by patches of dry, yellow grass covering the rocky ground in a golden haze. The occasional side-blotched lizard scurried away.

Then, backtracking down the trail and nearing a small boulder balanced atop a narrow stack of flat rocks, I saw another collared lizard. I approached slowly as the reptile looked out past the edge of his stone fortress. He noticed me, looked around, and rubbed the side of his mouth against the rock, much as a bird might rub its bill on a branch. To get a good photo, I climbed up on

Male eastern collared lizard

a shoulder of earth beside the rocks, a narrow gap between a tree and the boulder. Still he did not run, although he was keeping an eye on me. After the clicking of a couple of additional photos, this little dragon decided to retreat around the back of the rock and out of sight.

These two eastern collared lizards had both been adult males, and the males are more colorful than the females. They have big, muscular heads, strong legs, and long tails that can result in a total length of about a foot. The "collar" referred to in the name is really two black markings that partially encircle the neck. The collar does not cross the throat. In the spring, during breeding season, males may be a bright greenish turquoise on the back and legs, speckled in white and yellow. There may be yellow "socks" on their feet, and some males may have yellow rather than grayish heads. The male's dramatic colors may be accompanied by bold displays of head-bobbing when another male comes near. While most territorial disputes may be settled by these ritual displays, the big males are willing to fight with younger males.

Their feeding habits may be just as aggressive. While the diet of the eastern collared lizard includes lots of insects, they are quite willing to take smaller lizards and other small animals. Among the lizards of the American Southwest, this is a fierce little predator. And, in turn, collared lizards may be eaten by birds of prey, roadrunners, small mammals, and larger snakes.

When a predator approaches, the collared lizard scurries into crevices in the rocks and boulders, no longer an invincible Tyrannosaur but simply a lizard trying to avoid being eaten. And even though mine ultimately scrambled to the safety of some hidden rock crevice, he had been self-confident enough to watch me approach within about five feet while holding his ground.

We spent some time on the floor of the canyon after our hike and were able to see numerous bird species. In a clump of juniper a group of cedar waxwings searched for berries. With their smooth, airbrushed-looking shades of golden brown and gray and the patch of brilliant red on each wing, they are beautiful birds. The black mask and little crest at the top of the head made their identification pretty easy, even for me. At another spot, a pair of golden-fronted woodpeckers came and went, pausing long enough in a nearby tree for us to get a photo. These birds make use of open woodlands and brushland, and they eat not only lots of insects but fruit and nuts as well. While watching the woodpeckers, a female turkey walked into the area where I was sitting, not particularly concerned about my presence. We soon spotted another, and then before long the tom turkey (the male) came strutting by, gobbling and fanning out his feathers to impress his harem. He followed them around in a vain attempt to get some reaction, but the females were interested only in browsing for food on the ground. Perhaps his courtship achieved some results later, but the ladies appeared unimpressed while we were observing. When mating does occur, the hen lays from four to seventeen eggs in a shallow nest on the ground, according to the Cornell Lab of Ornithology.[4] After all that display and drama, the male does not participate in caring for the young, which follow the hen for a short time until they learn to forage for food on their own. Watching these turkeys and seeing the male's courtship display added to the richness of the time we spent at Palo Duro.

A Final Visit to Lake Meredith

Toward the end of our last full day in the Panhandle, we decided to return to the area west of Lake Meredith to see what might be on or around the road near sunset. It had been a warm day, maybe one of the earliest truly warm days this spring in the Panhandle. We could easily imagine any number of species out in the golden light of the setting sun. We did see a group of pronghorn, an animal that is often called an antelope but technically is not. It is found in Texas from the Trans-Pecos up into the Panhandle. The short grasslands surrounding the roads raised hopes that we might see a bullsnake or coachwhip. As it turns out, we were to see something that we prized even more than those. In the fading light of day a spikey little lizard was soaking up the last rays of the sun. It was a Texas horned lizard, an unusual treat reserved for our trips to localities with arid grasslands and lots of harvester ants. This one was fairly cooperative about being photographed, perhaps afraid to stir up these crazy humans who had done such a victory dance around their little horned treasure. Shortly afterward, we saw a second Texas horned lizard before darkness set in and temperatures began to drop rapidly. It was time to go back. This had been a wonderful few days, exploring a part of Texas that was still beautiful and fascinating, despite the drought.

9 Seven Nights on the Great Rattlesnake Highway in the Rolling Plains

Clint King

I'll sleep when I'm dead.
—*Warren Zevon*

THIS CHAPTER CONTAINS CONTENT of an extremely irresponsible and arguably dangerous nature. No attempt should be made to engage in these practices for the purpose of successful herping or otherwise. Driving while sleep-deprived for nights on end is not recommended by the Texas Department of Transportation, and abandoning moving vehicles in the middle of the roadway is downright stupid, especially in pursuit of rattlesnakes and other venomous species that should never be harassed in the first place. Energy drinks have yet to be evaluated by the Food and Drug Administration and are not guaranteed to keep one from falling asleep at the wheel. For that matter, using snake sightings as a stimulant is not appropriate insurance against death and destruction behind the wheel. All this aside, happy herping!

Night 1: A meager beginning

My headlights cut a path across the pitch-black asphalt as I leaned forward in the seat, eyes straining to pick up any sign of something reptilian on the roadway, but there was nothing. I was in King County along the eastern edge of the Rolling Plains that, just slightly north, begins to form the Texas Panhandle. It was the second weekend in May, and I was driving beneath the pale sliver of a barely visible crescent moon. Under normal conditions, I should have been raking in the herps, but such was not the case. It had been a strange spring in 2013, ironically, the year of the snake in the Chinese zodiac. It had been a warm winter, followed by an unusually late, cool, and dry spring. In fact, it had been the coolest and driest spring I could remember. Although it was only 9:00 p.m., the temperature had already dropped from the day's high of 81 degrees to 68 degrees at sundown. I drove on and on into the night, but aside from a diamond-backed watersnake found dead on the road I had failed to come across a single herp. (I was not surprised to find this watersnake—I am convinced the species could thrive anywhere, even a Walmart parking lot.)

The Great Rattlesnake Highway

Although the temperature and drought shifted the odds against me, I feared something much more sinister was to blame for the lack of herps—something irreversible: the human-altered landscape. Nearly every square inch of the county had been turned beneath the plow. The terrain was grass-green and as flat as a military buzz cut, without a single rock or tree as far as the eye could see. While this was no doubt a beautiful sight to the cotton, wheat, and cattle farmers, who make up the bulk of the area's human population, it was a bleak and disheartening one for the roving herper. There was nearly nothing to work with, habitat-wise. I felt like I was just wasting precious fuel.

So I turned the truck around and headed east toward Knox City, the county seat of Knox County, which would be my home away from home and central point of departure for the next eight days and seven nights. When I reached Knox City, I drove south into Haskell County, then headed southeast across what I hoped would eventually turn into some herp-worthy habitat. Unfortunately, this would not be the case. The pale luminescence from my headlights exposed more and more precisely geometrical green cropland. To top this off, the temperature had dropped down to 67. This search was downright pointless.

I was turning the truck toward home base to call it a night—then I saw it. It could have been a rock, but what would a rock be doing in this manicured reptile wasteland? I pulled over and went back to the spot, where a small, grayish lump of tubercular amphibian flesh greeted me. It turned out to be a Texas toad, a common species that replaces the Woodhouse's toad found to the east. Well, at least it was *something*. Still, it wasn't enough to keep me wandering against the wind. I continued due north as the mercury steadily dropped.

I was cruising along at seventy miles an hour when a lithe serpent form glowed in front of my high beams like a piece of white braided rope. Slamming the brakes, I wheeled back around and soon had a little male checkered gartersnake in hand. Checkered garters are great adapters. They are opportunistic feeders, exceptionally cold-tolerant, and capable of thriving in areas completely devoid of so much as a stick (areas equally devoid of nearly all other herps).

If the habitat wasn't ideal, what was I even doing out here? It's a fair question. Technically I was here on nonherping business, but I did have seven nights to indulge my sweet tooth for finding reptiles. I wasn't about to let one bad night slow me down. The week was still young; I just had to find some decent habitat.

Night 2: Slim pickings on the Brazos

I finished work early the next day with several hours of daylight to kill, so I drove as far away from the agricultural fields of Knox County as I could; down to the Clear Fork of the Brazos River, where I hoped to find a snake I had never seen before, the Brazos watersnake. I knew of a spot to safely and legally park—it was beneath a bridge along the county's northern border. I could pull the vehicle over and walk along the riverbank without worry of venturing onto private property.

The temperature was in the low eighties when I parked and picked my way down the steep embankment toward the water. The river was exceptionally low due to the drought, and a thick layer of algae covered the shallow, stagnant water that was passable by foot in most places. I honed in on a spot laden with flat, slippery slabs of river rock worn smooth by years of overpassing currents. Beneath the first one I found a juvenile watersnake. Unfortunately, it was another diamond-backed watersnake, not a Brazos River watersnake, but I hoped it was a good omen. I flipped in the area for an hour and a half, but aside from a couple of Texas spotted whiptail lizards, a variable groundsnake, a thousand Blanchard's cricket frogs, and metallic-green ground beetles, the site yielded little. Day soon turned into late evening, and the temperature dropped as quickly as the setting sun. It was already 74 degrees by the time darkness enveloped the landscape, and I had the sinking feeling that this night was going to be a repeat of my first night. The change in habitat was a vast improvement from the barren landscape of

Male ornate box turtle

Knox County, though hard-pressed by mesquite trees and prickly pear. The Brazos River wound through this mixture of rocky subdesert, thorn scrub, and grassland, interrupted by the occasional wide rectangular swatch of fertilized coastal Bermuda grass that befouled the landscape like an ugly gangrenous wound.

Back on the road, over the next few hours I found a western ribbonsnake, a western diamond-backed rattlesnake, and a western coachwhip, all common residents of such habitat, as well as a seldom-seen chelonian, the ornate box turtle—all, unfortunately, roadkill. The box turtle was the worst to see since females can take upward of ten years to reach full sexual maturity; even then, they may lay only one clutch of several precious eggs every year. To see one reduced to turtle jelly on the highway felt like a double shot of cyanide in the pit of my stomach. Making matters worse, that accursed temperature gauge in my truck already showed 67 degrees again. Angrily, I turned the truck around and headed back for Knox City with that now-familiar feeling of defeat.

Night 3: Hog heaven, herp hell
For the third night I decided to head south. The temperature climbed throughout the day to a high of 91 degrees, so my hopes were a little higher for spotting herps. Shaking things up a little, I planned to spend time in neighboring Haskell County, where I had previously picked out a nice twenty-mile stretch of dirt road along the southern county line. Judging from the

Rolling Plains habitat in Haskell County

topography, it looked like an ideal place to find a prairie rattlesnake (*Crotalus viridis*). This species is associated with a grassland milieu and tends to shun areas populated by its more habitat-generalist cousin, the western diamond-back. I hadn't seen a prairie rattlesnake alive in over a decade, and thus it was at the very top of my wish list for the trip. While common residents of the expansive Great Plains, I have found them only occasionally in Texas.

The West Texas sun was sinking low by the time I got to the dirt road. I saw only one herp, a spunky juvenile western diamondback that I mistook for a stick at first. It wasn't a total bust—I did come away with some great pictures of a red-tailed hawk perched on a fence post and saw a badger and several deer. I also saw over twenty feral hogs, some of which looked like they could have weighed over 150 pounds. These introduced animals wreak havoc on habitat and other wildlife and could have been part of the reason I didn't see more snakes, as their extremely varied diet includes snakes (as well as almost anything else they can crush into pulp). Their presence and ways of managing their population are controversial issues, but ones that need to be resolved. An introduction to the issues concerning feral hogs can be found at the Texas Parks and Wildlife Department website.[1]

I spent the remainder of the drive dodging white-tailed deer and wondering where all the snakes were hiding. The temperature ranged between 80 and 74 degrees, so that wasn't the culprit. I had a sneaking suspicion that the drought was partly to blame. Someone earlier in the day had informed me that the Miller Creek Reservoir, which supplies most of Knox County's public water, was going to be shut off by January if the area had not received adequate rainfall, bringing the drought problem into a much starker human perspective.

Night 4: The worm turns

Blessed storm clouds rolled in from the southwest as the sun set over the rolling hills and mesquite trees east of Haskell. The cell had dumped rain all over Abilene and was slowly working its way north. These were the favorable conditions I had been waiting on for four days. But the resident snakes had been waiting much longer than that. The storm was bound to cause a sudden drop in barometric pressure the hour before it unloaded, sending the snakes into fast-action mode, whereupon they would be zipping across the roadways at top speed, trying to outrun the low-lying, flood-prone areas for higher ground—at least that was the hope.

This weather fulfills a field herper's dreams, and it provides an added bonus: After the rains have passed, amphibians, seemingly nonexistent in the weeks and months before the shower, are likely to pop up suddenly to mingle on the still-wet asphalt.

My hunches were confirmed moments later when a monster western diamondback appeared on the pavement under the now-overcast skies. The fact that the snake was in high gear was a dead giveaway that things were about to get very snaky. Diamond-backed rattlesnakes are prone to lying motionless in the road, stretched out to absorb the warmth of the tarmac. Those on the move are usually found crawling slowly in rectilinear fashion, using their muscles to grip and pull themselves along in a straight line, not unlike the tracks on a bulldozer. But this snake was racing along like a startled coachwhip. By the time I stopped the vehicle, the huge crotalid was nothing but a disappearing string of rattles in the tall grass on the roadside.

From there on out, things only got better. I crossed into Throckmorton County and, once again, a pale, tubular object laden with scales crossed my path. This one wasn't getting away! There was barely enough daylight left to see without a flashlight, but I instantly recognized this small rattlesnake by its narrow head and olive-green, heart-shaped blotches. It was a western massasauga. This venomous grassland denizen has been one of my favorite finds since the age of ten, when I encountered my first specimen on the Wilson Prairie in southern Wise County.

I grabbed the rattler with my tongs and dropped it into a bucket—to be released later after photos had been taken. On with the show . . .

During the next hour, snakes came out of the mesquite woodwork. Western diamondbacks made up the bulk of the activity, but I also found several nonvenomous species, including a variable groundsnake, a diamond-backed watersnake, a coachwhip, and two large, beautifully adorned Great Plains ratsnakes. All except the massasauga had been moving at an alarming speed.

As quickly as the activity had begun, it shut off. The next hour failed to yield a single snake. Then the storms arrived, and the rain came down in buckets. It was toad time.

I turned the truck north in the direction of Knox City, intending to herp my way back in the rain, but after seeing only scores of giddy Texas toads, I blew right through Knox City and kept driving north, back into the hillier region of King County, where my adventure had first begun. Although Texas toads were still the prevalent species here, Couch's spadefoots were also common in all of their various color forms. As an icing on the anuran cake, a lively little Plains spadefoot made an unexpected appearance on the roadway back into Knox City. It had been a productive night on the Rolling Plains, and the rains were long overdue, especially for the drought-weary reptile and amphibian residents. But it was nearing 2:00 a.m., and work started at 7:00. It was time to wrap it up and wait on the next evening, when another band of late-spring showers was in the forecast. Things were going from bad to excellent.

Night 5: The Great Rattlesnake Highway

It had been a long, hot day in West Texas, with temperatures nearing 100. The cool front had finally passed on the coattails of a rapidly moving storm cell, and the sun was once again allowed to shine. And shine it had! As I watched the weather forecast, drinking a huge glass of iced tea that evening, there was little that could have removed me from my glued-on place on the La-Z-Boy. As I glanced at the radar, I heard the meteorologist caution that another storm warning was in effect for the area, but this storm would be in a collision course with the departing cool front, forming conditions that could potentially produce hail as well as tornadoes. This was bad news for herping yet again, unless, of course, I took off early and broke west of the storm—far, far west of the storm perhaps. Maybe as far as, say, thirty miles east of Lubbock. It was time to bid Massasaugaville good-bye and head deeper into prairie rattlesnake country, gas costs be damned.

My plan was to break out of Knox County to the northwest, cross King and Dickens Counties, then take FM 651 south of Crosbyton. This road cut straight through the heart of Crosby and Garza Counties from an elevated stretch of red-rock canyonland rife with diamondbacks into a vast expanse of downward-rolling shortgrass prairie still unmarred by agriculture. If I were going to find a prairie rattlesnake, this would be the most likely place. As an added bonus, the road eventually spilled out onto US Highway 380, where I could herp my way back in the direction of my temporary sleeping quarters.

I loaded up the work truck with cameras, flashlights, and pillowcases and broke west for the open road, hoping for a change, expecting the best, not fearing the worst . . .

Forty miles and a Texas horned lizard later, I turned south on 651. As the sun began to set, the eastern horizon piled higher and higher with dense cumulus clouds laden with moisture. I was counting on another sharp barometric pressure drop. Sure enough, as the shadows lengthened along the two-lane state highway and a dusky hue bathed the prairie to either side of me, herps sensed that change and began to move. These snakes were all western diamondbacks and checkered garters, the predominant species no matter what type of terrain I traversed. Before it got too dark I stopped to check out a drainage system on the side of the highway. Here with the aid of my flashlight I found Plains leopard frogs, western narrow-mouthed toads, and Texas toads, as well as a tiny yellow mud turtle the size of a nickel.

The night wore on and the temperature fell ever so slowly. I had seen almost a dozen snakes, but all of them had been either diamondbacks or garters. I was starting to think they had pushed everything else out of existence when I stopped on the bridge over McDonald Creek and found a lively Kansas glossy snake on the pavement. These lizard-eating, blotched colubrids are common western inhabitants of sandy areas where they can find prey and burrow easily. The glossy snake seemed to be the catalyst. After that it was like a great reptile spigot had been turned on, and snakes began to cross the highway in numbers I could have only wished for.

The farm road ended several glossy snakes later, and I turned eastbound on US Highway 380, in the direction of the storm, but it was still fifty or more miles away. As it turned out, this highway was an even better road than the secondary road had been. While this is seldom true of highways, this one was virtually traffic-free, with two wide lanes and a decent shoulder. It was sublime. Almost immediately, I slammed on the brakes for a tiny, wriggling serpent. To my amazement, it was a Chihuahuan hook-nosed snake. While not exactly rare, hook-nosed snakes are secretive, burrowing snakes, so they are difficult to find even within their range. They are highly fossorial, spending most of their lives hidden underground; they use their sharp-tipped, upturned rostral scale as a spade to dig up earth and ferret out the arachnid morsels that constitute the bulk of their diet. This little oddity was an even rarer sight here, as it had yet to be documented in the area.

As soon as I grabbed the snake, it broke into its unique defensive strategy. Coiling its tail into a tight spiral, it jabbed the end into a crook between my fingers and emitted a rapid flatulent sound from its cloaca while simultaneously smearing my hand with a vile mixture of urates and predigested

Chihuahuan hook-nosed snake

spiders. Presumably, a predator might be more likely to release a snake that engages in this startling behavior. This tactic, known as cloacal popping, is caused by the snake sucking in air and then letting it back out in a series of short bursts. Now I was herping!

By the end of the night, I had found a total of thirty-four snakes, the majority of which were diamondbacks and glossies. I also found Great Plains ratsnakes, bullsnakes, and several western massasaugas. I clocked the last specimen of the evening, a gorgeous hybrid between the desert kingsnake and the speckled kingsnake at 3:24 a.m., just east of Knox City. Best of all, I had two more nights to find my elusive prairie rattler; while I had yet to come across one, I finally had a pretty good idea of where to start looking.

Night 6: It's raining snakes!
I had driven 377 miles the previous night, and if I had had it my way, I would have put at least that many more on the poor work truck the following night. As my good fortune would have it, yet another stream of storms was due in the exact place where they had moved through the night before. So armed with Visine and energy drinks, I once again made the great escape from work in the late evening. With only three hours of sleep under my belt, I was going to need some help. Hopefully the adrenaline rush that comes every time I see scales in the headlights would provide both the physical and mental stimuli I would need to make another long and productive road cruise.

I departed at seven o'clock and the temperature was still 102 degrees. It was hot enough for those undulating lines of heat to shimmer off the piping

Juvenile Texas horned lizard

hot asphalt, giving one the impression of a mirage on the horizon line. So it came as a surprise to find a juvenile Texas horned lizard sunning itself on the tarmac with what I can only describe as a quite contented lacertilian smile on its pudgy, harvester-ant-stuffed face. The road tar was impossible to hold my own finger on for more than a second or two, but the lizard never budged. I feared if it sat there much longer it was going to either melt into the pavement or become glued there by a passing ranch truck, so I escorted the little saurian safely to the roadside with my hook where it could resume its sunning on rockier but safer ground.

As I had expected, it was ten o'clock before the temps dropped to a level sustainable for the other, less heat-tolerant reptiles to surface. As the hours passed without herps and the gas needle dropped steadily, I wondered why I had left so early and why I was so bent on exhausting my energy supply on this sixth night, when any sane person would be in bed getting some much-needed rest. I could almost envision myself in some quaint, white room occupying a folding chair in a group circle amid the usual innocuous confections of coffee and donuts, waiting my turn to stand and say, "Hello, my name is Clint and I'm a herp-a-holic. It's been twenty-one days since my last road-cruise . . ."

My musing was shattered by the wonderful sight of red, black, and yellow scales winding slowly across the pavement. I ground the brake pedal into the floorboard and soon had a wriggling long-nosed snake in trade for new brake shoes and pads. I have always held these lizard-loving nocturnal gems in high regard. Truth be known, they are my favorite colubrids, hands down.

Long-nosed snake

I bagged the long-nosed snake and hit the road again. By this time, I had put a hundred miles between me and Knox City. As the next hour passed, I saw only a dead box turtle and a live checkered gartersnake. An interesting and uncommon mammalian find was a badger shuffling across the highway for an instant before disappearing back into the realm of darkness beyond the high beams. Robust, fearless predators, badgers belong to the mustelid family, kin to weasels, skunks, and ferrets, and are powerful diggers as well as avid snake-eaters.

Garza County passed behind me to the west, and just as I crossed over the Kent County line, there it was: a three-foot-long crotalid stretched out full length in the road. Although I had become complacent due to the lack of snake activity and was driving way too fast, I could tell that this snake didn't have the characteristic black and white ringed tail of a western diamond-back. It had to be a prairie rattler! (Though without seeing it, I couldn't be sure.)

I swung the truck around as quickly as I could and sped back to the place where I had seen the snake, but it was gone. I kicked myself for not being more alert as I reluctantly crept back onto the highway at a snail's pace, shaking my head as I thought about the rattler that had gone ghost on me. My eyes were open wide now, scanning my surroundings. It was a good thing, too, or I would have missed the next snake: a male Plains hog-nosed snake. Lying between the white line and the roadside grass on the shoulder, it could easily have been mistaken for a short stick. These are the western counter-

Plains hog-nosed snake

The belly of the Plains hog-nosed snake is black with patches of orange color.

part of the eastern hog-nosed snake back home. Smaller and more strongly patterned, with a more upturned, spade-like snout, they more closely resemble rattlesnakes than the eastern hognoses. This was another surprising find. Hognoses are almost always found in the daytime, but it was 11:38 p.m. Apparently this snake had failed to read the field guides.

I took US 380 east, and the herping opportunities opened up again just as they had the previous night. Diamondbacks and massasaugas were everywhere. Glossy snakes and Great Plains ratsnakes made up the bulk of the colubrid sightings. The best part of all: there were no other cars, which meant almost every snake was alive. By the end of the night I had racked up twenty-five snakes, including another beautiful kingsnake hybrid in Haskell County. It had been crawling on the surface at 1:17 a.m.

The temperature was still around 80 degrees when I pulled over at 2:35 a.m. for the last snake of the night, a small western diamondback whose stomach was distended from a large meal. It had been a glorious night of herping on the Rolling Plains, but little did I know that the best was yet to come.

Night 7: *Viridis* or bust

> Seek, and ye shall find.
> —*Matthew 7:7*

It had been another 100-degree day in Knox County, and I was running on a total of about seven hours of sleep and 500-plus miles of driving in the last three days. I was tired, sweaty, hungry, and road-weary, but I couldn't stop. I had not found a prairie rattler, and this just would not stand. It was my final rendezvous with the Rolling Plains in all of its nocturnal glory and consequently my last chance to locate the target of my obsession. I had already been fortunate enough to find a multitude of both common and uncommon species, some of which I hadn't seen in over a decade, including some sightings that went down as county records and even a range extension, but still my thirst had not been satiated. And so, in what had become my new routine, I pulled out and gassed up an hour and a half before dark. My final battle plan involved heading northwest, skirting yet another spring storm that was slowly rumbling north over Knox, King, and Foard Counties and spending the first early hours of the night in the southern panhandle of Motley County near the town of Matador. After this I would cruise back down 651 and then 380, hopefully one *viridis* the richer. As I headed out of town and into King County, the sky began to take on an ominous amber tone, and a thick gray band of nebulous clouds edged in a sulfur color swelled up in my rear view. Somewhere out there, a prairie rattlesnake was sensing the changes in humidity, temperature, and barometric pressure and was emerging from its daytime snooze-spot to prowl. Hopefully our paths would cross.

If the previous two nights had been wonderful, they were only a precursor to this last evening on the road. The approaching storm worked its magic both quickly and efficiently, dropping the baking temps to more herp-comfortable levels and cloaking the open grasslands in a shady, humid bowl of cloud cover. Even before dark I began seeing reptiles. Coachwhips, checkered garters, and Texas horned lizards were just notches on the belt, as were a handful of Great Plains ratsnakes and western massasaugas. As I passed into Dickens County, the landscape became rockier and "canyon-esque." Just before the sun set I witnessed a golden eagle gliding low over the tops of the mesquite trees, its six-foot wingspan spread to full length as it scanned the view below for a juicy coachwhip or jackrabbit.

I turned the truck northward through a disturbing swath of agricultural land just as darkness swooped in. Suspense was high as I sucked down another energy drink, eyes peering intently for a break in the ground. As I crossed over into Motley County, the grass gradually grew taller, and I saw the now-familiar silhouettes of mesquite trees creeping back into the habitat at roadside. No sooner had I witnessed this conversion than I also spied a tiny serpent meandering across the road. I wheeled around and back-tracked slowly but couldn't find the creature. Finally, in my angst, I resorted to pulling over and getting out to look down the road with my flashlight. The instant I turned the light on and aimed it at the ground, my beam fell upon a large massasauga emerging from the grass. This wasn't the snake I had seen earlier; it was much too large and venomous! After escorting the little pit viper to the relative safety of the grass, I resumed my search for the missing colubrid. To my surprise, I found it—a tiny variable groundsnake. This was one of the prettiest examples I had seen. It was a straw-yellow color, with dark black crescent-shaped moons running from nape to tail tip. A thin vermillion vertebral line ran between the bands, as if it had been painted on first, further enhancing the beauty and intricacy of this otherwise diminutive beast, which was all of five or six inches in total length.

For the third night in a row the massasaugas and glossy snakes dominated the road. These were seconded by the familiar diamondbacks, for which I likewise stopped only to shoo them out of danger from passing traffic, not that cars seemed to be posing much of a problem. I was the only person on the road. Maybe I had finally reached a herper's version of Heaven, Mecca, Nirvana . . .

This went on until almost eleven o' clock, when I turned around to try a new spot. Why, fellow herpers may ask? Well, blame it on *viridis*. Sure, I was seeing tons of snakes, and most of them were rattlesnakes. But the fact that there were two species of abundant rattlesnakes in the vicinity told me that the prairie rattlers were not the dominant species here. In other words, I was in good rattlesnake country, just not good prairie rattlesnake country. Since I was already in the lower Panhandle, I figured traveling south and west would put me in better favor of finding my quarry.

I drove back to Dickenson and then broke due west. I stopped for gas in Crosbyton and checked the map (yes, I still use a paper map). A thin strip of state highway snaked southward through what looked like a vast open stretch of what I hoped was shortgrass prairie and not farmland. The road was twenty-three miles long. That seemed like a pretty good place to spend the remainder of my last excursion. I would either find a prairie rattler there or die from lack of sleep trying.

Five miles south of Crosbyton the state road rose sharply along both sides, giving me the impression of driving on a hilltop. Still, in the shadow of the headlights I could see that the grass was not just short, it was as if God himself had issued it a military buzz cut. And then there was a snake lying along the side parallel with the white line. I caught only a glimpse of it, and it looked promisingly crotaline. I stopped the truck at the side of the highway, threw it into park, and bailed out with tongs in hand.

The light danced along the asphalt, bouncing as I ran back to the spot where I had seen the snake. It was still there, and the strong blotched pattern of chestnut brown on tan keeled scales told me that at long last my search for a prairie rattlesnake had come to its blessed end. The snake remained motionless until I grasped it gently at midbody with the tongs. Then the "Jekyll-and-Hyde" effect that is typical of the species came into play. Rattles whirred, and the snake turned into a live, loose electric wire. There was no way I was going to get photos of a now-enraged rattlesnake at night on a hilltop highway with my truck parked at the side of the road. So I dropped my unhappy prize into a container until the light of the following day, when I could take all the pictures I wanted.

I was done. My seven-night search for *viridis* had finally come to an end. I had found my treasure, which was even more satisfying since I didn't see another snake moving in the next two hours. It was time to head back to Knox City for some sleep. The only problem was that any way I sliced it, Knox City was almost two hours away.

I drove on south without seeing a thing—snake or human. This, coupled with the hum of the highway, was beginning to lull me into a dangerous, exhaustion-induced trance. I had been down this wicked road before. Having pressed my body to the ultimate limit of sleep deprivation, I would be lucky not to end up in a fiery ball of steel and rubber.

I somehow made it to 380 and was traveling eastbound on the Great Rattlesnake Highway when the trance was once again broken by a light-hued tricolored snake stretched out full length. Like no energy drink could, this brought me instantly awake, and I jumped out to find a beautiful specimen of a long-nosed snake. While almost all examples of this serpent consist of

Prairie rattlesnake

Prairie rattlesnake in a defensive position

some degree of red, pink, or orange in the pattern, this particular jewel was predominantly red.

After the longnose, the skies opened up and a steady downpour of snakes followed me as if some divinely inspired cloud had been draped over the highway for miles. In fact, snakes were more numerous on this last night than on any other night of the trip. Aside from the usual steady stream of

Western milksnake

glossies, massasaugas, ratsnakes, and diamondbacks, I found an additional *viridis*, another more typically colored longnose, a bullsnake, two garters, and a dead eastern yellow-bellied racer. Most notable was a western milk-snake (previously known as the Central Plains milksnake), which crossed my path just east of the city of Haskell. Even though it was 2:50 in the morning, I paused for a good half hour to photograph this seldom-seen gem of the plains in a rock cut at roadside. By the time I got back to Knox City, it was 4:30 a.m. While I still had some nonherp-related work to do, as well as the photographing and releasing of a few specimens, the only thing on my mind was sleep. I had gotten off to a shaky start, but it had ended up being one of the most successful trips of my life. I had seen over a hundred snakes and, most importantly, had found my prairie rattlesnake. As I headed for home the following evening, another band of dark clouds began to build up in my rearview mirror along the western skyline. In spite of all of the miles and herps I had put behind me, my mind couldn't help but wonder what might be out there crawling on the roads tonight. Did I mention I am a herp-a-holic?

A reminder: collecting or moving herps from the pavement is not cur-rently a permissible activity. See the chapter titled "Final Thoughts: Getting Started Field Herping" for a discussion of how the legality of road hunting has changed in recent years.

10 At the Doorstep of the Trans-Pecos

Clint King

The wilderness has a way of renewing a man's soul
—*William H. Stephens*

ON THE WAY TO THE DESERTS of the Trans-Pecos, there is a transitional landscape where the Edwards Plateau begins to yield to the arid, rocky terrain of the Chihuahuan Desert. As one traverses through it, the habitat is reminiscent of both ecoregions. Expanses of gravel, creosote, and mesquite are broken here and there by limestone hillsides that often shelter small groves of live oak and juniper. The presence of oaks and junipers whispers to travelers of a last chance to find water in any sizable amount. Jagged canyon beds and ravines carved from years of erosion brought on by seasonal flash floods are adorned with a mixture of leafy green plants and desert succulents. It is the Edwards Plateau's last stand.

When people began laying claim to these remote sections of the state in search of oil and other resources, they required modern roads and highways to get from place to place quickly. The hills were dynamited so that roads could cut through rather than go around them, leaving a narrow strip of asphalt centered between two high walls. The faces of such rock cuts, over time, crack and crumble with exposure to the elements, and these cracks provide deep holes and fissures where wildlife can seek refuge from the insurmountable summer heat as well as winter cold and spring rain. Herpers have discovered that searching these cuts at night with aid of headlamps or flashlights allows them to find those rarely seen, secretive species.

Juno Road

Val Verde County will always hold a special place in my mind as my introduction to the Trans-Pecos region of Texas. It was the location of my first official herp trip. I was eighteen years old, and the Dallas–Fort Worth Herpetological Society was just learning to crawl. Its president, the late Steve Campbell, and Michael Price, then president of the West Texas Herpetological Society, had proposed a joint field outing in late May. I had just graduated from high school and could think of no better way to celebrate my newfound freedom than to take to the open road in search of all those desert gems I had only

207

read about in field guides by Tennant and Dixon. One in particular, the long-nosed snake, was at the top of my wish list. Despite being a common species in many parts of its range, I had yet to find one.

I can remember that first nocturnal road cruise down Juno Road as vividly as if it were yesterday. We had all agreed to meet up at a hotel in the small town of Ozona, which lies some considerable distance to the southwest of San Angelo. Members of the two herpetological societies had traveled from different regions of the state to join up in the first field outing of the year. After general introductions all around, we paired up into vehicles. The evening sun cast ever-lengthening shadows across the parking lot, and we knew those herps wouldn't wait—nor could I. I drew the good fortune of carpooling with Steve Levey. Although this was our first acquaintance, it didn't take long before we were chatting it up and swapping old snake stories as if we had known each other for decades. As we traveled down the highway, the luminescent twin beams of his car's headlights piercing the darkness, our casual conversation was interrupted by a brilliantly colored serpentine form lying in the center of the two-lane highway. Steve hit the brakes, and before the car could come to a complete stop, I had barreled out of the passenger-side door, feet flying, my flashlight bouncing in nervous skitters as I raced toward what I already knew was nothing short of some reptilian miracle. It was a brilliantly patterned Blair's phase gray-banded kingsnake—a *Lampropeltis alterna*, the most coveted reptile in the Trans-Pecos. It was my first live snake in the field in West Texas, and it hadn't taken more than an hour to find it. With shaking hands, I reached out and gently grasped the exquisite creature, which responded with a firm though harmless clamp on my index finger. I couldn't wait to get back and show off my newfound prize to the others, who would undoubtedly be green with envy. I was ecstatic to the point of disbelief.

As it turned out, we were among the last to arrive back at the motel, the majority of herpers having already given up for the night. Steve Campbell was standing in the doorway of my room as I threw my bags in; a quirky smile spread across his bearded face as his eyes fell upon the wriggling pillowcase I was undoubtedly brandishing just a little too proudly in my free hand.

"What ya got in there, King?" he inquired.

"Oh, nothing. Just a little snake we picked up on Juno."

"See anything good?"

"Oh, you know, a gopher snake, a few diamondbacks."

Steve was a professional fisherman of sorts for Texas Parks and Wildlife, so I had a bit of fun baiting my line before reeling him in. "Oh yeah, and this . . ."

Clint and his first gray-banded kingsnake

I casually unknotted the top of the pillowcase and extracted the snake, holding it under Steve's nose like it was the world's largest diamond. It would be quite undignified to repeat his response as he shook his head at my luck, but I will say it was accompanied by a finger gesture and a low, guttural chuckle. "And this is your first night in the Trans-Pecos?" he said, knowing full well that it was. "That's right," I replied nonchalantly, to which Steve repeated the aforementioned obscenity.

"Well, that's beginner's luck for you," he said as I handed him the handsome specimen. "And to think you came out here looking for your first long-nosed snake."

"Yeah," I deadpanned, "that would have been cool if it had been a long-nose instead of this kingsnake."

Steve caught on instantly. "I know," he said, "We'll have to print you a T-shirt that says 'I came to West Texas looking for long-nosed snakes and all I got was this lousy *alterna*.'"

That trip will likely always be one of my most treasured memories afield. It was when I got to know Michael Price and Justin Garza of the West Texas Herpetological Society, who are not only living storehouses of knowledge on the local herpetofauna but respected photographers and naturalists with excellent field ethics who hold conservation in high regard. Steve Campbell introduced me to Pepe's Cafe, home of fine Mexican cuisine in Ozona (which still stands to this day; I seldom, if ever, miss the chance to visit Pepe's when I find myself en route to the Trans-Pecos). Later that day, the Pecos River greeted me with a wonderful day of trading herp tales and chasing down arid land ribbon snakes below what was then the Pandale Store, and numerous inside jokes were born live and wriggling as I became acquainted with local hot spots. These included the Pandale dirt road and the Fort Lancaster rock cuts, where species I had previously known only from childhood books came alive before my very eyes. For an eighteen-year-old herper still wet behind the ears, I felt as if I were walking through the Promised Land among giants.

Juno Road, fourteen years later

The thin two-lane blacktop stretched before me like a gentle undulating ribbon, its colors muted by the disappearing sun barely visible over the western hills—a vibrant slit of tangerine. The dusky, pastel hues of rose, vermillion, and periwinkle that made up the creative evening masterpiece in the sky above me would all too soon be wiped clean as the canvas gave way to nightfall in Crockett County and then Val Verde County, south of the town of Ozona.

It was after nine o'clock by the time I made it to the first cut. I pulled the car over as safely as I could on the grassy shoulder, cut off the engine, grabbed my snake tongs, headlamp, and flashlight, and exited the vehicle. Once the interior light cut off, I paused for a brief moment to stare up at the night sky. It was a cloudless night in mid-May and as dark as pitch. Billions of stars twinkled overhead, as if God had tossed a pocketful of diamonds into the air. The wide openness of West Texas, coupled with its clean air and general lack of artificial lighting along the horizon in any direction makes it, hands down, one of the best places for star-gazing in the country. This has always been my ritual at the first cut: get out, kill all the lights, and just stare up into that vast expanse of creation that always defies my attempts to contain its magnitude. I send up a quick prayer of thanks and guidance to that ageless Maker of the stars, then click on the headlamp and it's go-time.

As seasoned West Texas field herpers know, there are a few tricks to upping the ante on one's success along the cuts. A lot of it depends on the exact species that you are looking for. For example, mottled rock rattlesnakes emerge from the crevices at dusk when they are on the move until they find a suitable flat place to coil and ambush their prey. So if rock rattlers are on the desired wish list, it helps to walk the cut bases in late evening and early night, then move along the top of the cut, shining the light down at the exposed shelves as the night wears on. Of course the principal reason for most "cut-shiners" is the gray-banded kingsnake, and this is well understood. For a herper it is almost an unmatched feeling to be walking along in the darkness, a single light beam piercing the night along a seemingly unending succession of light gray rocks, cracks, and root systems, and then suddenly to have the pattern broken by the thin, wiry trunk of a gray-banded kingsnake in search of sleeping lizards, the brightly alternating saddles of orange and soft gray broken by thin borders of black and white. For a brief moment it seems unreal, as if the snake isn't really there or was perhaps painted there on the rocks, and then the tongue flicks, or the snake finds traction along the rough surface of the rock wall and pulls itself up an inch or two, and reality suddenly kicks in in the form of a rush of adrenaline as the herper finally comes across his or her "diamond in the rough."

While gray-banded kingsnakes are one of our most beautiful native serpents, one does not have to strike "*alterna* gold" every time in order to be a successful cut-shiner. This is a good thing, as graybands, while not exactly rare, are seldom found even in areas of favorable habitat in perfect weather. Fortunately, there are a host of other creatures that make use of the roadcuts, from lizards (which can often be photographed at night as they sleep unawares along the crevice edges) to a variety of snakes, invertebrates, and small mammals. And while snakes sometimes flat-out refuse to move on certain nights for both known and unknown reasons, I have yet to venture out into the roadcuts when I didn't find something of interest.

The typical way to find snakes on a roadcut is to start at one end and walk along the base of the cut on the road's shoulder. Scan the rock face from bottom to top slowly, paying careful attention to shadows. Watch for a bit of movement or anything that looks out of place. The shadows of overlapping sheets of rock or the gnarled roots of an exposed juniper tree can look astonishingly similar to the muscular trunk of a snake, and more than once I have had to actually clamber up the cut in order to make sure the thing I was looking at was not a snake.

One advantage of cut-shining over road-cruising is that it is a perfectly legal method for the average person interested in observing herps in the wild, provided a few minimum requirements are met. Although I was under the wing of a scientific collecting permit, this is not required for general herping by the average naturalist. All the State of Texas requires for cut-shining at roadsides is a valid Texas hunting license, a reptile and amphibian permit ("stamp") that can be bought with the hunting license, a reflective safety vest, and an adherence to the standard road laws of the state (i.e., parking the vehicle in a safe place and not engaging in any reckless activity). It is important to remember that you cannot shine your light from inside the vehicle, as this falls under the definition of "spotlighting" and can come with a steep fine from a game warden.

Another advantage (and this is just personal opinion) is this: a snake found in its natural element is worth two on the road. Even common species such as Texas nightsnakes and western diamondbacks seem to take on a different light when found in the cuts, actively engaged in their nocturnal forays. While it is true that a herper can usually find more snakes in a single night by road-cruising, the ones I find in the cuts are always far more memorable, as I have a chance to stop and observe them at my leisure without having to worry about an approaching vehicle bearing down on me before I can get out the camera.

Roadcut safety is an important issue that cannot be stressed enough. The Chihuahuan Desert is an unforgiving land that, while full of life and beauty and magnificence, is seldom synonymous with the word "safe." Imagine walking around slippery rock talus along cliff edges in total darkness where virtually every living thing is equipped with some sort of thorn, fang, or stinger with which to defend itself, and you can easily envision a few of the dangers associated with this activity. While most of the potential dangers can be thwarted by a good dose of common sense (how much I personally possess is still a disputable matter), there are a few insights well known and preached by seasoned cut-shiners that have helped us all avoid trouble on the rocks. The last thing you want to be faced with is a nasty fall or a venomous snakebite when the nearest hospital is sometimes hundreds of miles away.

The first general rule is to always park your vehicle as far over on the shoulder as possible. While traffic is usually light on the little-traveled back roads, what traffic you will encounter may be in the form of eighteen-wheelers barreling down steep mountain grades at eighty miles an hour at two o'clock in the morning, whizzing by you with all the ferocity of a runaway locomotive. Park your car too close to the white line and you put the ball in the court of whoever is behind the wheel of that semi.

Upon exiting the vehicle, it is a good idea to lock your doors. While you are not likely to encounter anyone out walking the cuts, aside from fellow herpers, keep in mind that you are very close to the border and that car-jacking and drug trafficking can occur in the area, especially in the Big Bend region. Some herpers swear by carrying personal protection such as a handgun just in case of an encounter with someone with bad intentions. While I don't personally find this necessary, it is definitely understandable, as several of my friends who have found themselves in precarious situations out there can attest.

When you are walking the cuts, a number of safe field practices will cut down on the chance of something going awry. For one thing, never put your hands or feet down without first scanning the area with your flashlight. For this reason, I find a headlamp to be a helpful addition to my handheld light. Rattlesnakes are notorious for lying coiled at the bases of the cuts, and it is all too easy to neglect watching where you are walking in the excitement of scanning the rocks at eye level. Also, broad-banded copperheads (until recently known as Trans-Pecos copperheads) and rock rattlers are prone to draping their bodies across the tops of low-lying bushes that grow at waist level from fissures in the rock, and it is a wise idea to keep your arms, legs, and body clear of these areas until you check them out.

Be careful of falling rock as well, as this is probably the most common danger associated with cut-shining. The crumbling nature of limestone and the flaking nature of granite both make for slippery footing, and while this is a no-brainer while walking along and not finding anything, it can all too quickly go out the window once a specimen has been spotted and the desire to secure it before it can escape takes priority. Many times I have sent my arms and legs scrambling up a steep cut side only to slide back down to the bottom. Once, in the Christmas Mountains of Brewster County, I actually lost my footing on a pile of granite slivers and rolled over fifty yards head over heels across all manner of desert lovelies such as cholla, ocotillo, and catclaw.

On this particular night, I shined the first cut and immediately began to see signs of life. Two mice skittered up the rock face ahead of my flashlight, their tiny toe pads sending minute pebbles clattering around my feet. Desert millipedes were busy crawling and feeding on vegetation that grew from the rock crevices. A large black scorpion munched on the posterior of a cricket, and a female black widow spider darted for cover from the center of her lazy web. I was back! This was West Texas herping at its finest! And while I had yet to encounter any actual herps, I savored the sweet anticipation, knowing that I had hours and hours ahead of me in which to search.

This is a unique aspect of West Texas herping. Whereas reptiles in most other areas of the state are generally active between dusk and midnight, with peak activity between 9:00 and 11:00 p.m., West Texas herps party all night long. I have found snakes as late (or maybe I should say early) as 4:30 a.m. To further complicate matters, a second volley of species makes its appearance in the early-morning hours just after sunrise, leaving herpers with the option of either rapidly rearranging their sleep patterns (i.e., sleeping between noon and early evening) or picking and choosing which specimens are higher on the priority list to see. I always go with the option All of the Above, since everything is of high priority on my wish list and I have discovered that "when in West Texas, do as the wildlife does." I usually herp from about an hour or two before dark until 8:00 a.m., although I have been called an obsessive radical by certain unnamed family members and field partners.

The first side of the cut produced only the mice and arthropods, so I walked across the road and began scanning the opposite cut. I had made it to the very end without seeing anything reptilian (which happens often; cut-shining requires more than a grain of both faith and patience) when my light beam fell on a small, grayish-white serpent partially emerged from beneath a large rock. It was a mottled rock rattlesnake, a personal favorite! This one was a small male, and he buzzed his disapproval as I gently lifted him from the cut and onto flat ground where I could better maneuver him for a picture.

Rock rattlesnakes vary in coloration across their range. When hunting for rock rattlesnakes, a good general rule of thumb is that the color of the snake will usually match the color of the rocks. For example, rock rattlers from the reddish granite rock formations of the Davis Mountains are often pinkish or reddish gray, whereas those from the chalk-white limestone hills of the eastern border of the Trans Pecos are much lighter-hued. In my opinion, there is nothing finer than coming across a mottled or banded rock rattlesnake in situ in its mountain home. The camouflage that nature has equipped these astounding little serpents with is nothing short of amazing, and I will often resist the urge to grab the snake with tongs before it can make its escape in favor of sitting down in the darkness and simply watching it for a few moments. These encounters never fail to mesmerize me.

The rock rattlesnake is a member of the genus *Crotalus*, which is generally composed of heavy-bodied, longer species such as the western diamond-backed rattlesnake, prairie rattlesnake, and eastern black-tailed rattlesnake, all occupants of one region or another across the Trans-Pecos. However, the comparatively diminutive rock rattlers differ from their formidable-looking cousins both in size and habits. Being creatures principally of montane habitats, they seldom grow larger than two and a half feet in length. Unlike most rattlesnakes, their patterns do not conform to a series of blotches or diamonds. Instead, they can best be described as ringed in thin alternating bands of often sharply contrasting light and dark hues. They are high-strung, nervous little snakes, although they possess an uncanny degree of curiosity, often making a buzzing retreat into some deep crevice at the

Mottled rock rattlesnake

first sign of danger, only to resurface with head up and tongue flicking several minutes later as if trying to get a good look at whatever disturbed them. Rock rattlesnakes are either diurnal or nocturnal, depending on season. On cool overcast days or early-summer mornings they can be found in the first few hours after sunrise, thermoregulating on flat, exposed shelves of rock. On warm nights in late spring and early summer the rock rattlesnake can be found abroad engaged in one of two methods of hunting: either coiled in ambush along a rock face or in low-lying brush or actively foraging for the small mice and lizards that make up the bulk of its diet. Rock rattlesnakes have also been known to consume a variety of other prey items, both endothermic and ectothermic, including fledgling birds, smaller snakes, and centipedes in the genus *Scolopendra*. Their venom is a complex mixture of both hemotoxic and neurotoxic peptides, with certain specific populations yielding considerably more toxic venom than others. The rock rattlers of the Val Verde County area are known for having a particularly "hot" venom; while seldom life-threatening, a bite from one of these serpents is always a serious medical emergency.

As the night rolled on, the infamous Juno Road began to pay off like a loose slot machine. Crevice spiny lizards slept in every cut, their backward-pointing, shingled pine-cone-like scales keeping them wedged safely within cracks, often with only their black and white banded tails protruding. Ornate tree lizards, in contrast, slept relatively exposed to danger, either clinging loosely to the rock surface or clenching dried twigs of creosote on the ends of bushes. At Baker's Crossing, where the Devil's River gurgles along the western edge of the road beneath a steep hillside beautifully adorned with stands of live oak, a symphony of hardy amphibian species could be heard calling. Here my flashlight picked out a slumbering rough greensnake in a bush. This is a species I am used to finding in a variety of habitats in the eastern portion of the state, from dense Piney Woods to Post Oak Savannah, hardwood forest, and even suburban backyards, but I was taken aback at its presence here in this transitional desert hill country.

The half-mile, steep, winding cut on the east side of the road south of Baker's Crossing is usually my final search on Juno. I got out of the car and paused briefly to breathe in the splendid silent isolation, only to have it broken by the most unearthly sound I had ever heard in the desert. A loud grunt that quickly dissolved into a muffled growl rose up from the pitch blackness on the rolling hillside behind me. The unidentifiable call perked up my senses immediately, but before my mind could go through the list of native birds, frogs, and mammals that could be its source, it broke into an alien howl that rose in pitch until it became a deafening scream. The sound sent chills up my spine, and for a moment I considered that old mythical bane of Mexican goat farmers, the deadly blood-sucking chupacabra. I turned around to face the darkness, fully expecting to see the telltale twin pair of glowing scarlet orbs penetrating my own before falling under the hypnotic gaze of the legendary beast, but, alas, there was only the night. I waited for several seconds, considered returning to my car, and then thought much better of it. After all, this was often the sweetest cut on the entire road. It had yielded many beautiful specimens of rock rattlesnake in years past, and to bypass it due to a case of the supernatural willies was definitely not in my nature. But as I turned around, the silence was once again shattered by a repeat of that hackle-raising snort-growl-howl-scream. This time I whirled around, and while no red eyes could be seen staring back at me, the crash of something large as it dashed through fallen live oak leaves told me that whatever it was had been close enough to be watching. It was then that the part of my brain devoted to science and rational thought overpowered my unnatural and superstitious case of the heebie-jeebies, and I focused my attention back at the round patch of rock face illuminated by my flashlight.

Several minutes later, when the sound came back in full force, I had long since run down the checklist of native fauna and didn't even turn around. I was glad that I hadn't, too, for no sooner had the final scream of the mysterious creature died away than my eyes picked up the last few inches of tail of a brilliant gray and orange serpent at the base of the cut. Yep, it was another Blair's phase gray-banded kingsnake. I leapt up in excitement, voicing my

Gray-banded kingsnake

enthusiasm into the night, and the sound of crackling leaves behind me was more like a whisper this time as I scooped up this prized creature and positioned it on the rock face for a photograph.

Pandale Road

From Juno Road I headed to a second famous herping hot spot: Pandale Road. Located in western Val Verde County, the terrain can best be described as transitional desert with a splash of Edwards Plateau flair. The entire road is over sixty miles in length. It runs from US Highway 90 near Langtry to the west end of Ozona. The road's northern end is paved but turns to caliche gravel some ten miles north of the Pecos River. Well known for its mottled rock rattlesnake population, this was the site where I had first been introduced to the species. The Pandale dirt road is equally well known for its ruggedness. Many a herper's vehicle has been reduced to a clanking, clattering box on wheels, and more than a few have been rendered inoperable, including my own on more than one occasion. I have rarely run the road without suffering a flat tire at best and have also hit two deer and knocked out an alternator. To add insult to vehicular injury, there are no inhabited towns along its sixty-mile stretch, and the few vehicles that do travel down this lonely stretch of Texas are either local ranchers or herpers. Most West Texas herpers are familiar with the "Pandale Curse," but the tiny winding track full of steep grades, washouts, and razor-sharp chunks of rock can hold many blessings for those foolhardy or fearless enough to brave it in search of reptilian treasure.

Trans-Pecos black-headed snake

While I had no desire to attempt a run down the dirt part of Pandale on this particular night, I did know of a series of choice rock cuts on the road's more vehicle-friendly northern end. Driving from Juno to Pandale makes for a long night, and it was well after 1:00 a.m. by the time I made it to the cuts. I shined for the good part of an hour, finding a hog-nosed skunk and ringtail (two of the area's more uncommon nocturnal mammal species), but the herps were absent. Then around 3:00 a.m. I spied what I at first thought was a large millipede winding its way along the top of a cut. Now giant desert millipedes are a dime a dozen out west, making their appearance both day and night on virtually every rock and bush, but something about this particular diplopod didn't look exactly right. Was it a hallucination brought on by sleep deprivation, or was that millipede wearing a black and white bowtie? I scrambled up the side of the cut, sending crumbling limestone skittering down beneath my shoes. It was pointless. The side was just too steep to gain footing. I slid back down to the bottom and then made a second run at it. This time I grabbed onto an exposed root about ten feet up the cut, hoping it would hold. With my free hand I reached up and grabbed what I had already identified as a Trans-Pecos black-headed snake just as it sensed my presence and began to seek refuge. Once I had secured the snake between two fingers, I released my hold on the root and slid haphazardly back down the sloped side of the cut to the roadside.

A member of the genus *Tantilla*, which consists of mostly diminutive, fossorial Mexican species under six inches in length, the Trans-Pecos black-headed snake is the largest and least-common species. This one was nearly a foot and a half in length, with smooth, shiny tan scales and a buttercream-

Rock cuts at the Fort Lancaster Scenic Overlook

colored underside. There are two variants of the species: the first possesses a solid black head and neck, and the second a black collar broken by white edges. This particular specimen was of the latter phase. It was the first one I had ever found.

Black-headed snakes are predators of a variety of arthropods, but their chief prey seems to be centipedes. The Trans-Pecos black-headed snake is the only species large enough to prey upon the giant centipedes of the genus *Scolopendra*, which it attacks and overpowers using its mildly toxic rear fangs. While capable of subduing invertebrates, the venom is completely harmless to humans, and I held this magnificent serpentine gem in my hands for several minutes before photographing it and releasing it under a large boulder. It had been a wonderful night of rock-cut-shining at the gateway to the Trans-Pecos. While I hadn't seen a great number of herps, the ones I had seen had been beautiful and uncommon species. It was time to head to Fort Lancaster and try to get a few hours of sleep before venturing into the heart of the desert.

Thirty miles west of Ozona, the Fort Lancaster Scenic Overlook is a great public herp spot. About a half mile in elevation, from this vantage point one can look out across the western desert lowland for miles and catch spectacular sunsets. I had arrived a little late for that, though, as the sun would be evident on the opposite horizon within a few hours' time. I figured I would have to rough the night in the car since I had failed to bring any overnight gear, but I was no stranger to car camping. After kicking back the seat,

I got as comfortable as I could to catch a few winks. Needless to say, it was a long night; I was dozing off in five-minute increments while Warren Zevon repeated the words to "Carmelita" through my stereo. The morning sunrise soon found a road-weary, sleep-deprived herper trying to massage the stiffness out of his neck before dining on his breakfast of champions: a bologna sandwich and a lukewarm can of Mountain Dew.

Sanderson, Texas—A herper's home away from home

Sanderson, a tiny town in Terrell County, is known for two things: cacti and snakes. It is the self-proclaimed "Cactus Capital of Texas," and rightly so. It is also snake friendly. While not exactly selling points for a *Wheel of Fortune* vacation prize package, it is one of the few towns in the state where a connoisseur of all things thorny and scaly won't raise so much as an eyebrow among most of the locals. This is largely due to local motel owners and operators Roy and Ruth Engledorff, who run the Outback Oasis, probably the most snake-friendly motel in the United States. The place screams "herps" the moment one walks into the office. Every square inch of the walls bears some kind of reptile-related memorabilia, and a small room inside offers an impressive display of live specimens of native herpetofauna. Snakes are welcome in the rooms here, provided they are properly secured, and even the housekeeping staff treats squirming pillowcases on the floor and buckets marked "VENOMOUS" with relative indifference. The Outback Oasis is well known in the herpetological community, and on the motel's patio between May and August it is common to meet herpers from across the United States, most in search of their own gray-banded kingsnake, which can be found with some frequency in the area. In recent years the town has further embraced its snaky notoriety by hosting Sanderson Snake Days, an annual festival in June. Herpetological speakers, live music, and even a trade show all take place in honor of the lowly serpent and all of its countless admirers from near and far. And behind it all sits Roy Engledorff, a friendly guy with a humble smile who is more apt to be found shining the rock cuts on US Highway 285 than he is basking in the limelight.

The Outback has always been a favorite haven of mine since my earliest expeditions into the Trans-Pecos, and I learned much of what I know about rock-cut herping from Roy and the throng of *alterna* hunters who flock to the Outback on their annual summer pilgrimages. Fond memories of popping tops on the patio, my ears aflame with a thousand snake stories after a long night of cut-shining, are but one of the many fringe benefits of hunting out west, and even on snakeless nights the Outback Oasis truly lives up to its name. Back in the day, one could simply pull up into the parking lot unan-

The Outback Oasis in Sanderson, a gathering spot for herpers

nounced and be guaranteed a room, but nowadays the motel is in such high demand during peak herping months that it is necessary to make reservations months in advance.

I had secured accommodations the previous winter, so I knew my room would be waiting and I could afford to take advantage of a leisurely early-morning road cruise, tired as I was. In the dry land of Terrell County, diurnal creatures are most often found out and about during the cool early-morning hours before ten o'clock, and the drive from Fort Lancaster to Sanderson is almost always certain to turn up a plethora of lizards as well as a few snakes. This day was no different. I saw whiptail lizards darting nervously at roadside in great numbers. The genus contains a dizzying complex of species of similar size and pattern that, with over a dozen different types native to the Chihuahuan Desert alone, can give even experts trouble at exact identification. Some species are parthenogenetic (all-female species capable of self-reproduction), and all are wary, sun-loving reptiles that are common in every ecoregion throughout the western half of the state.

A young western coachwhip was the first snake of the morning to cross my path. While they are usually seen only momentarily as they glide effortlessly into the roadside grass, it was still cool enough to render this one sluggish, and I pulled over and succeeded in apprehending the little creature long enough to take a photograph and receive a series of shallow, superficial bites to my wrist from its tiny teeth. Soon after that I pulled over for an adult mountain patch-nosed snake, another diurnal desert speedster that is tough to run down, but the reptile had likewise not had a chance to fully warm up, and I simply reached down and plucked the gray and black striped colubrid from the pavement and positioned it for a quick picture.

Dryden, Texas—Daytime road-cruising with a whipsnake

Daytime road-cruising is not without its advantages. For one thing it is perfectly legal, provided you have the license and stamp and you observe all the general rules of the road (use your flashers, park a safe distance from the roadway, don't run out in rush-hour traffic wielding a snake hook like an escaped mental patient with a bad case of road rage, and so on). To tell the truth, my expectations weren't exactly high for what I might find in Dryden. I am just stubborn as a granite wall and wouldn't give up until the area coughed up something scaly and wiggling. So I rose early, as planned, and headed twenty miles east of Sanderson along US 90, stopping several times to walk a series of rock cuts, my eyes scanning the flat surfaces of exposed rock for a basking rock rattler.

I didn't find any, but I did come across a Big Bend spotted whiptail caught in the messy web of a black widow spider; I marveled at the virulency of the venom and strength of the silk from a spider the size of a marble that could overpower a lizard several inches in length. A Great Plains skink was another welcome find as it basked in a patch of sunlight, allowing me to get unusually close for a photograph. Clad in its handsome juvenile coloration of ebony black with tan edges and white labial scales, the sunlight reflecting from its shiny body, I counted myself fortunate to make its acquaintance. Next came a tiny neonate ornate tree lizard. Well, the lizards were moving. That was always a great sign. Back on the road, I came across a regal ring-necked snake, the first snake of the morning, but unfortunately it had already met an untimely end, a vehicular casualty. But at least it meant things were starting to crawl.

I made the turn at Dryden and headed north on State Highway 349. I hadn't gotten far when I spied a black snake stretched out in the road with its head held high. This makes for an easy identification in the Trans-Pecos, as there is only one snake that fits these criteria—diurnal; long, thin, and black, with its head raised. I recognized it as a Central Texas whipsnake.

This snake was lying in full sun on the road with its head up, fully alert, its large eyes already locked on the Pontiac G6 that was slowly rolling to a stop twenty-five yards away. Seasoned herpers are familiar with the usually futile effort at running down whipsnakes on roadways. The idea is to get the vehicle stopped before the snake spooks. Then approach as slowly as possible, eyes locked on the snake. Like a gunfighter from the Old West, both combat-

Central Texas whipsnake

ants stand their ground, except that you are gradually, ever so slowly closing that wide open space between you and it. At some point, you know the snake is going to bolt, but you cross your fingers and get as close as you can before breaking into a mad dash just as the serpent realizes it is being stalked and makes for the nearest fence line. Nine out of ten times, you lose. I have seen whipsnakes disappear on completely open ground without a bush or burrow in sight. It's almost as if they wink out into some unseen dimension as soon as they leave the tarmac. Occasionally one will go up a bush or beneath a large rock, but don't count on it. By the time it hits dirt, it is as good as gone. That is why I was shocked when this particular snake let me walk up to within three feet of it. The head was still up, big eyes locked onto mine, but it hadn't so much as flinched. I sent up a quick prayer, counted to three, lunged forward, skidding on my knees. It took off like a rocket, but I managed to grab the last few inches of tail and the whipsnake was mine! The asphalt had ripped the knees out of both of my pants legs and shaved off the first layer of flesh as well, and the free bleeding complemented the bites I was receiving to my forearms as the terrified serpent began to thrash and strike simultaneously. But as they say, "Love hurts," and I was too busy laughing at my unlikely victory to notice the pain much. I positioned the erratic whipsnake in a bush along the fence line and it posed with its neck resting comfortably on a strand of rusty barbwire for several minutes while my Canon clicked away. Thanking him for his eventual cooperation, I left him to resume his lizard hunting and made for the car.

Independence Creek, at the border between Terrell and Val Verde Counties

My next stop was the bridge at Independence Creek. I couldn't explore beyond the boundaries of the fence line (another good general rule of daytime road-cruising: No trespassing!) While it is sometimes easier to ask forgiveness than permission (a suggestion once given to me by a herper who will remain anonymous), forgiveness that involves law enforcement, shotguns, or court fees are not my idea of happy herping. Still, the part of the creek under the bridge was fair game. Independence Creek is virtually the only water source within a hundred square miles that is semipermanent, and even it can run dry in the middle of June. But with the recent monsoons the creek was full and flowing. Clear water bubbled over rocks worn smooth by years of trickle. Guadalupe bass darted in the shadowy realms of shallow pools along the banks. Cricket frogs and Rio Grande leopard frogs made grand departures into the safety of the water ahead of my boot steps. The water was so clear that I could see them dive in, plunge to the bottom, then double back and bury themselves in the thick gray mud just beneath the surface at bankside. In the dense grass that grew here arid land ribbonsnakes were plentiful, and I managed to grab one and position it for a photograph before releasing it back into the creek, where I watched with childlike fascination as its yellow and brown striped body made expanding ripples along the creek's surface.

After exploring the creek, I headed back for the car and was greeted by a nicely patterned western diamond-backed rattlesnake on the bridge. Far-

Arid land ribbonsnake

ther up the road I moved a large Texas horned lizard. From there I turned onto FM 2400, where a pink western coachwhip disappeared as if through a wormhole into that inaccessible dimension open only to such snakes. A Great Plains ratsnake followed shortly after, and the morning was topped off nicely with another mountain patchnose at the junction of 2400 and 285. I had more than made up for getting skunked the previous night.

As late afternoon gave way to evening, I found myself pondering the question of where to go in search of herps for the night. This question can be answered in one of two ways. One can simply pick a good-looking road with favorable habitat or known locale where herps are abundant, or one can go tech and get on the Internet and look up weather conditions. I have found the latter to be much more productive. There is a certain science to phenomenal herping; nights where herps move everywhere and all night long. A lot of it has to do with good habitat, true, but even in good habitat adverse weather conditions can stir up the pot for an evening of skunking. There are nights when weather conditions are unfavorable for hundreds of miles in all directions, but in the Trans-Pecos weather can change on a dime. It can be storming in one location and bone-dry thirty miles away. In general, nocturnal herps prefer high humidity and low barometric pressure. In fact, a mass of high pressure over a large area can send snakes to shelter in their underground hiding places for weeks. On the flip side, a low-pressure cell moving in can bring about the exact opposite reaction, especially during the early spring when tornadic activity is included. On these nights I have seen upwards of thirty snakes in the span of three or four hours. Of course, driving around picking up snakes during periods of severe weather is questionable, but then again picking up snakes at all is questionable to most people, so I'll leave it at that.

Some herpers also swear by moon cycles, claiming when the moon is full, herps are less likely to venture out, as they are more likely to be seen by nocturnal predators. While this may bear some grain of truth, most nocturnal predators are equipped with excellent night vision and may rely very little on moonlight anyway. I have personally found the moon phase to be insignificant when it comes to herping, and some of my best finds have been on clear nights under a full moon. Various other factors such as wind, rainfall, and cold fronts affect certain species, while other species seem unaffected. For example, many species of snakes are surprisingly cold tolerant. Kansas glossy snakes and black-tailed rattlers are notorious for being surface-active even when the temperature has fallen into the low sixties, and amphibians (especially salamanders) actually prefer cooler temperatures as low as 45 degrees. Elevation also plays a key factor in a herp population's tolerance of heat or cold. In the Davis Mountains of Jeff Davis County, daytime temps in summer average in the mid-nineties, but at night the temperature normally drops rapidly. Where it may be 85 to 90 degrees at midnight on the desert flats some 100 miles to the south, points of high elevation such as the Davis and Chisos Mountains (4,000–6,000 feet above sea level) can be 50 to 60 degrees. In these montane environments, many species have adapted to be surface-active in these chilly temperatures.

11 The Chihuahuan Desert

THE TRANS-PECOS REGION IS DEFINED by the Pecos River. It flows out of New Mexico, runs southeast to Del Rio, and joins the Rio Grande. It cuts through the desert as a clear stream, sometimes shallow and sometimes gathering in pools over the limestone riverbed. West of the river is desert landscape dotted with mountains that were formed either by volcanic action or by limestone reefs under an ancient sea. In the Trans-Pecos two great geological formations meet. Some of the mountains are the southernmost part of the Rocky Mountain range. However, near Marathon there are exposed hills that are part of the much older Ouachita Range, formed hundreds of millions of years ago before the great age of dinosaurs. Between the isolated mountain ranges are miles of Chihuahuan Desert, generally flat, rocky, or gravelly land scarred by arroyos and dry stream beds that fill during sudden thunderstorms in the summer. This desert extends northward into New Mexico and stretches for many miles south into Mexico.

The great river—the Rio Grande—separates the United States and Mexico. The Rio Grande flows east through this region, dips far to the south in Presidio and Brewster Counties, and then takes a northward bend before again dropping off to the south toward Del Rio. This is the "Big Bend" of West Texas, and the river forms the southern boundary of Big Bend Ranch State Park, Big Bend National Park, and the Black Gap Wildlife Management Area. These state and federally designated places together protect about 1,899 square miles of desert and mountains. Additionally, large portions of the surrounding area contain undeveloped ranchland. The Trans-Pecos is radically different from the rest of Texas, open and uncrowded and largely unchanged by human activity. The desert feels vast and open, extending to the horizon or meeting a line of hills in the hazy distance. The highway unrolls across the desert for miles, unbroken by gas stations, businesses, or towns.

Just as the prairie is sometimes mistaken for a simple expanse of "just grass," the Chihuahuan Desert might be misunderstood as a barren place of gravel and scattered cacti. That is, until you visit. The lowest, flattest region,

227

A view of the Chisos Mountains

called the "shrub desert formation" in Wauer and Fleming's *Naturalist's Big Bend*,[1] is mostly treeless but supports a diversity of low-growing plants such as creosote bush, lechuguilla, and cacti. Creosote bush is a small shrub with little round leaves that have the characteristic creosote smell when crushed. Lechuguilla is one of the desert's agave species, with thick, succulent leaves growing in a rosette around the center. This plant is extremely common, and the rosette of leaves resembles a bunch of green bananas viewed upside-down, with leaves gently curved and pointing upward. Among the most interesting and beautiful plants in the desert is ocotillo, which sends unbranching stems as high as twenty feet in the air; its beautiful red blooms are timed to coincide with hummingbird migration.[2] The long, gangly stems originate from a clump at ground level and are covered with spines as well as small, rounded leaves that sprout after rainfall. Other noteworthy plants include the various yuccas that may bear a dense cluster of stiff, sharp leaves at the top of a shaggy trunk. Within Big Bend National Park the area known as Dagger Flats boasts a number of species of this succulent plant, including the giant dagger yucca. Of course, the Trans-Pecos includes numerous cacti, such as the familiar prickly pear.

Greater rainfall is associated with higher elevation, and as the land rises above the shrub desert formation, we see grasslands mixed with other plants. This is the sotol-grassland formation. Sotol is an evergreen shrub that grows in big clumps up to waist high, with many long, flat, flexible leaves. The sotol-grassland formation includes grasses and many other plant species.

One of the cacti, the cane cholla or tree cholla, has jointed sections growing off a woody stem, reaching as much as five feet in height and looking like a cactus that thought it was a shrub. Its big magenta flowers are beautiful.

As you move up into the foothills and enter the mountains, the plant communities shift toward those needing a cooler, wetter climate. Higher elevations bring cooler temperatures, and the mountains may squeeze moisture out of the air, so the rainfall in the mountains is higher than that of the surrounding desert. Up in the Chisos Mountains there are woodlands with Emory oak, alligator juniper, and pinyon pine, among other tree species. Scattered in these woodlands are Parry agaves, with rosettes of large bluish-green leaves, each ending in a sharp spike.

We have traveled to the Trans-Pecos many times, usually for only a handful of days, and we have never been able to get enough. We have taken nighttime walks under the black dome of the sky, with its limitless field of stars, in nearly complete silence except for the crunch of our steps and the sound of our breathing. We have hiked mountain trails within a garden of trees, agaves, flowers, and ocotillo, looking out across great distances or down into mountain meadows. And we have walked across the desert floor, watching lizards skittering among the rocks and cacti or seeing the black flash of a whipsnake slithering under a sheltering rock, and felt the dry desert heat that is intense but not oppressive. The Trans-Pecos region is like an exotic country, and herpers talk about it with near-religious reverence.

A night walk in the desert / SMITH

It was a dark night, and Clint and I were walking through the desert. Occasionally, toward the horizon, distant lightning illuminated storm clouds, the small flashes arriving soundlessly over distances of fifty or sixty miles. In our patch of desert, north of Terlingua near the Christmas Mountains, everything was quiet and still. Our flashlights illuminated one ocotillo after another, their tall, fingerlike branches pale against the dark desert. Ahead a line of scales stretched across the path, as a thirty-inch rattlesnake inched along toward some unknown destination. On the gravelly soil the pattern of pale-bordered, rounded diamonds on a lighter beige background did not seem out of place. However, failing to notice this Mohave rattlesnake could be a tragic mistake out here on a night like this. While its look-alike cousin, the western diamond-backed rattlesnake, can deliver a dangerous dose of tissue-destroying venom, many populations of Mohave rattlers add a generous dose of neurotoxins to the mix of peptides in their venom. Being bitten by one could shut down the reflexes that keep us breathing and cause bruising, swelling, and other symptoms of rattlesnake envenomation.

However, like other rattlesnakes, Mohaves just want to go about their business and will stay out of trouble if given half a chance. Clint and I hovered over this one and took several photos as it pulled itself into an inconspicuous bunch, head half hidden under a coil. We did not take its shy nature for granted; both of us have seen rattlesnakes either freeze in place or pull into the smallest space possible, only to lash out furiously if pestering continues. We moved on, letting this reptile return to its travels. Perhaps it was going to a hunting spot where it would wait beside a rodent trail, hoping for a mouse or rat to show up for dinner.

As I walked along the dirt track, shining the flashlight this way and that, Clint was thirty or forty yards away, investigating a nearby arroyo and restlessly poking his flashlight into mammal burrows and shining it along dry creek beds. Later he told me about turning up a huge female tarantula, which he photographed from a perch on a nearby boulder while a coyote howled from somewhere so far away it could have been in the next county. Periodically we each looked up at the night sky, which can be as fine and clear and limitless here as any place on earth. An infinity of stars is scattered from horizon to horizon in a sky so black that the awesome depth of it is apparent. When there is haze, it seems like a ceiling to the sky, but on these clear nights you look out into a universe into which you imagine that you could reach deeply, as if through an open window. The thicker band of stars, the Milky Way, stretched from one edge of the sky to the other, millions of tiny pinpoints of light.

We also found a little Texas banded gecko scampering across the desert floor between an ocotillo and a creosote bush. With their fine, granular skin and expressive eyes, these lizards can seem out of place in such a harsh environment. Their eyelids are generally outlined in a light color and frame the eyes in a curved, vaguely feminine shape. While they can dart quickly, they move deliberately as they climb effortlessly along ridges and rock piles. No doubt this one was hunting spiders and insects common in the desert; when it finds one, the gecko may run and grab it or may approach it with head held high and pointed down for a quick jab. The banded gecko's tail contains valuable fat reserves but is also easily broken off by predators. In fact, when cornered, the little lizard holds its tail up and rapidly waves it back and forth, creating a distracting target for predators hoping to make a meal off the gecko.

The distant lightning drew nearer, though the scale of the Big Bend landscape makes it difficult for city folks to estimate distance. The thunder grew audible, and we considered hiking back to the car, as a storm might flood the arroyos and make leaving impossible. Clint reminded me that being stuck

Texas banded gecko, near the Christmas Mountains

here overnight, far from creating a problem, might be the perfect outcome, and I had to agree. Our night walk was a great way to experience this region. So often herpers drive the lonely highways here, finding snakes but missing out on the quiet as the tires hum on the pavement. The Chihuahuan Desert may be glimpsed out the car window, but walking in it, especially at night, is a radically different thing. This is a unique part of Texas, a place of extreme temperatures, volcanic landscapes, and yet rich with desert plants and creatures. It attracts a variety of humans as well—small communities of artists and eccentrics in places like Terlingua along with ranchers and others who love the solitude and wide-open spaces.

Lizards and snakes in the desert heat / SMITH

We have been in the lower elevations of the Chihuahuan Desert mostly at night because temperatures are more moderate at that time and most of the animals of the shrub desert become active after sundown. In summer the sun and heat are intense across the miles of rock and gravel, creosote bush and cacti. Temperatures routinely reach over 100 degrees, and reptiles have few defenses against overheating except to find shelter from the midday sun. However, there is reptilian activity—within limits—on summer days here. Several lizard species can be seen foraging around the bases of plants, shifting between sunlight and shade. Daytime is also when you might find one of the legendary pink western coachwhips of the Big Bend.

The coachwhip is a snake species we have touched on throughout this book. In the Big Thicket it was the beautiful, satiny-black eastern coachwhip; in the Rolling Plains it was the sandy, reddish-brown serpent that Clint described capturing a Great Plains skink. In the Big Bend some of the western coachwhips occur in a bright, reddish-pink form, a striking sight as the snake slips among the catclaw and yucca at seemingly impossible speeds. A charismatic species, it makes for a good story because it is a long, alert, lightning-fast predator that often inspires comparison to hawks and eagles. The coachwhip cruises the desert floor over sunbaked rocks and through cactus mounds, hunting lizards and other snakes, but it is not immune to the scorching temperatures. In its foraging activity it alternates its time in full sunlight with time exploring a thorn thicket or down a burrow where it remains in the shade long enough to keep from seriously overheating.

One typical encounter happened in Big Bend National Park on the Grapevine Hills Road. I had taken a couple of friends, Casey and Shelsea, to introduce them to the park and surrounding areas. As we made our way slowly up the dirt road near a small arroyo, I saw a flash of red cross the road. Casey saw it, too, and was momentarily disoriented because it was gone before he could really take in what it was. We flew out of the car as soon as I could pull to stop. Five feet of what looked like a slender snake with the world's worst sunburn had vanished. We encircled the bush closest to where the snake had disappeared, hoping it was still there. Sometimes a coachwhip tries to hide at the base of a plant or ascends into the low branches. I also scanned the surrounding rocks, cacti, and creosote bush, but there was no snake to be found. And that is how these encounters often turn out.

Earlier that same day we got a nice look at one of the coachwhip's favorite prey species—the Chihuahuan greater earless lizard. We were walking around an area off the Grapevine Hills Road where a trailhead leads back among some hills and rocks. A small shadow of a lizard darted under the meager shade of a creosote bush. The lizard was a male, and while not in breeding colors it was nevertheless a pretty reptile. Although they are wary and very fast, a little patience and a telephoto lens can be used to get a decent photo. It tolerated my gradual approach, watching me carefully but not darting off.

These lizards are well adapted to their hot, sandy habitats, with no external ear opening and a lower jaw that closes a bit back of the upper jaw, making it easier to push under sandy soil without forcing dirt into the mouth. There is some resemblance to the closely related Texas greater earless lizard, found in the central and northern parts of the state, but the Chihuahuan subspecies has a much more colorful pattern. Males have two large black crescents starting on the flanks and wrapping down to the belly, and these may be edged in blue. From these crescents forward, males tend to have a series of sandy-orange spots or speckles up to the shoulders. From the

Chihuahuan greater earless lizard

crescents backward, males have a wash of greenish, yellowish, or blue color, especially during breeding season. Just as female birds are often drab compared with males, the females of this lizard have less color but may have a suggestion of dark crescent markings on the back and a yellow or peach wash of color on the sides and venter. They actively forage during the day for beetles, spiders, flies, and other insects, running them down or even jumping into the air to catch them. Temperatures up to about 105 degrees are workable for them, but even these lizards are most active in the morning and late afternoon, sitting out the hottest part of the day under vegetation or burrowed under sand.

The previous day our travels had taken us through the sotol-grassland formation in the foothills of the Chisos Mountains. A short walk among the big green sprays of sotol plants produced a small flurry of movement to one side. This was our cue to freeze and look around carefully to identify what critter our movements had spooked. In this case, it was a Big Bend spotted whiptail. This boldly spotted and striped lizard spends its days nervously poking into leaf litter and under rocks in search of termites, grasshoppers, and other invertebrates. Like the earless lizard, its natural history involves warming up in the daytime heat to hunt or run away from predators, but it shifts into shade or underground burrows to avoid overheating. It is another wary, lightning-fast reptile that can be observed closely with binoculars or a telephoto lens.

In each of these encounters, we would not have considered collecting these animals, even if we had been fast enough to catch them. First, we were

Big Bend spotted whiptail

A pair of round-tailed horned lizards courting

within Big Bend National Park, where collecting of herps, invertebrates, cacti, or anything else is not allowed. Second, we believe our experience is just as rewarding without collecting. The magic of these desert lizards is how they move about in their surroundings, not just how striking their color patterns are and how they feel when held in the hand. We think that watching and photographing them results in the most satisfying encounters.

Horned lizards can also be found during parts of the day, but the commonest one in the Big Bend area may be the round-tailed horned lizard. They are less than three inches long, rounded, and camouflaged to match the surrounding rocks, and they even have shaded areas mimicking the shadows at the edge of a small stone. You're not hallucinating if you think you just saw that rock move. Ants make up over two-thirds of their diets, and they prefer smaller ant species such as the honeypot ants.

Back in 2003 a companion and I spotted activity in a rocky area north of Big Bend National Park off State Highway 118. It was a pair of round-tailed horned lizards, a male courting a female and attempting to mate with her. He darted to her and briefly mounted, and then she ran forward a short distance. One possibility is that our presence was disrupting their activity, or she might not have been receptive. In any case, watching this bit of courtship was an interesting and memorable privilege.

Herping Highway 118 and finding a place to stay / KING

As I headed south toward the Christmas Mountains that are the gateway to the Big Bend region, my anticipation grew with the setting sun. I made a brief stop to run down a bright red coachwhip on the desert flats north of Study Butte, but the energetic four-foot serpent quickly reminded me I was not a kid anymore. A stout, heavy-bodied western diamondback made for a much easier encounter. By 8:00 p.m., a thunderstorm was steadily growing to a head to my west. That is when a second coachwhip crossed my path, and with the sudden drop in barometric pressure I was eager to get checked into the Longhorn Ranch Motel and get back on the road.

When staying in the Big Bend country there are a surprising number of options as far as lodging is concerned. Most of my friends and cohorts have their traditional sleeping quarters. Those who don't mind splurging a little can stay in the Chisos Mountain Lodge in the park. Located at one of the highest points of elevation, it is a delightful stay in a cozy cabin intentionally devoid of a television, although if collecting specimens is included in one's regimen, it would be wise to find lodging outside of the park's boundaries, as the collecting or possession of any specimens of native flora or fauna is strictly forbidden without proper permits, even if the specimen was collected in a perfectly legal manner outside of the park. For those more adventurous souls the park also offers campsites, from primitive spots to those with hookups.

More popular places (especially among gray-band hunters who have no intention of actually entering the park premises) are the string of inexpensive, independently operated local motels along Highway 118 and FM 170, where herpers can find snakes crawling across the parking lots. Two of the most popular of these lodgings are the Wild Horse Station and the Longhorn Ranch Motel, both located on Highway 118 about ten miles north of Study Butte. Both motels are quite used to naturalists visiting and do not frown upon snake collecting or keeping snakes in the rooms, provided you fore-warn the staff, of course. The Longhorn Ranch has always been my preferred choice, as the proprietor also runs the local café and doesn't seem to mind my pulling in at three o'clock in the morning and checking all of the lights outside of the rooms for insects with a high-beam flashlight.

Of course, a third option is just pulling over by the roadside and sleeping in the car. While I wouldn't recommend this, it has been an oft-employed strategy borne of necessity on those trips when I had either failed to make prior arrangements or simply herped so long and hard that I needed a few winks to reenergize. This is not the safest way to go when herping in the Big Bend, as vehicles and visitors do go missing from time to time, but the gas station at the junction of Highway 118 and FM 170 has proven a reliable spot on at least one occasion when I just simply ran out of energy and could no longer function properly behind the wheel.

I headed down Highway 118, having long since passed the last remnant of desert-encroaching grassland. Here the terrain was flat, crumbling lime-stone, giving way to predominantly succulents with the occasional jutted, low-topped rocky outcrop of white limestone full of cracks and fissures that I knew harbored a multitude of nocturnal species awaiting darkness. There are thirteen cuts of this nature before one dips into the truly montane region that makes up the southern section of Brewster County north of the Rio Grande. As I passed cut after cut, I reminisced about herpetological gems found here in the past.

In 2004 I had the good fortune of finding a dark phase gray-banded kingsnake of the "*alterna*" morph. It was solid black with an orange nuchal blotch. At first I had mistaken it for a strip of black tire rubber, but my bet-ter judgment had taken over and I had wheeled around to find this most unusual specimen lying in the middle of the road between two low cuts.

On another night, ten years later, this same cut had produced a tiny Texas nightsnake along with several Texas banded geckos. Several species of similar geckos are found across the American Southwest, but only two are native to Texas. The Texas banded gecko is the smaller and more common of the two, found across the Trans-Pecos from El Paso to Del Rio and even occurring in pockets throughout the Tamaulipan thorn scrub of the Rio Grande Val-ley. The other species, the secretive and uncommon reticulate banded gecko, is a similarly marked, though much larger gecko. It is restricted to northern Mexico and the Big Bend region of Texas and is almost never found north of the Christmas Mountains. The creature is so seldom encountered that it went undiscovered until 1956, when a specimen turned up in a mouse trap. No further specimens were found until 1971. While seen more frequently today, it is still one of the area's rarest natural treasures and is listed on the Texas Parks and Wildlife Department's threatened species list and therefore protected from capture.

Until recently, my friend Scott Robinson and I had an ongoing annual tradition of vacationing in the Big Bend together. Scott is a captive breeder of bullsnakes, a well-rounded naturalist, and a beast in the field with a seemingly superhuman stamina that allows him to herp all night and hike all day with minimal rest and sustenance. A few years ago, on one of these trips, we passed a van full of herpers farther down this road, the lights from their headlamps cutting bright swatches of light across the pale, vertical limestone rock surface, no doubt in search of that elusive *alterna*. We pulled up alongside them just as one of them extracted a large colubrid snake from the rock face. Scott and I climbed out to see what it was exactly: a four-foot adult desert kingsnake. Kingsnakes are well known for their ability and willingness to overpower and consume other snakes, including venomous species, although in truth they are not specialist feeders and are instead opportunistic, constricting and wolfing down almost anything that will fit between their elastic jaws. The desert kingsnake, as it occurs in the Trans-Pecos, is a real beauty. It can best be described as a shiny black snake sprinkled with gold dust, with a solid black "sock" that encompasses its head and the first several inches of its neck. The other herpers were a family unit, and the young boy, who was only a year or two older than my own son, was particularly ecstatic about finding this uncommon desert treasure. Still, he was a little hesitant about holding it, but after some encouragement from Scott and me as well as his father, he mustered up his courage and let the gentle, nonvenomous constrictor climb across his arms before placing it back onto the cut.

My reminiscences were cut short as I neared the Longhorn Ranch Motel. In typical Trans-Pecos resident custom, the proprietor was nowhere to be seen. Guests are often left with notes on the front door stating, "Gone to church. Be back in a few," or "Key is in basket. Will return Saturday morning." Such is the unhurried, informal lifestyle common among residents of the region. Far from being annoying (at least in my opinion), I find myself envying these folks, who seem to live life unfettered by the bustle of living in a city. Being without urban amenities sometimes seems a small price to pay for such a laidback lifestyle.

Santa Elena Canyon / KING

On a trip with Scott Robinson a few years back, I admitted that I had spent little time around Santa Elena Canyon. Scott assured me that my unfamiliarity with the canyon was nothing short of a personal sin. Santa Elena

The Rio Grande emerging from Santa Elena Canyon

Canyon is a twenty-eight-mile drive south from the main road through Big Bend National Park. The canyon walls tower hundreds of feet above the Rio Grande, and Mexico is literally a stone's throw away. We made a brief stop to walk through Tuff Canyon, which is Santa Elena's baby cousin, born of lava and ash rather than the limestone that forms Santa Elena. It is a small gulch by comparison, barely a half-mile long and twenty-five yards wide; we searched it for broad-banded copperheads. While I didn't turn any up among the mats of fallen cane and poplar, I did get a chance to photograph more common side-blotched lizards than either of us cared to count.

We spent the rest of the day in Santa Elena Canyon. After laying eyes upon it, I instantly fell in love with the place. The process by which it was made has been described as the gradual forcing of a limestone cake upward against the knife of the Rio Grande, which cut through the rock as it was thrust upward over millions of years. Rocky mud beds supporting thick stands of cane and introduced salt cedar, which the park is trying to eradicate, border the winding river. We found Texas spiny softshell turtles paddling leisurely in the water and sunning themselves on exposed mudbanks, and the ever-present side-blotched lizards peered out from sun-exposed cracks in the rock walls. The dried sand uphill from the riverbank provided excellent digging opportunities for several species of whiptail lizards, including the common checkered, the little striped, and the Big Bend spotted, and every stray clump of grass seemed to be privately owned by one of these nervous little sun-lovers.

The mudbank was the hub of the local insect fauna as well. Common mestra butterflies floated alongside lemon-yellow cloudless sulphurs and least skippers, and shiny tiger beetles, like zipping shards of colored metal, chased wasps and smaller insects below. A myriad of dragon and damselflies added even more color to the dazzling scene.

At some point, I had the bright idea to hunt for broad-banded copperheads in the deep jungle of cane that grew along the riverbank. I slogged through mud so thick that it clumped along the edges of my shoes, achieving the equivalent of lead weights around my ankles. As if this were not enough, the cane stalks themselves grew less than a foot apart, creating a mass of vegetation impossible to penetrate. Of course, I had to try. There were life-listers at stake, hypothetically hiding just out of sight beneath the layers of dried deadfall and glue-like mud. I slowly picked and pushed my way in. I had progressed only a few feet before I felt a burning sensation on my arms and neck. As another dried cane stalk snapped in my wake, its hollow center exploded, releasing a shower of stinging ants like some wicked piñata and forcing me to retreat. It appeared that the copperheads would win the day.

The River Road / KING

The River Road (FM 170) is one of those fabled roads well known in the specialized world of Texas herpetology. It sprouts out on a westward course from the base of the Christmas Mountains in southern Brewster County, following the Rio Grande, hence its nickname. The road cuts across the relatively low-lying flats between the towns of Terlingua and Lajitas, then gradually rises in elevation, resulting in some steep grades. The River Road is well paved, thankfully, but it is often nauseatingly winding, with a sheer drop-off several hundred feet into the river on one side and an ascending granite rock face on the other. Forty winks, or even one prolonged one for that matter, could put a driver in a very treacherous situation indeed, but for the dedicated road-cruiser the River Road can't be beat. It is well known for its unusual color phases of a host of desert species, including but not limited to speckled *alterna* phase gray-banded kingsnakes, strongly patterned mottled rock rattlesnakes, and "blonde" phase Trans-Pecos ratsnakes, not to mention such rarities as the Texas lyresnake and the Trans-Pecos black-headed snake. It is a must-drive for anyone spending any amount of time herping in the Big Bend.

In a rock cut just east of the rural, sixty-inhabitant ghost town of Terlingua I came upon not one, not two, but three examples of the Trans-Pecos ratsnake, a stunning straw-to-caramel-colored species with bulging eyes and intricate, H-shaped, jet-black markings running the length of its back. This

The River Road (FM 170), with the Rio Grande beyond

is one of the most attractive species native to the Chihuahuan Desert, and, as my good friend Scott Robinson has often put it, "A road cruise in the Bend doesn't qualify as herping until you've found your first *suboc*" (a reference to the species name, *subocularis*). This is one of the largest nonvenomous serpents in the desert, with adults achieving maximum lengths of well over five feet. In spite of its size, this powerful constrictor is a skillful scaler of even the smoothest vertical rock surfaces, and specimens are sometimes found by the aid of a spotlight, their pale, slender trunks seemingly glued to unreachable rock walls by means of astounding ventral musculature. I had found dozens of examples of this species in the field in times past, but this was the first time I had seen three specimens within several feet of each other.

On another drive on a different night, Scott and I had a bittersweet sighting of this ratsnake. We pulled over to let a Border Patrol cruiser pass in Lajitas, and a few miles down the road we regretted it, as it succeeded in running over a blonde phase Trans-Pecos ratsnake. The blonde phase of *Bogertophis subocularis* is a handsome, straw-yellow serpent with a series of irregular tannish-green blotches that replace the normal black H pattern. This was a first encounter with this color pattern for both of us. It was a painful experience to watch it dying of a broken neck in front of us. But such is the game of road-cruising, and after a few postmortem photos of this unfortunate rarity we left it to rest in peace at roadside and pressed on.

In early September of 2016, Michael and I had a memorable drive on the River Road from Ruidosa, a tiny community in Presidio County, to Lajitas

Trans-Pecos ratsnake

Blonde color phase of the Trans-Pecos ratsnake

and back. We started out from the gravel road to Chinati Hot Springs, the pale sliver of an early waning crescent moon visible high above an exquisite desert sunset, where it would soon hang like an ornament above a spectacular parade of twinkling stars. Desert sunsets are always beautiful beyond description, but this particular evening it was unbelievably gorgeous. Thin bands of sunlight expanded in parallel bars from piles of condensed cumulus clouds, their soft, subdued corners edged in vibrant orange fire from their lavender centers as the sun slowly slipped into obscurity behind the mountains, providing an almost celestial view.

On the way to Presidio we began to see our first snakes. The ever-present western diamond-backed rattlesnake was first, followed by a small Great Plains ratsnake that had been clipped by a car and was doomed to the fate of being disposed of by the morning's cleanup crew of avian, mammalian, and invertebrate scavengers.

A Mohave rattlesnake was next on the scene. These are creatures of variable dispositions. Some immediately assume a defensive coil with a noisy whir of rattles as soon as they are approached. Others remain motionless with their tails flicking in short, random twitches of barely audible sound, their violet-black tongues held menacingly over the thick, triangular head as they size up the situation by smell. Luckily, this was one of the latter individuals, and it allowed us the pleasure of photographing it at roadside as it coiled in hesitant patience in front of the flashes of our cameras. In coloration the species closely resembles the western diamondback, being clad in a series of diamond-shaped blotches running from the nape to several inches above the tail. Aside from differences in head scalation, an easily discernable characteristic is the width of spacing between the black and white bands on the tail. The Mohave's white rings are noticeably wider than the black ones, whereas the diamondback has rings of equal width.

We crossed paths with a second diamondback, this one a tiny young-of-the-year. Afterward a Trans Pecos ratsnake materialized out of the darkness, its straw-yellow and black pattern easily recognizable from our position in the front seats. We slipped it into a pillowcase for a prospective photo session the next day and continued following the desert highway.

As we passed through Presidio, in the distance the lights of nearby Ojinaga, Mexico, shone like a thousand halogen balls of illumination in the otherwise ink-black oblivion surrounding us. Off into the interior of the desert's black heart we set, eyes scanning the road as it stretched ahead on a southeastward course, following the Rio Grande.

As sometimes happens when herping in the Southwest, there was a brief lull in reptilian activity between 9:30 and 11:00 p.m., and we found only a small Texas nightsnake. This is when the greenhorn herpers often give up and retire to their places of lodging for a few cold ones on the porch before hitting the sack, reflecting on their mediocre early night of cruising and chalking it up to fate. This is usually a mistake—the real party starts after midnight in the Trans-Pecos.

Broad-banded copperhead, River Road

We came around a curve with the high granite rock wall towering up into the starlit abyss to our left and a swath of bone-white river sediment and dense stands of cane to our right. A blend of orange and maroon bands, made all the more vibrant in the glow of the headlights, was moving along the shoulder here, and I instantly recognized the Trans-Pecos region's version of the copperhead, even though in fifteen-plus years of herping the River Road I had never seen a single specimen. I called it out, and Michael hit the brakes and whipped the car into the riparian scree. I sprang from the passenger seat, flashlight and snake hook in hand, while the tires were still trying to maintain traction. To my surprise, there in front of me lay not one but two copperheads, both large adults well over two feet long. These handsome pit vipers, which were until recently described as a subspecies under the name *Agkistrodon contortrix pictigaster* (*pictigaster* meaning "painted belly"), are splendidly marked creatures, ringed in pleasing cross bands on top and squarish blocks of maroon and white on the stomach. Michael set about getting the first one in the bucket (we had the relevant license and the reptile and amphibian stamp that allows this) while I conducted a primitive roadside experiment. In North Texas the copperhead is a much more common sight than it is out west, and oftentimes the presence of one specimen can mean others are in the immediate vicinity. Walking in a widening circle radiating from the initial specimens, I scanned the ground with a flashlight and headlamp. Within a minute, I had located a third copperhead crawling

Mottled rock rattlesnake, River Road

slowly along the smooth river stones. I had gone from a fifteen-year drought to three specimens on my life list in a three-minute period. Encountering these absurd twists of fate is one of the things that keeps my herping balanced precariously between hobby and obsession.

On a rock cut just outside the town of Lajitas, Michael found a huge Big Bend dark scorpion, *Diplocentrus whitei*; on another cut, popularly known among gray-band connoisseurs as "the Big Hill," I found a stunning example of the mottled rock rattlesnake as it actively slid between the piles of granite talus patrolling for sleeping lizards.

A steady procession of sightings followed until the wee hours of the morning—black-tailed rattlesnakes, diamondbacks, a long-nosed snake, and a glossy snake. It was three o'clock in the morning when we finally completed the eighty-five-mile journey back to the lodge. The desert had given up twenty-three snakes.

Late-summer herping at Chinati Hot Springs, 2016 / KING

The desert stretched before Michael and me in a splendid carpet of rocks, cacti, and creosote bush as we drove along FM 170 north from Presidio. To our left, the land dropped away toward the Rio Grande and beyond it was a line of mountains just over the border into Mexico. To our right, hills and ridges rose gradually toward the Chinati Mountains. Sandwiched in this arid cradle, there was no escaping the feeling of being infinitesimally small.

This would become a fantastically successful trip, memorable both for the wildlife and for the people. We stayed at Chinati Hot Springs, a cozy place tucked away in the high desert at the edge of an arroyo and a short distance from the mountains. Our original wish was to visit the new Chinati Mountains State Natural Area, an area of 38,137 acres within the mountain range, but it is not yet open to the public. For now, we would spend a couple of days in the nearby desert. That area felt familiar, with ocotillo, creosote bush, and catclaw growing out of gravelly soil along ridgetops and low hills. Earless and side-blotched lizards ran from the bases of lechuguilla and prickly pear cactus. While we were there, the daytime highs did not climb higher than the mid-nineties, and in the dry desert air this felt warm but never oppressive. After driving the last jarring seven miles on a gravel road roughly scraped over the desert hills, we arrived at the hot springs. We checked in, met the proprietor, Dianne, and the security guard (her cat), and expressed how jealous we were that they live in this splendid oasis.

That first night we drove down the River Road and saw twenty-three snakes, as described earlier. We returned to the hot springs around three in the morning, tired and happy. Back at the cabin, I set up a blacklight and sheet in an attempt to survey the moths, beetles, and other nocturnal insects flying around. Afterward, we sat briefly at a picnic table and gazed up into the immense magnitude of the Milky Way and constellations, which appeared in vivid brightness on such a dark, clear night. Occasional meteors streaked across the scene before fizzing out and fading as if they had never been. And out in the darkness, hidden from our eyes, something lovely and elusive was on the prowl. It was the holy grail of Chihuahuan Desert reptiles, at least in my mind, and our paths were going to cross. But this day was done, and we rose from our seat beside the lonely arroyo and reluctantly called it a night.

A lyre in the kitchen / SMITH

During the day, Clint and I walked the arroyo that winds beside Chinati Hot Springs. It is spring-fed, and the manager of the property said it always has some water in it. The clear water flowed in a small, thin stream, sometimes gathering in small pools and in other places before disappearing under the gravel, to reemerge ten or twenty feet farther down the arroyo.

This permanent spring makes it possible for a healthy population of small frogs to breed. We saw an egg mass, small tadpoles, and a just-metamorphosed froglet, and speculated that these were probably canyon treefrogs. A population of frogs and tadpoles, in turn, supports many western black-necked gartersnakes. On my first walk in the arroyo I spotted one as soon as I got there, motionless in less than an inch of flowing water. Perhaps it was waiting to ambush a tadpole or just resting between hunting forays. Its body was contoured around the larger pebbles, a bright, creamy yellow stripe running all the way down its back to the tail tip and a white stripe along each side, just above the belly. The next day Clint and I watched another one poking under a small stone in the wet gravel, trying to wedge underneath it to get at something. Although we tried not to disturb it, the snake caught sight of us and quickly swam with graceful undulations across a small pool to hide underneath a grassy outcrop. When we investigated the small stone that the snake had tried to push under, sure enough, a froglet was hidden underneath.

The lodgings at the hot springs have a communal kitchen, with sinks, oven and cooktops, refrigerator, and, most importantly, a couple of coffee-makers. Clint and I walked into the kitchen to make coffee and were greeted warmly and enthusiastically by other guests making breakfast. Jan and Cheyenne, their two boys, and their family friend Symantha were from Alpine, a place where Clint and I both fondly imagine living. Cheyenne is a nurse at the medical center there, and they both confirmed that if it's not the perfect place to live, it comes close. During our conversation our search for snakes naturally came up, and we regaled them with our adventures of the previous night. Symantha was instantly intrigued. A bright, friendly teenager, Symantha eagerly recounted her recent experiences at an animal care camp where the ball python had become her favorite. She talked about an unfortunate childhood encounter with a small captive javelina that had injured her arm. Apparently the experience had not discouraged her interest in wildlife in the slightest degree.

Our plan was to photograph some venomous snakes later in the day. When we collect venomous snakes for photographs, we usually aren't eager to reveal that to everyone. We do not want to make people anxious about the neighbors with a rock rattlesnake and some copperheads. However, Symantha was excited about seeing these snakes, and a couple of other families staying at the place expressed interest in seeing them. So later in the day an entourage of people joined us at a spot where we could safely position the snakes for photos. We did not let anyone assist or get too close, but several people took their own photos, and we were glad to let everyone see and appreciate these wonderful animals.

I also showed Symantha the Trans-Pecos ratsnake we had picked up the night before, and she was instantly in love with this gentle and graceful serpent. She named him Clyde and handled the snake like a pro, supporting him and making slow and predictable movements with him. For his part, Clyde behaved in typical Trans-Pecos ratsnake fashion, with no attempts to nip despite being taken from the wild less than twenty-four hours before. Symantha could hardly let this snake out of her presence, though she did respect his need to go back into the bag and rest.

As night fell, the kitchen was a busy place. Jan had a brisket cooking, and as he described the spices he had rubbed it with, we were grateful for his invitation to share dinner. Jan recalled his Cajun heritage, and we talked about what makes the best boudin. Outside, their friend Mike was setting up his camera to photograph the stars, and he helped educate us about taking nighttime photographs. And this was a great night sky for it, with the Milky Way stretching across the heavens in an irregular, silvery band. Meanwhile, Clint was blacklighting for insects, attracting lots of species to a sheet on which a UV bulb had been positioned. Symantha proved to be a valuable field assistant—she spotted sphinx moths and caught them almost as easily as Clint. Between the light and warmth of the kitchen and the beautiful darkness of the Chihuahuan Desert, this night seemed perfect. We were surrounded by generous, friendly people, chasing insects under the mesquite tree and down toward the cottonwoods near the water; it was like a carefree memory from childhood. People like Symantha, with her energy, curiosity, and her delight in her ability to find insects with the best of them, give us hope that members of a new generation will care enough about the natural world to protect it.

The next morning, as we were preparing to leave, we heard a knock on the door—it was Symantha. Excitedly she informed us that a snake had been spotted over by the kitchen. Could we come and check it out? Of course, we immediately grabbed a hook and followed her. As we searched around the porch, Cheyenne said the snake was actually in the kitchen. We opened the screen door and found a little bundle of reptilian coils tucked between the screen and the door jamb. It was a Texas lyresnake, a rarely seen gem of a snake that Clint and I had hoped to see for years! All this time, we had been searching rock faces along roadcuts in the middle of the night, and here one was in the kitchen at Chinati Hot Springs!

It may not be that these snakes are rare—just hard to find.[3] Their big, bulging eyes with elliptical pupils show how adapted they are for nighttime activity. Lyresnake habitat includes rocky mountainsides with layers of broken rock or talus to hide in and to explore in search of their lizard prey. They have been known to try other cuisine—bats, birds, or other snakes—but lizards are the mainstay. Once the lyresnake grabs the lizard, the serpent works the lizard to the back of its mouth, where it uses enlarged, grooved fangs to puncture the prey and secrete a toxin to immobilize the victim. These snakes are not dangerous to us because the venom is not reported to cause significant harm to humans.

Symantha was fascinated with it and wanted to give it a name, despite the fact that we were going to take some photos and immediately release it (the

Texas lyresnake

Closer view of the Texas lyresnake

species is protected in Texas). Since it was a juvenile snake whose sex was hard to determine, she said it had to be a name that could apply to either gender and immediately christened the snake "Sam." The perfect name for it! We took several photos, and Symantha released it along the rock walls of the arroyo, where it will hopefully stay away from the cat that prowls the property. We can hope that we might see it again, all grown up, some day when we return to Chinati Hot Springs.

Reticulate banded gecko

El Patio and then one last surprise in the roadcuts / KING

When you are in the area, there is only one restaurant to include on the "must visit" list, particularly if you are inclined toward authentic Mexican cuisine. El Patio, located in Presidio, fifty-plus miles west of the FM 170–Highway 118 junction at Study Butte, is well worth the drive. Several of my field partners and I have made it a tradition to go at least once if we find ourselves within a 100-mile radius. En route to El Patio once, Michael and I found a juvenile Big Bend patch-nosed snake—a reminder that occasionally the flan comes with unexpected frosting.

El Patio is a small, easily overlooked two-room building, but the food is huge, and that is what really counts. After fresh-squeezed lemonade or perhaps a Negro Modelo, traditional tortilla soup, and tacos alambre (the house's signature dish), herps temporarily drift to distant regions of a herper's mind. It doesn't take much—one glance out at the quickly sinking sun—to feel a sudden urge to gobble up the final bites of a chile relleno or a honey-drizzled, cinnamon-sprinkled sopapilla and hit the highway once again.

After yet another wonderful dining experience that was a year in the waiting, I found myself once again staring out that same window as I dipped my final homemade tortilla in a fiery salsa. Sometime after leaving El Patio, I pulled over at roadside to examine a checkered gartersnake that was on the pavement in search of frogs and toads. I have found this species to be quite common in the region just east of Presidio, so its appearance here was

Mule Ears, Big Bend National Park

no surprise. As darkness fell once again, Couch's spadefoot toads began to appear en masse, a result of the recent seasonal rainfall. Western diamond-backs, Texas nightsnakes, and another juvenile Great Plains ratsnake soon followed. However, the temperature cooled rapidly on this second night in the Big Bend, and soon after midnight I returned to the Longhorn Ranch Motel, where I found a great consolation prize. Stuck to the wall beneath the light outside my room, I spied a giant root borer (*Derobrachus* sp.), the larg-est coleopteran native to the United States. At nearly two and a half inches in length, these sturdy, fearsome-looking beetles, with shiny brown elytra, long, saw-toothed antennae, and bolt cutters for mandibles, are quite conspicuous seasonal residents of the Southwest, where they emerge from the roots of palo verde with the late-summer rains.

I tried to get some rest. Honestly, I did. But this was my final night in the Big Bend, and I couldn't help but wonder what might be lurking in the cuts while I sat in my room wasting time sleeping. Eventually my curiosity could be ignored no longer, and I opted for a second late-night run to the nearby Christmas Mountains to see what the cuts would provide. To my glee, the front had passed, and a rush of warm air was heating the desert back up to 80 degrees. With my spirits now lifted, I strapped on the headlamp and made for the nearest cut, where I immediately came upon another nightsnake making its way across the base of a fallen chunk of granite. Minutes later, I found a subadult black-tailed rattlesnake. Soon after, the western diamond-backs came out in full force once again, and I turned up six neonates on the roadway. Finally, I approached the final cut—a massive section of rock that had been blasted from the center of a large hill. No sooner had I flicked on my flashlight than the beam fell upon a velvet-skinned lizard creeping slowly among the rocks like a silent phantom. But this lizard was much too large to be a Texas banded gecko. It was the reticulate banded gecko! This species is almost never seen except on warm, humid nights after a rainstorm, which explained its presence there. For well over a decade I had searched in vain for this species, and there it was only a few feet away from me. In years past I had often scrutinized each banded gecko I encountered, making sure it wasn't the coveted reticulate species, but now that I was seeing the real deal, there was no mistaking it. I took several dozen photographs of this rarely seen desert dweller as it scampered among the dried tangles of a dead creosote bush.

It had been a phenomenal trip, with the best definitely saved for last. But I had an eleven-hour drive ahead of me in the morning, so I took one last parting shot of the reticulate banded gecko and then watched it disappear into the realm of darkness beyond the beam of my light. I headed back to the motel, weary to my very core and yet still reluctant to leave this beautiful, sacred region of Texas for another year.

12 The Mountains of the Trans-Pecos

FOR AN AREA THAT MANY OF US ASSOCIATE with quiet and serenity, the Trans-Pecos originated from dramatic changes and explosive mountain-building. After the formation of the Ouachita Mountains, there was a long period during which the area was part of an inland sea, and huge amounts of limestone were deposited throughout the area. Around the Texas–New Mexico border, a gigantic limestone reef formed, which would later result in the Guadalupe Mountains. Then, at the close of the Cretaceous period, there was a time of uplift that created some of the canyons such as Santa Elena and also helped raise the Guadalupe Mountains. The earth's crust then relaxed and pulled apart some, resulting in great intrusions of lava up through the rocks, forming the Chisos and Davis Mountains.[1]

The Chisos Mountains, located roughly in the central part of Big Bend National Park, reach between 7,400 and 7,825 feet at the tallest peaks. This is the only mountain range completely contained within a national park. There are tall columns and cliff faces of reddish volcanic rock as well as woodlands consisting of Emory oak, alligator juniper, and pinyon pine on the slopes. Within these woodlands are shrubs, cacti, and big blue-green agaves. Here and there, ferns grow in protected spots, able to survive because of the cooler, wetter mountain climate. On rocky mountain slopes and small grassy meadows there may be ocotillo and lechuguilla, reminders of the desert flats below. Numerous hiking trails snake around the mountains, ranging from relatively short and easy to long and challenging. Even at higher altitudes, on trails that can be steep, it is often possible to walk a little distance, stop and appreciate a flower, lizard, or butterfly, take a few photos, and then climb a bit more. A leisurely hike such as this can make the trails more manageable and rewarding. The air is sweet and relatively cool most of the time—but on clear days the sun's radiance is relentless, even if the air is not too hot. Bring plenty of water!

About 100 miles north of Big Bend National Park, the Davis Mountains rise out of the surrounding desert to elevations of 5,000 to more than 8,000 feet. In places there are grassy mountain slopes dotted with trees as well as cool montane woodlands. On one of our trips the desert flats near Study Butte baked in 103-degree heat, but up in the Davis Mountains it was in the range of 85 to 90 degrees. The Nature Conservancy in Texas owns 32,000 acres within those mountains, and another 65,830 acres of adjoining land is in the form of conservation easements. While the nearby Davis Mountains State Park provides camping, the Nature Conservancy property is more protected and undisturbed. The Davis Mountains shelter several species of rare plants, serve as a migratory route for numerous birds, are a source of groundwater for the surrounding area, and provide crystal clear views of the sky—the McDonald Observatory is located here.

The Guadalupe Mountains are at the border between Texas and New Mexico; like the Davis and Chisos Mountains, they rise up out of the desert to form "sky islands." Because of their elevation, the temperatures are generally cooler than the surrounding desert, and they squeeze more rain out of the moisture that moves through the area. At higher elevations there are woodlands with oak, juniper, and pine trees, and springs emerge from the rocks. These "islands" in the desert tend to isolate populations of plants and animals that cannot live on the desert flats. The Texas part of the Guadalupe range is protected as a national park. Much of it has been designated a wilderness area, and as such there are only limited roads or facilities, just at the margins of the park. Once those of us who are not serious backpackers get past the inconvenience of that fact, it seems wise: the high country in the Guadalupes will be preserved without pollution (except that which arrives by air), litter, or traffic. The park imposes relatively few rules and modest fees, meaning that the toughest part of planning a trip there is the travel and then deciding where to stay. There are no gas stations or motels anywhere near the main access points.

Going herping in these places is based on the idea that "herping" does not necessarily mean "collecting." You won't find houses built into the sides of these mountains or convenience stores, and you won't get shot by hunters. The trade-off for being able to walk through these amazing places is that you are not allowed to change them or take away from them. Would we rather see a reptile or amphibian in the habitat in which it evolved instead of on the pavement or under a trash pile? You bet! We support the protection of parks, refuges, and preserves.

Lost Mine Trail, Big Bend National Park

The Chisos Mountains

The Lost Mine Trail / KING

The towering red granite of the majestic Chisos stood before Scott Robinson and me, promising in their silent solitude. Like ants, we began marching up the trail to the Lost Mine under a beautiful blue early June sky. By noon the temperature would be too hot for hiking, but for the next three and a half hours the natural world was our oyster. And my eyes were already busy scanning the ground for that pearl. It was a gorgeous morning in Big Bend National Park, with a soft breeze whisking around us. The Lost Mine Trail begins at 5,800 feet in elevation and is not terribly difficult, spanning barely over a mile. However, that mile ends up at the top of the mountain, so it is a steep mile. In the heat of midday it would be rough indeed, but it looked like our timing—about 8:00 a.m.—was perfect.

View from the Lost Mine Trail

Large common checkered whiptails foraged along the sides of the trail-head among immense patches of prickly pear, whose lemon-yellow blooms were alive with the buzzing of early insects. Butterflies, bees, scarabs, and buprestids jostled for position among the pollen-swollen flowers. South-western fence lizards hung, head down, from seemingly every juniper trunk and sun-exposed boulder face. Overhead, turkey vultures rode wind currents. Small coveys of scaled quail, with crests resembling wisps of cotton, bobbed along in nervous unison as the pebbles beneath our feet gave away our intrusive presence. I leaned down and removed the cast skin of a Baird's ratsnake from a hole at trailside. Nearly a decade ago my wife, Amber, and I had watched in fascination as a large adult of this species crossed the trail in front of us not far from this exact spot. But today Scott and I arrived too late. Baird's ratsnakes are not commonly seen and are generally found in canyons and higher-elevation woodlands. Adults come in complex shades of gray, gold, and orange, generally with four vague, dark stripes down the body. Some may be predominantly gray but with hints of orange or gold, while others may be more brownish gold or a subdued shade of orange, occasion-ally with the color shading toward gray approaching the tail.

Hikers in the Chisos Mountains will see periodic signs asking visitors to stay on the trails even when they turn back and forth on a hillside to make a gentler ascent (these zigzags are known as switchbacks). It might be quicker to cut across the exposed hillside rather than follow the switchbacks, but we hope you won't. These delicate microhabitats are naturally eroded away by early-spring and late-summer rainfall and baked dry by the desert sun

Baird's ratsnake

between rains. This makes for a fragile and vulnerable ecosystem, and a single misplaced footstep could mean a major alteration in habitat. For this reason, sticking to the trails should always be in the Big Bend hiker's code of ethics, no matter how tempting the urge to stray may be.

Birdsong filled the air the higher we climbed. Black-headed grosbeaks, white-winged doves, canyon wrens, and blue-gray gnatcatchers provided a variety of melodious whistles, cheeps, and chirps—sweet music to any naturalist's ears. The scent of prickly pear blossoms mixed with the pungent juniper complemented this aural symphony. A magnificent two-tailed swallowtail butterfly drifted by on lazy, gently flapping wings of ebony and gold. I always look out for these butterflies, one of the largest in the United States, whenever I find myself in the higher elevations of the Trans-Pecos. I usually do not have to look too hard; they dwarf every other species with a wingspan of over five inches. On the other end of the lepidopteran spectrum, a host of tiny marine blue butterflies, one of the nation's smallest species, visited goldenrod clusters alongside beetles of the genus *Sternithocornis*, which are excellent wasp mimics, so much so that Scott batted at one as it buzzed over his shoulder. Only by swatting it gently to the ground were we able to tell it was indeed the suspected beetle and not a wasp.

The trail took a sharp turn to the left as the mountain loomed ever higher in front of us. My ears detected a slight rustling sound near my feet.

Mottled rock rattlesnake, Lost Mine Trail

Expecting another fence lizard, I glanced down to find a mottled rock rattlesnake slipping into a pile of dried juniper brush. Scott was right behind me, and we managed to snap several pictures of this pit viper, a personal favorite of mine, from a safe distance. Its camouflage was unbelievable, the body composed of slightly varying shades of gray that made it all but invisible among the granite and dead juniper. Several hikers stopped to see what we were photographing, and we were glad to find them interested in the snake. We missed no opportunity to brag on and commend these marvelous animals, so perfectly at home here in their native mountain range.

We left the little rattler to resume its morning hunt for lizards and continued climbing ever higher. I stopped for the better part of an hour between a cleft in two rocks that had been weathered smooth by years of seasonal monsoons, forming a perfect stone chair. Sitting on the edge of this mountaintop and staring out across the vast Chihuahuan Desert below, I could make out the watchtower tip of Emory Peak, the highest point of elevation in the Big Bend. The vantage point was so splendid, so natural and overwhelming, that I couldn't help but feel divinely inspired, and for a brief moment in time herping took a backseat to sheer awe.

By 10:30 we had reached the top, a high flat mesa shrouded by short, stubby junipers. A Mexican jay flew in close enough for us to snap some great photographs, and its lack of caution at our presence was evidence that this particular bird had been visiting the Chisos Mountain Lodge and had probably learned to glean scraps from well-intentioned hikers.

On the side of a boulder I spied a short-lined skink. Skinks are timid, skittish lizards with short, stubby legs and glossy, smooth scales that lie flat and closely compacted, resulting in an incredibly slippery animal that is difficult to grab and even harder to hold without harming them. But my camera posed little threat to this one, and I was able to snap a series of nice shots before it grew wary of my presence and slipped back into the labyrinth of stacked granite. On the walk back down the trail I spotted the last half of another skink species, the Great Plains skink, before it disappeared into the crumbling soil around the partially exposed roots of a stand of prickly pears.

The Window Trail / KING

Early in the morning, a bright orange sun began peeking its way over the top of the desert foothills, as Scott and I loaded our hiking gear and set off for the park. As we drove, we were blanketed in a dense shroud of fog, which I had never before seen in the valley. Our destination for the day was the Window Trail, a five-mile trek leading from the Chisos Mountains Lodge to a spring-fed canyon deep in the mountains. The trail ends at a spectacular view of the valley below from between two giant slabs of rock, dove-gray and worn smooth by hundreds of years of running water.

We made it to the trailhead by nine, and already the sun pierced through the thick fog in tiny slivers of golden light. We parked at the lodge, slung on our backpacks and cameras, and set off on the trail. In little time I flipped up our first herp of the day, a Texas banded gecko.

Within the hour the fog had dissipated under the overbearing influence of the sun, and the lizards responded accordingly, emerging from their sleeping quarters to bask on the warming rocks. Little striped whiptails were the first to make an appearance, followed by a Big Bend tree lizard and several common side-blotched lizards. The hike through the canyon bed and up to the window proved well worth it by the time we reached the top, if only for the view itself. From this point one can gaze out into the awesome wonder of the valley below that is the Big Bend. Here clouds of two-tailed swallowtails and Mexican queen butterflies sipped mud from the rocky stream pools where tadpoles of the canyon tree frog metamorphosed. It is here, in this pristine flood of visual and aural montane wonder, that one can find an array of animal and plant species that are specially adapted to life at high altitudes. We saw Del Carmen white-tailed deer as well as two grasshopper species, the ornately patterned rainbow grasshopper and the beautiful blue-winged grasshopper, whose names speak for themselves.

The hike revealed several other unique arthropods, including a vinegaroon, a large desert arachnid that looks more at home in a Ridley Scott film.

Madera Creek, Davis Mountains

This relative of the scorpion has no venom but can deliver a strong pinch and can discharge a fine spray of acetic and octanoic acid from a long, whip-like appendage protruding from the end of its bulbous black abdomen. Acetic acid is basically vinegar, hence the name "vinegaroon." The chemical is harmless but noxious-smelling.

The Davis Mountains

Madera Canyon / SMITH

Mountain breezes and a small creek gurgling over volcanic rock—could this really be Texas? We made our way across Madera Creek and up the other side, among ponderosa pine, Emory oak, alligator juniper, and rocky outcrops, in the Davis Mountains near Mount Livermore. As Clint walked near a small stream tributary, he called out, "*Lepidus!*" There, amid the low vegetation and gravelly soil, a mottled rock rattlesnake was stretched out. Like many of the rock rattlesnakes in the Davis Mountains, this one had a bit more color than its pale gray cousins from the limestone hillsides and road-cuts in other parts of the Trans-Pecos. It was a grayish tan with dark, jagged crossbands at spaced intervals down the back. There was a hint of orange color toward the belly. Between each of the darker, olive-brown crossbands were mottled lighter and darker colors, suggesting secondary crossbands. The snake began to make his way onward and away from the intruders, but

Mottled rock rattlesnake, Davis Mountains

we were insistent on getting a photo. He resisted our invitation, and it took a couple of minutes of hooking and rehooking this snake to move him a few feet to an exposed area where we tried to get him to stay still. He continued his attempts to crawl away, buzzing his rattle intermittently. Then, after snapping a few pictures, we let him move up to a crevice where he promptly tucked himself inside.

We have seen our share of rock rattlesnakes while road-cruising at night, shining roadcuts, or lifting rocks during the day. Seeing the snake moving about in midday made this encounter something special. Rock rattlesnakes are secretive, using rock ledges and crevices as refuges, and they are more often seen at night or at the beginning or end of the day when temperatures permit. These small rattlesnakes are also well camouflaged, and most people who are not used to looking for them will overlook them.

We had already seen a number of lizards and snakes in this mountain locality, part of the Nature Conservancy's Davis Mountains Preserve. When we arrived at the property, we talked with project director Chris Pipes about activities on the preserve. He told us about the various research and teaching programs taking place there. A group was there that day studying rare plants, and master naturalists as well as university researchers regularly visit. When Chris dropped us off near Mount Livermore, he immediately scooped up a little horned lizard and said, "Here's a *hernandesi*." What luck! There in front of us was a neonate greater short-horned lizard!

Investigating the rocks and vegetation in the creek, we saw several young western black-necked garter snakes, one of which ate a young canyon treefrog

Juvenile greater short-horned lizard

while we watched. These garter snakes are closely associated with water sources in West Texas, and their diet appears to consist almost exclusively of amphibians. Amid the large clumps of grass and rocks in the little creek that goes through Madera Canyon, treefrog tadpoles were swimming in abundance. Newly metamorphosed treefrogs hopped near the water's edge, providing relatively easy pickings for the garter snakes. We found a number of hatchling lizards of the genus *Sceloporus*, almost surely southwestern fence lizards. These are mostly terrestrial lizards—fast and often seen more or less as a blur as they dart from one shelter to another. We saw an adult and managed to get a passable photograph as it paused before dashing off. In several places we saw juveniles of one species of whiptail lizard, whose pale yellow stripes were in bold contrast to the almost black background.

As we walked back, there was a crevice spiny lizard on a rock face above a pool in the creek. These are large lizards, growing up to eleven inches or so in length, with a conspicuous dark band around the neck. The scales are keeled, and each one comes to a point, making them truly "spiny" lizards. They are expert at gripping rock faces with their claws and can run vertically at the same stunning speed as they can sprint overland. After we got a photo of this one, it scrambled up into a crevice and disappeared.

The action below, in the creek, was interesting as well. One of the black-necked garters took flight across the pool, swimming in fast, graceful curves. It reached the edge of the rock wall and stopped in a clump of vegetation. It reminded me of a young black-necked gartersnake foraging in a pool in the Davis Mountains some years ago. Seeing a rippling disturbance in the water, I approached for a closer look. The little garter, about a year old, was

Western black-necked gartersnake eating a canyon treefrog

going after the canyon treefrog tadpoles and had already gorged on a couple. The snake had been foraging in the shallows and, upon seeing me, had taken off for the other side of the pool. They are beautiful little snakes, even if not as dramatically pretty as their eastern cousins from the Edwards Plateau. Between the three yellow lines going down the back are a series of bold black spots that usually fuse into a zigzag pattern.

As the sun got lower, we began to walk back, trading comments about this having been one of the best outings ever. This was not about the species seen, as we have seen almost all the herps before, with the exception of the greater short-horned lizard. Rather, it was about the total experience of the mountains, the woodlands, the warm sun and cool breezes, and seeing such an abundance of herp species in their natural settings. The preserve was one of those increasingly rare outposts of beauty and solitude that seem to be a whole world away from the craziness of human society. The sky was clean and clear, and the mountains signified that this was a place where things change on a geological time scale. What is here will still be here tomorrow.

We were indebted to the Nature Conservancy for allowing us to visit. Far from being locked away from people, the Davis Mountains Preserve is used a great deal. However, this appears to be done with the conservancy's careful stewardship to protect this great place for future generations.

Davis Mountains

Bucketloads of snakes and insect interludes in the wild Davis Mountains / KING

On a solo trip to the Trans-Pecos in late summer of 2015, I found it impossible to resist the call of the Davis Mountains. After checking the radar, I noticed a long line of storms moving westward from the Fort Stockton area toward Jeff Davis County. I hoped that they would bring enough rain to adequately soak the ground and dry up in time for evening, bringing temps back up out of the inevitable cool-down of the storm. Thick layers of stratus clouds began to pile up overhead the farther west I drove, and by the time I got to the grassland valley town of Marathon, the rain had begun to spatter my windshield in random droplets.

As I drove north of Alpine, up State Highway 118, the day was heating up nicely, and just as I had suspected, the area had received plenty of rainfall, as evidenced by the wide puddles of water that had accumulated in low spots on the highway. I passed through the quaint mountain town of Fort Davis, which feels like a brief drive into a Wild West version of a Norman Rockwell painting, and then broke north, where the exquisitely spectacular monolithic red granite walls grew up from the surrounding grassland. Temperatures here are generally cooler than those in the desert flats, although it was currently 93 degrees. I stopped at a roadside park for the dreaded bologna sandwich (thankfully, my supply was beginning to run low), and while I ate I walked among towering cottonwoods that provided ample shade for the meager picnic tables. Ornate tree lizards were everywhere. In my experience, this is the most common lizard species in the Davis Mountains, and it is not unusual to find two or three dozen of these wily little bark-colored reptiles on a typical evening walk among the rocks. I also found a flame skimmer resting on a low-lying cottonwood leaf. This is one of the most beautiful of our native dragonflies, with its neon-orange body and rust-colored wings. After the last bites of whatever mystery meat makes up bologna, I was back on the road, my car pointed in the direction of the Buffalo Trail Scout Ranch.

The ranch is a private facility located just south of Balmorhea off Highway 17 in the northern end of Jeff Davis County. While it is not accessible to the public, the road that leads up to the gate is, and it is here that many a choice specimen of sought-after serpent can be found. Years ago a friend and I had made our virgin journey to the fabled road. Unaware of the land laws, we had unknowingly ventured onto a private section of the ranch. Seeing no signs advising us otherwise, we had driven to the end of the road, where we had parked the truck and hiked up into the canyons with headlamps and flashlights. While the herp count wasn't exactly mind-blowing, the night will always stand out in my memory as one of my favorites in the Davis Mountains. We found tadpoles and calling and breeding adults of the elusive canyon treefrog, a brilliantly banded orange and black scolopendrid centipede, and a long-nosed snake. The icing on the cake had been my first Chihuahuan hook-nosed snake, which we had the privilege of watching as it chased down a small spider.

But those days were long gone, and it was unlikely that I would ever get access to the heart of the scout ranch again. So that night I would have to be content with driving the only part I legally could: the road that leads up to the ranch. There was still some daylight left, so I took advantage of the situation by stopping at a roadside park where I knew I stood a good chance of finding some jeweled scarabs of the genus *Chrysina*. These marvelous beetles have always been a personal favorite. Chiefly Mexican and Central American in range, a handful of species occur far enough north to slip over into the southwestern United States. Here they occur only in areas of high elevation, and each species feeds solely on specific trees, so finding them can require a bit of research and luck. However, once you find a good spot, it tends to pay off well. *Chrysina* beetles are most active in mid to late summer, when they fly from several hours before dusk until late into the night. Large and conspicuous in flight, the sight of a jeweled scarab buzzing lazily through the oak and juniper trees with the last rays of sunlight glinting off of its metallic emerald wing covers is an experience not soon forgotten for a beetle enthusiast.

Pulling into the picnic area, I noticed a large white van and several people with long aerial nets assembled beneath the nearby trees; all of them were looking up into the lower canopy. I had little doubt as to what they were

Jeweled scarab beetle, Davis Mountains

doing. As I approached the group, I greeted them with a question I already knew the answer to: "Found any *Chrysina*?"

The guy closest to me broke into a wide smile. "Yeah, lots of *woodi*, but we're really hoping to find *gloriosa*." I nodded. "You and me both," I replied. The Wood's jeweled scarab feeds mainly on hardwood leaves, while the glorious scarab nibbles on juniper needles. The potential for finding both was high here, as both types of tree grew in abundance.

As it turned out, the group was a party of entomologists from Texas A&M University who were there to set up their equipment for black lighting at the picnic spot. Insects are attracted to the ultraviolet rays emitted by black and mercury vapor (blue) lights; when a background for one or more of the lights is created by stringing up a white sheet between two trees or laying it across an area of flat ground in favorable habitat, the number and diversity of insects that come to the sheet can be downright staggering. As the entomologists prepped the site, I got to know them better. Josh McDermitt, a lepidopterist, was looking forward to the incredible diversity of moth species that the Davis Mountains had to offer. No stranger to the area, he was remarkably well versed in native insect identification. While I may not be able to identify much in the small moth department, I know a *Chrysina* when I see one, and by the evening's end I had pointed out upward of a half dozen as they buzzed around the lower branches of the trees growing in a neat row along the edge of the pull-in spot.

Finally, it was time to hit the road. I told the team my plans, and they invited me to stop by whenever I felt like it to check out whatever the black lights brought forth. As an amateur entomologist going on twenty-five years now, as well as the owner and operator of a dried insect specimen collection that long ago surpassed the definition of hoarding, I wholeheartedly agreed and promised to stop by whenever the herping got a bit slow—not knowing at the time just how fast-paced that night would turn out to be.

Highway 17 begins a steady incline as you climb higher into the Davis Mountains. The terrain becomes rockier and the boulders more massive and closely compacted. But between peaks the continually upward-reaching stretches of grassland resemble some great botanical sea, approaching the red granite foothills before sliding back, as if governed by the same lunar cycle that controls the coastal tides. It is here that the road to the scout ranch branches off at a westward slant from the highway. Just before I could make the turn, the corner of my eye fell upon a snake at roadside. There was little space to pull over, but I made way and soon had another mountain patch-nosed snake in hand. This one had just swallowed a meal that was much larger than the circumference of its body, and its engorged state had rendered it sluggish enough to grab before it could pull its vanishing act. The old adage "Your eyes are bigger than your stomach" doesn't seem to apply to snakes. Like a tennis ball somehow fits into a stretched sock, it is amazing how much lizard you can get into a foot-and-a-half-long patchnose the diameter of a Sharpie. As I positioned the snake for a quick photograph, I happened to glance down at my shoes; between them lay a young whipsnake that had been run over. "See there," I scolded the little striped glutton, "you lie in the road with a full stomach and that's what will become of you." One could question the sanity of a grown man talking to snakes in the middle of a mountain back road, knowing full well they are physically incapable of hearing as well as comprehending what was being said to them, but then again some people dress their dogs in Christmas sweaters, so I'll offer no apology.

As darkness fell, I drove up and down the ranch road, but nothing crossed my path. Tiring quickly of turning around so frequently on the narrow, mile-long trek, I abandoned the area for the farm road where I had found the patchnose less than an hour before. Here the humidity from the previous days' rainfall, coupled with the higher-than-average temperatures, brewed up an excellent recipe for nocturnal road cruising. It is a recipe that is seldom cooked up at such high elevations; I have spent more than my fair share of nights getting skunked in the Davises. But tonight was about to make up for all of those. Western diamond-backed rattlesnakes popped up all over the road. From tiny button-tailed neonates to three- and four-foot-long adults, they were definitely the most common finds of the night. By the time I made it back down the mountain to town, I had seen over a half dozen of them.

Any herper in his right mind would have turned right back around and given that road another pass without a second thought, but keep in mind that I literally talk to snakes, so whether I am of sound mind remains a matter of opinion. Like a fool I thought, "I wonder what's moving on 118?" Highway 118 is a well-known herp road. It runs from Big Bend National Park to Alpine for over eighty miles, then continues another twenty up through the middle of Davis Mountains State Park, where it keeps going north of Jeff Davis County to who-knows-where. From the sandy gravel banks of the Rio Grande River to the juniper-studded bluffs of these picturesque sky islands, it is a must-cruise for anyone in search of reptiles and amphibians in the Trans-Pecos. My wife always scolds me for finding a good road where the herps are moving, then deciding that if that road is hopping, the next one that pops into my mind could be even better. It doesn't make much sense, but that is often how my mind works, usually to my discredit. While the eastern side of the mountain was experiencing atypically perfect herping conditions, the western side turned out to be a dishearteningly normal night in August. As I climbed toward the entrance to the state park, the temperature dropped sharply. It was now 59 degrees, and aside from a red-spotted toad and a rock rattlesnake that had been dead for several hours, I saw nothing. I could picture my wife's raised eyebrows in my mind: "You had to screw it up." Well, maybe not. After all, it was but a short drive back to the other road, where the snakes had been moving. Time was suddenly of the essence.

I dipped back into the convergence north of town, headed back up Highway 17, and immediately noticed the temperature climb again. It was in the mid-seventies several minutes later when I pulled up on another rattlesnake. This was no western diamondback. It was a beautiful eastern black-tailed rattlesnake (formerly known as the northern black-tailed rattlesnake). Blacktails are quite common throughout the Trans-Pecos, from Juno Road to the Big Bend. They occur at higher elevations than most of the state's other native rattlesnakes and thus are able to remain surface-active at cooler temperatures. It is not uncommon to find blacktails out and about in the low sixties. While most montane species of animals tend to be smaller than those found at lower elevations, the black-tailed rattlesnake can grow to be well over four feet long and as big around as a soda can. They possess the longest fangs of any of Texas' native venomous serpents, although they are as a general rule quite passive and reluctant to bite. Beset by a variable amount of black pigmentation scattered in a loose chainlike pattern on a background that ranges from tannish to olive-gray, with a solid black tail and a black "mask" about the face, they are among our handsomest snakes.

Eastern black-tailed rattlesnake

I was elated, to say the least, about making a long-overdue reacquaintance with my beloved black-tailed rattlers, and the mountain would not let me down on this night. I would find four of them before I made it back up to the picnic spot, where I decided to take a brief rest and see how my newfound friends from Texas A&M were faring with insects.

I could see the black lights glowing in the darkness from afar, like mysterious bars of purple illumination floating in some black abyss. I chuckled to myself as I pulled up, imagining some local rancher on his way home suddenly transfixed by their unexpected appearance. Was it a previously undescribed extension of the Marfa Lights phenomenon? The lonely ghosts of some phantom band of outlaws from the days when Texas was young? Aliens? Or maybe it was just some mescaline-charged mountain hippies partying off the grid? I could picture the rattling old pickup truck stopping only briefly in the road before hightailing it for the safety of home.

I pulled in and hopped out where Josh and the other members of his party were busy plucking selected insects from white bedsheets suspended between tree trunks in front of the lights. If it was a favorable night for herps, it was a spectacular night for bugs. Every square inch of the sheets was covered by something bearing six legs. As a naturalist with a keen interest in both reptiles and insects, I often find myself torn between two worlds. Both are highly active on these humid, moonless nights after a storm. So it's either one or the other. Long ago I discovered a sort of solution. I would set up a black light and sheet around dusk in my yard or campsite, leave it to draw in the bugs for a few hours while I herped, then return around midnight with a fold-out chair and a jar. After all the herp activity had shut down, I could enjoy the wee hours with a parade of silk moths and beetles. Since many of the largest and showiest species mate in the hours before dawn, it all works out splendidly well—except for that annoying little problem of sleep deprivation. But of course coffee is a godsend, providing you don't mind picking the odd stray bug out of your cup.

The insect team had been raking them in. Not only had they found over a dozen examples of *Chrysina woodi*, they had managed to call up a *gloriosa*, described by *Simon & Schuster's Guide to Insects* as "the most beautiful beetle in North America."[2] It is a not a large species, typically the size of those somber-colored brown May beetles—popularly known as June bugs—that take over porch lights in late spring, but what it lacks in size it makes up for with its coat of many colors. The glorious scarab is adorned with alternating stripes of metallic green and silver, looking more like a tiny figure sculpted from precious metal than an actual living organism. I had never seen one and was quite envious of their luck.

"How about you?" Josh asked. "Finding any snakes?"

"Oh yeah," I said. "Some nice blacktails and tons of *atrox*" (western diamondbacks).

"Help yourself to whatever you want from the sheets," he said.

I needed no second bidding. This was the equivalent of a kid walking into that intriguing, fantastical candy store in the mall and the clerk saying, "Take whatever you want, kid. It's on me."

At first it was sensory overload: there were literally thousands of insects flying and crawling around the lights—so many that some of the tiniest-winged ones began to go up my nose, in my ears, and down my throat. More than once I gagged and spat out some unseen gnat or minute moth, but so it goes in the world of insect collecting. Eventually I selected a dozen particular species. When collecting any organism, even those as abundant as our six- and eight-legged friends with whom we share this planet, a bit of etiquette is always in good order. The old maxim "Never harvest more than you need" applies anywhere and everywhere. Universities are certainly apt to find good reason for collecting larger quantities of invertebrates; they are researchers of biological animal and plant associations and ultimately concerned with conservation of the species as a whole. I, on the other hand, being a private collector, try to limit my collection to a few examples of species of special interest to myself. The exception is when the specimen is a record for that county or documents a range extension. Rhinoceros beetles, a species I have in the past had trouble locating, were one of the most common visitors to the sheets that night, and I picked out a few of the largest males with the longest horns. Rhino beetles look like a June beetle on steroids. Bulky and dark brown, built like a miniature tank, the elongated curved horns of the males are thought to be used principally in combat rituals over the attention of nearby females, with the victor being the first one to flip the other one over onto its back. I also picked up a nice Wood's scarab and several long-horned beetles of the family Cerambycidae.

With some reluctance I returned to the road to finish off the night's herping. I hadn't gone a mile when I pulled over for a small Great Plains ratsnake, followed by a dark-colored long-nosed snake. Western diamondbacks continued to move as if fleeing from snake hunters from the Sweetwater roundup, and I helped most cross the roadway in spite of the general lack of automobile traffic. I hit the Boy Scout road once more, but it produced only a single neonate diamondback, so I decided to finish off the night by cruising up and down Highway 17. It turned out to be a good move: a four-foot-long Trans-Pecos ratsnake the color of a stick of butter immediately came into view, its bug-eyed head held several inches from the ground as it tested the surrounding air for particles of kangaroo rat scent.

By this time it was nearing one o'clock in the morning, so I made a final stop at the picnic area to say good-bye to Josh and the A&M students. I was glad I did, for Josh had saved me a special prize: a flag moth. These large, aptly named lepidopterans were unknown to me prior to this night, and I was taken aback by the brilliantly patterned black, white, and orange moth with the four-inch wingspan. I tucked the specimen into a glassine envelope, picked up a few more moths for my collection, and helped the team break down their setup before wishing them well and heading back for the lengthy drive to Sanderson. It was two o' clock in the morning by the time I made it down from the Davis Mountains. The temperature had finally fallen, but the snakes seemed to pay it little mind. I found a Mohave rattler, four more diamondbacks, a gopher snake, a western black-necked gartersnake, and two desert kingsnakes before the night finally shut down. In spite of all the action, I took full advantage of a strong cup of black coffee the moment I stopped for gas. With a quickly downed boost of caffeine, a false sense of youthful vigor flowed through my veins, and in spite of a brisk wind that had picked up, I shined cuts all the way down US 90 from Alpine to Sanderson, trying in vain to milk them for one last specimen. Knowing when to be contented is admittedly one of my weak points whenever I am out in the field, although the sight of the Outback Oasis coming into view as the sun rose on the eastern horizon held more contentment than I could have ever imagined it would at the start of the night. It had been one of those great evenings that come few and far between in this inhospitable land prone to adverse weather conditions and extended spells of drought. At last I could succumb to the numbing effects of total fatigue in my motel room.

The Guadalupe Mountains
A hike into McKittrick Canyon, September 3, 2013 / SMITH

Along the eastern slopes of the Guadalupe Mountains and up near the New Mexico border is McKittrick Canyon, one of the main attractions of Guadalupe Mountains National Park. A trail leads from the visitor center back about 3.5 miles into the canyon, crisscrossing an intermittently spring-fed stream that winds back into the mountains. This would be our introduction to one of the great mountain ranges of the Trans-Pecos.

Clint and I started our hike in high spirits. At 8:30 a.m. (Mountain Time) it was sunny and warm as we descended into the stream bed along a narrow trail surrounded by cacti, yucca, and alligator juniper. The stream was dry at this location, and we followed the trail out of the streambed and onto a fairly flat, rolling area. One of the things we encountered quickly was a mysterious tree with a red, twisted trunk and red-orange branches. If you are not familiar with it, the tree has a psychedelic appearance that could make you question your senses. As we later discovered, this was the Texas madrone tree, which the park brochure describes as a relic of cooler and wetter times. Other specimens farther along the trail had peeling bark, exposing a pale, dense, smooth wood.

We saw whiptail lizards and southwestern fence lizards. Although they are wary little reptiles, able to dart under a catclaw bush or skitter around to the backside of a boulder, we managed to photograph them a few times. Predators must either be fast and alert, like the Central Texas whipsnake that we glimpsed, or else stealthy and able to find them at night when escape is much harder.

Along the trail it became apparent that we were at a high elevation comparable to that of Denver, and while it was not excessively hot, the desert sun was bright and warm. We huffed and puffed along and pulled out the water bottle frequently but sparingly, knowing that we would be thirsty again before our hike was over. We walked past shoulder-high sotols with big green sprays of serrated leaves and around alligator juniper and stunted gray oak trees. Magically, the trail opened out into a creek bed with clear flowing water. While the water was shallow, it was still a beautiful oasis. Up in these mountains where there is almost no water, the butterflies are drawn to places like this, and they fluttered around us in a profusion of yellows. Clint

McKittrick Canyon, Guadalupe Mountains

soon came across a Big Bend tree lizard with beautiful turquoise color on the belly and chin. These mottled lizards are often seen in trees and branches, where their dorsal color is an almost perfect camouflage and gives no hint of the exquisite colors on the lizard's underside.

The trail took us back up and a little apart from the creek bed, through a montane woodland with oak, pinyon pine, juniper, and madrone, with big blue agaves growing in groups here and there. As we walked along the path, motion on the ground caught our eyes. Moving along in fits and starts, a Great Plains skink, probably eight inches long, darted from the base of an agave to the sheltering dead leaves at the bottom of a sotol. We could glimpse the lizard's yellowish scales edged in black, which blended with the dappled sunlight on grasses and leaves. There was no way to catch the skink for a photo, as we certainly were not going to risk injuring the lizard or tearing up the sotol; we were just grateful to get a brief look at it before it disappeared.

The creek bent back around to meet the trail, and in this spot were more pools of crystal-clear water. Within one of these shallow pools, as if hanging suspended an inch or so above the limestone bottom, was a fairly large speckled fish. We admired its streamlined form and subtle colors without knowing quite what we were seeing. Later we learned that ranchers long ago introduced rainbow trout into McKittrick Creek, and this is the only place in Texas with an established population of these fish. The introduction of these

A female Chihuahuan greater earless lizard

nonnative fish has taken an unfortunate toll on leopard frogs in the area, as the tadpoles and smaller frogs make excellent meals for the fish.

Several hours had passed and our water was running low, so we began the return hike. We continued seeing lizards, including the large crevice spiny lizard as we reached the trailhead. Tired, dehydrated, but happy with all we had experienced, we wondered if the Guadalupe Mountains had anything that could top this.

Exploring the lower slopes, September 4, 2013 / SMITH

We started the next day walking a short loop trail at the Pine Springs area. This place was once a stopover for the Butterfield Stage Mail Route, and there are ruins of a couple of the station's walls. The trail features plants of the area, such as Apache plume, alligator juniper, soaptree yucca, cholla cactus, and the gray oak, a fairly small oak with grayish-green leaves. The lizards there were accustomed to people and allowed us to approach quite close. One Chihuahuan greater earless lizard sat motionless on the path as we circled it, finding good photographic angles and clicking away.

Later, exploring the area around the historic Frijole Ranch, we saw many more of these earless lizards. True to the "earless" name, these common lizards have no external ear openings. They are heat-tolerant, so we saw them out on rocks and gravel in midday. The color along the lizard's head and back is beige-gray, and a series of rounded faint blotches may become evident at the tail. Underneath, the tail is white with several black bars or spots. When alarmed, these lizards often run several feet and then stop, curl the tail up, and wave it. This moving pattern of black and white certainly might distract a predator so that an attack would be directed toward the tail. These lizards seem almost to hold their ground at times, sitting atop a rock and doing the push-ups that males use to assert their territory. One of these sat on a rock close by while I took a number of pictures, almost daring me to try to catch it.

Smith Spring in light and darkness, September 5, 2013 / SMITH

From the Frijole Ranch, a trail leads up the mountainside to Smith Spring. Above it is the sheer upthrust of the mountain, and below it is the eastern slope, dropping down to the desert floor below. As any source of water in these mountains is likely to be a magnet for wildlife, we resolved to hike up to the spring. The climb is not too difficult, though it is challenging if you are over sixty and not in good shape (one of us is speaking from experience!). The slope is rocky and dotted with sprays of green sotol and soaptree yucca with crowns of spiky green leaves on trunks covered with the dead, downward-pointing yellow leaves of earlier growth. Here and there an agave grows, sending up its towering stalk with branches at the top for flower heads. Prickly pear cactus is common, as is the cholla cactus. Clumps of yellow flowers grow in the midst of all this.

As the hike progressed, we climbed between two hillsides that formed a little canyon with large boulders strewn along the trail. On one side the slope dropped away, while on the other it rose more steeply as we got closer to the sheer rock mountainsides. The cacti grew closer together, and the sun continued to bear down on us—then abruptly the trail entered a montane woodland and we arrived at our destination.

I wrote the following while sitting at the spring: "Here, at N31°55.109 / W104°48.397, is Smith Spring, one of the most magical places I have seen in Texas, tucked away in the mountainside and surrounded by desert. In the dappled shade beneath oaks, Texas madrone, and other trees is a crystal-clear pool of springwater collected in a bowl of limestone boulders and ringed by maidenhair fern. A low branch from a big-toothed maple shades part of the pool. Small water bugs zigzag a pattern in the water's surface on one side, as a couple of water striders paddle their leisurely way across what might be a sheet of glass suspended over the rocks below. The pool and the flowers around it are a magnet for butterflies like Mexican yellows, sleepy orange, and southern dogfaces, which dance and flutter around the vegetation, in

Maidenhair fern at Smith Spring

and out of sunlight. While I stood at the pool, a morning sphinx moth visited the flowers, hovering as it extended its proboscis to gather nectar. It then skimmed the surface of the pool two times and flew away.

"One wall of what almost seems like a big, open room is composed of layers and blocks of limestone, with the occasional small alcove where yuccas take root and grow. Another wall is a jumble of boulders and chinkapin oak, ponderosa pine, madrones, and other tree species. The water flows gently through a small gorge, allowing a mountain woodland to grow before giving way to a rocky arroyo.

"At first it is tempting to say that it is utterly silent here. But the truth is that the lack of noises from people and their machines allows for the music of this place to be heard. There is the sighing of the wind in the trees, the gurgle of springwater flowing over rocks, and the occasional humming of bees."

Clint soon captured another Big Bend tree lizard, its mottled charcoal and gray-brown pattern mimicking the tree bark on which it is usually found.

Color on the belly and chin of a male Big Bend tree lizard

Who could have guessed the bright metallic blue of the belly and green on its chin? It was a beautiful little reptile.

We decided that the best way to increase our chances of seeing some of the snakes of the region was to do a night hike up to the spring. We checked with the park staff to make sure that such a thing was permissible, and then we returned to the Frijole Ranch at sunset.

The hour before nightfall is a peaceful, almost magical time anywhere in the Trans-Pecos, as the arid landscape slowly comes to life like a flower head opening to greet the day. Tranquility sets in, and the ears and eyes take in a world of natural wonders usually hidden during the midday heat. The air gradually fills with the chirps and hums of bats, insects, and birdsong. If one is observant, the ground too begins to crawl with reptiles, arthropods, and small mammals that have spent the daylight hours hiding in some cool subterranean shelter, out of sight and mind.

The first thing we discovered on our night walk is this: when you are on the eastern slope of a mountain range, the sunsets may not be spectacular. The sun simply disappeared behind the mountains, casting a huge shadow over the landscape. The sky darkened slowly to night, and that was it. We started our hike in the shadow of the mountains and used flashlights as it got darker to make our way up to Smith Spring. As we made our way down the gravel path, a scurrying movement caught Clint's eye, and he ran up ahead to find a large solifugid, or sun spider, running hectically across the caliche. At over two inches in length, including the eight legs and two pairs of jaws that not even a mother solifugid could love, these ravenous shrews of the invertebrate world look like something out of a science fiction movie. Imagine a scorpion crossed with a spider and then dipped in a big vat of hideous and you've got a halfway accurate mental image of one. While they could never win a beauty contest, they are nevertheless fascinating creatures. Like all solifugids, this one was in a rush to get somewhere and devour something of equal or lesser size, so after a brief photo shoot we left it to continue on its journey.

On the lower portion of the trail, before nightfall, Clint found a large vinegaroon emerging from its burrow under a sheltering rock. He held this coal-black, menacing-looking arachnid and even put it on his face, hamming it up for the camera. Luckily he did not get a dose of the vinegaroon's trademark chemical defense. Clint replaced it under its rock, from which it would no doubt emerge later in the night to search for small invertebrates on which to feed. Vinegaroons can be quite common in rocky areas replete with patches of native brush, which they can burrow beneath, and we would see five before the night was over. By that time Clint's hands would smell like a third-grade volcano experiment gone wrong since he insisted on handling each and every one of them before releasing them.

We worked our way up the trail fairly quickly, hoping to get to the spring before it was fully dark. We focused on the trail in front of us because we not only hoped to find rattlesnakes but wanted to find them without stepping on them. Calling it a trail might be overstating it. The way was a bare track in the rocky ground, ranging from a few inches to a foot and a half in width. For a time, it ran just a few feet from the steep drop-off of an arroyo. The first thirty feet down was more or less vertical, and in places we could look down on pine trees whose tops did not reach eye level. Farther up the slope the arroyo became shallower and the trail descended into it, came back up, and later crossed it when it was nothing more than a rocky ravine.

As the climb became steeper, we passed large rocks and threaded our way between huge boulders. There were numerous cracks and fissures along the bases of the larger boulders, which consequently made excellent sites for rattlesnakes to coil quietly in wait of a passing meal. Although we gave these spots extra attention, we were unable to turn up any specimens of the local main attractions, the mottled rock rattlesnake and the eastern black-tailed rattlesnake. However, on several occasions we found crevice spiny lizards living up to their names perfectly, tucked away in crevices and sleeping.

Now in complete darkness, the trail wound around boulders and through patches of mountain woodland, and we kept thinking we had reached the spring, only to climb farther. Eventually we ducked under tree branches and emerged into the relatively flat area around the spring. Our flashlight beams illuminated flat rocks, low-growing branches, and then the clear pool. Outside of the flashlight's reach it was inky black.

Smith's black-headed snake

We turned off the flashlights for a moment to soak in the darkness and depth of this secluded place. This may have been the first time that we could recall being outside and unable to see our hands in front of our faces. Looking upward, we could barely make out patches of sky, which were slightly less black than the tree limbs that reached overhead. We were immersed in deep, impenetrable black. This isolated, sheltered place felt no less safe now than it had when we visited it in daylight. We sat in the darkness, breathing in the mountain air, listening to the low gurgle of water, and enjoying the experience. The combination of openness and deep darkness made for a rare and enjoyable few minutes. Was this what the Apaches might have felt when they stared up at this same sky several hundred years in the past, perhaps and quite possibly from this very same spot? For a few moments we felt as if we had traveled back in time to some bygone age—before fences and houses and cars and electric lights left their stain on the landscape.

Eventually, though, Clint's compulsive desire to herp regained its firm hold on his inner being, and he turned the light back on and shattered the dream state that had previously entranced him. He scanned the huge rock face that bordered the eastern side of the spring and almost immediately found a huge scolopendrid centipede. At nearly seven inches in length, with more legs than a marching band and fangs that would make Bela Lugosi shrink back in fear, these imposing beasts have few fans, even among naturalists. Clint has always enjoyed the company of these wicked-looking creatures, although even he prefers to keep his bare hands at a safe distance.

The centipede quickly faded away as the flashlight beam fell upon another seven-inch-long cold-blooded creature of the night, and this one had scales! Clint could see only the last inch or so of its tail, the end of which had been stubbed by some unknown predator in the snake's past. Making a quick grab

Red-orange ventral scales of the southwestern black-headed snake

before it could disappear entirely into the crevice, Clint pulled out a Smith's black-headed snake. These small, secretive snakes prefer to burrow under rocks or other ground cover in search of the small invertebrates that make up their diet.

Smith's black-headed snake bears a resemblance to the more common plains black-headed snake at first glance, but it can be distinguished without too much difficulty by a less tapering black crown bordered by a thin cream-colored row of scales above the nape. The general ground color is a light tan, with a bright red-orange venter. While capturing the black-headed snake was a simple task, photographing the wiry little serpent on a rocky incline in total darkness was incredibly difficult. But eventually Clint was able to snag several passable shots, after which we released the snake to resume its search for centipedes. As for ourselves, our time had almost run its course, and as much as we wanted to stay, we had to get some sleep if we were to function properly the next day. So with no small amount of regret we descended from the spring and made our way back to the valley below.

Final Thoughts:
Getting Started Field Herping

Michael Smith

Now that you've "taken the tour," are you ready to go field herping? Some readers may already be field herpers, and we tip our hats to those folks and wish them lots of success in future outings. For those who have not been field herping, here are a few ideas about getting started, with an emphasis on staying safe, having a great time, and adding to your knowledge.

For those first few trips it is better to look and take photos without trying to capture most herps. With snakes, of course, it is essential for you to know if a specimen is venomous before trying to capture it. Additionally, keep in mind that nonvenomous snakes often bite when captured, and bites from larger species like bullsnakes or big watersnakes hurt even if it's just a scratch. Turtles sometimes bite when grabbed, and even a mud turtle or box turtle can give an uncomfortable pinch. Of course, the American alligator is off-limits for handling, both because of its legal protection and the obvious danger from this large reptile.

It is also important to remember that being grabbed by an inexperienced person can be harmful to the animal. Lizard tails may break off, other kinds of injuries can occur, and the herp may be excessively stressed. Amphibians have delicate skin designed to allow some water to pass through it, and these animals are particularly vulnerable to contact with toxins and diseases. Herpers who have insect repellant on their hands would likely poison a salamander or frog if they handled it. Additionally, a fungal infection, chytridiomycosis, which attacks the skin, is decimating amphibians worldwide. If humans handle an infected animal, they can transmit the infection to the next amphibian—or amphibians—they handle.

As we have mentioned in several chapters, much can be learned simply by watching. Suppose we see a kingsnake on a rock ledge. If we remain still and observe, we will see how a creature with no hands or feet can be an expert climber, anchoring itself in two or three places with a curve of its body while moving up the ledge. We may be able to watch which crevices it explores, looking for food. If we made a dash for the snake as soon as we saw it, all we might observe is how it tries to escape when threatened. That is not to say that you should always be a purist who never captures anything. To tell the truth, most of us really like to capture and examine herps up close, so we have to remind ourselves of how nice it can be to simply watch.

Choosing a place

Where can you go to see herps? Depending on what you want to see, the answer might be "out your back door." In many parts of Texas it is still possible to find a toad sitting in the garden after dark. Toads are taken for granted, despite having interesting faces, eyes with horizontally elliptical pupils, and lightning-fast gulps when an unsuspecting cricket comes by. In many backyards, various lizards may visit trees and fences. In South and East Texas, there is the green anole, a brilliant green lizard that can turn dark brown. Lucky homeowners in those same, wetter parts of the state may see a little emerald-green lump of frog stuck to a window or a large leaf. By day, these green treefrogs hunker down and sleep while adhering to smooth surfaces. In much of Texas there is the prickly, brown and gray Texas spiny lizard that camouflages well on a tree trunk. More of these backyard herps are found in places that are near parks or in suburban areas and with fewer free-roaming cats and less pesticide use.

Backyard herping only goes so far, and restless herpers thumb through field guides and dream of more exotic places. So where else can we go? Most of the undeveloped land in Texas is behind private fences, but there are places scattered around the state where we can wander without trespassing. The chapters in this book describe state and national parks, wildlife management areas, wildlife refuges, and preserves that are great places to visit. It is not appropriate—and may be illegal—to capture herps and take them home from many such places. However, we can find and photograph them while enjoying some very beautiful places. Keep in mind that some places, including refuges held by the Nature Conservancy or Audubon Society, may not be open all the time and may limit where visitors may go. Please check in at these places and follow their guidelines so that sensitive areas are not damaged. It is important to protect areas for future visitors.

Ranchers may be understandably reluctant to welcome everyone who shows up and wants to visit, but in some cases a friendly conversation or polite inquiry will get you behind the fence. Just remember that landowners have to think about whether visitors will get hurt, harm livestock, or start fires while on their land. They do not owe us access to their property, and if we are lucky enough to be invited onto their land, we must act responsibly.

The rough earthsnake, a common backyard snake in much of Texas

Woodhouse's toad, found in many yards and gardens

Roads create public rights-of-way through the land, and herpers have spent many nights under the stars examining roadcuts where snakes explore crevices in the exposed rock. Similarly, roads may give access to ponds and wetlands where frogs and toads call at night. However, as discussed below, you must have a hunting license and a reptile and amphibian stamp to "road hunt." Might it be legal to simply walk along rights-of-way to look and take photographs? It is unclear how a game warden might interpret this, though possession of collecting containers and snake hooks would likely make the officer decide that you were "hunting." If you walk along rights-of-way at night, remember that this activity must be done with a great deal of caution, since roadsides place us in the immediate vicinity of cars and trucks driving by. Herpers should not get on the roadway in front of traffic and certainly should not shine lights into cars or nearby houses.

Finding herps once you're there

If you have decided on a destination, there are several things you must do to have a successful trip. Suppose you want to go to the Big Bend and your list of "must see" herps includes rock rattlesnakes, Texas horned lizards, those beautiful pink coachwhips, Mexican hog-nosed snakes, and the eastern Chihuahuan green toad. The more you know about these species' natural histories, the more successful you're likely to be. For example, hog-nosed snakes are best seen at the very beginning and end of the day, and driving in certain localities at dawn has been the recommended approach (and perhaps walking along a right-of-way would be successful). Rock rattlesnakes are largely nocturnal and are often found around rock cuts or areas with rocky outcrops. Horned lizards are daytime critters, but even they have their limits, so it helps to know the temperature ranges they prefer. Since Texas horned lizards like to gobble up harvester ants, walk the areas around harvester mounds. Experienced herpers may know specific localities and conditions that are best for finding a target species. Reading about, exploring, and hanging out with experienced field herpers are ideal ways to get to know how these animals live and therefore how best to find them.

It seems like an odd contradiction for people who love unspoiled nature to go out looking for trash piles. We have a love-hate relationship with trash piles. We may love an area and admire its unspoiled beauty and, at the same time, wish for a pile of discarded tin or plywood somewhere in it because herps may be resting beneath it. Trash piles, however unsightly, provide artificial cover for herps, and flipping tin or boards is a common way to find snakes, lizards, or amphibians that have taken refuge. *Do not flip tin, boards, rocks, or such items with your hands*! You will know what we mean the first time you flip a piece of tin and find a large diamond-backed rattlesnake beneath it. Grabbing with your hands exposes fingers to venomous snakebite, rusty nails, scorpions, and potentially dangerous spider bites. Good herping trips do not end at the hospital!

The ideal tool for flipping cover is the "snake stick" or "snake hook," a tool about the size of a golf club but with an L-shaped piece where the head of the

Amber shows how to use a snake hook to lift a board.

golf club would be. There are ways to improvise a hook that will serve, but if you plan to do this a lot, invest in a commercial field hook. The kind we prefer has an aircraft aluminum shaft and a titanium hook—it is lightweight yet strong. For those who have the necessary training and experience, it is also useful for moving and positioning venomous snakes.

When a board, a rock, or a log sits undisturbed for enough time, it makes an excellent shelter for herps and other animals. If a field herper comes through and rolls the log over and leaves it that way, the usefulness of that shelter is affected. Please put the log back the way it was! The same goes for any other cover. It's discouraging to walk through an area and find every suitable rock flipped over. Responsible field herpers try to leave an area just as they found it so that the quality of the habitat for everything that lives there is just as good as when the field herpers arrived.

When you do flip something and find a herp beneath, you may have some time to admire it and take a photograph. This depends somewhat on the temperature and the species. At cooler temperatures, many reptiles move more slowly and may simply remain motionless and hope you don't see them. On a warmer day, snakes that depend on speedy escapes (like garter-snakes or racers and coachwhips) may race off after only a glimpse. In our experience, many venomous snakes freeze in place and can be photographed and admired safely before the cover is gently lowered back into position. If you are inexperienced, please take an experienced person with you when you are searching for herps. However, suppose you are alone and you flip cover to find a venomous snake. There's no reason to be afraid. Keep your cool, lower the cover back down, and move away (you weren't picking up that cover with your fingers, were you?).

Laws related to field herping
A number of laws regulate what herpers may do and protect certain species from being collected. Unfortunately, none of those laws can protect an animal from being run over on the highway or killed by fearful or malicious humans. As of 2017 in Texas, forty-two species and subspecies of herps are either state or federally protected as threatened or endangered (see appendix). Texas Parks and Wildlife Department regulations, which have the status of law, prohibit the "taking, possession, transportation, or sale" of any of these animals without a special permit.

The regulations allow some collection of nonprotected herps from the wild, but only by persons who have a hunting license. If you have a valid hunting license, you can collect up to six specimens for personal use. A nongame collector's permit must be obtained in order to have more than six of a given species. Additionally, species on a "white list" can be sold if the seller has a nongame dealer's permit, whereas species on a "black list" may not be "collected or possessed for commercial purposes." (Readers can check these lists by visiting http://www.tpwd.state.tx.us/business/permits /land/wildlife/commercial/ and clicking on Texas Administrative Code regulations Regarding Commercial Nongame Permits.) In the last few years, most Texas turtle species have been added to the black list because their life history makes them especially vulnerable to overcollecting. Turtles are slow to mature, have low reproductive rates, and depend on adults living and breeding for a long time in order to keep their numbers from dropping. The only native turtles one is allowed to buy and sell are red-eared sliders, snapping turtles, and the softshell turtles. Furthermore, commercial collection of these turtles is allowed only on private land and water (and then only with a permit).

"Road hunting," a popular method of field herping, was outlawed in Texas a few years ago, but recent changes in the law have made some road-hunting activities legal again. Road hunting traditionally involved driving on the smallest, most deserted roads and either finding herps as they crossed the roads or parking the car and walking along roadcuts to look for snakes or lizards. This was usually done at night or at dawn or dusk. With recent changes in the law, parking the car and walking along the shoulder and right-of-way is allowed, provided we wear a reflective vest and have a hunting license with a reptile and amphibian stamp from the Texas Parks and Wildlife Department. However, collecting a snake from the pavement is not allowed. We suppose that the authorities would allow us to stand on the right-of-way and cheer the snake, frog, or turtle on, hoping it moves off the pavement without being hit by a car or truck. Again, sadly, there is no prohibition on running them over.

Based on all the hobbyists, students, and professionals who have spent time road hunting, we have a great number of the locality records that tell us where species can be found. A large number of preserved specimens used in the scientific study of herps came from those of us who drove the roads. When I was a young teen, my parents would drive me out to the Benbrook-Aledo Road, where a great many western massasauga rattlesnakes were located. These small snakes are venomous but pose little threat unless you pick them up. I moved quite a few of them off the road so that they would not be run over. We also found kingsnakes, bullsnakes, and other species. I kept careful notes and would salvage specimens that had been run over, donating them to the local museum.

Road hunting, as currently allowed by the Texas Parks and Wildlife Department, is valuable in places where there are roadcuts that leave exposed rock surfaces and crevices where lizards may be tucked away and snakes may be looking for them. It also may be useful for examining roadside ditches for amphibians. However, we do not recommend walking in areas with grassy rights-of-way where you cannot see the ground. You are unlikely to find anything and instead are at risk of hidden hazards. There are limited viable alternatives for hunting some nocturnal species. Presuming we have access to private land, walking across the landscape in the darkness produces fewer sightings but has its own rewards. Such a walk gives us a glimpse into the nocturnal world in which these animals live.

About venomous snakebites

Chances are, you will never be bitten by a venomous snake, even if you spend time in the field looking for reptiles and amphibians. According to a *Dallas News* article (citing the Texas Poison Center Network), in 2012 there were 951 reported snakebites in Texas.[1] In that same year, there were over 26 million people in Texas,[2] meaning that a citizen's chance of snakebite was roughly 0.004 percent that year.

And if you are bitten by a venomous snake, your chances of dying are extremely low. Andy Price's excellent book, *Venomous Snakes of Texas*, reported that there were only five snakebite fatalities in Texas between 1997 and 2005.[3] The annual mortality from lightning strikes was considerably higher. You are literally more likely to be killed by lightning than by venomous snakebite.

Even though, statistically, venomous snakebites are not common and death from a venomous snakebite is even rarer, if you go field herping, you are putting yourself in harm's way a little more than the average person. The more knowledge and experience a field herper has, the more he or she may know how to safely observe and photograph venomous snakes without incident. Time after time (but not *every* time!) we have been impressed by how a venomous snake either tries to get away, or freezes, hoping you will not notice it. You have a tremendous advantage if you see the snake before stepping on it or accidentally putting your hand near it (*again, do not flip with your hands!*). If you do come across a venomous snake, keep a reasonable distance and do not harass it.

Once you have encountered Texas' venomous snakes a number of times, the biggest potential mistake you could make, and the one we struggle not to make, is to feel overly safe and get too close, either to take a photo or for any other purpose. A close, detailed photo can be a great thing to have, but getting too close and "trusting" the snake is one of the most dangerous things you can do. Do not tell yourself that a motionless snake is being friendly or will not hurt you. In an interaction with a venomous snake that is still (almost always a pit viper, as coralsnakes are usually too nervous to stay put), it is likely that the snake is stressed and is freezing in place in the hope that you will go away. The snake is likely gauging how much danger you represent and at what point it is more likely to survive by trying to bite you rather than freezing. If you get too close with a camera, the snake can switch strategies in an instant and strike at you.

It should go without saying that you should never try daredevil stunts with venomous snakes or interact with them while drinking. It *should* go without saying, but it is widely known that venomous snakebites are more common with folks who enjoy taking risks and getting the resulting adrenaline rush. A few beers may decrease one's judgment and one's reaction times, so don't drink while herping. Really, 90 percent of you don't need to hear this, but we hope the remaining 10 percent will listen!

What if, despite heeding all our warnings, you are bitten while out in the field? Let's review some important steps to take:

1. **Can you positively identify whether the snake was venomous?**
   If you are not positive, then err on the safe side and assume it may be venomous. If someone can quickly and safely take a photo for later positive identification, do that. Pit-viper bites generally result

in immediate pain (like a wasp sting or worse) and rapid swelling. A nonvenomous snakebite hurts a little from the scratches made by the snake's small, sharp, recurved teeth, but should not sting or burn. The bite of a coralsnake may not produce much pain, so do not use pain as a sure way to tell if the snake was venomous. Nonvenomous snakebites may leave one or more rows of small punctures or scratches (there are four rows of teeth in the upper jaw and palate and two rows in the lower jaw, but they may not all make contact). A venomous snakebite should additionally leave two larger punctures, representing the fangs. However, in the heat of the moment it may not be easy to analyze the punctures, and fang marks might be missed.

2. **Immediately remove any rings and watches.** Swelling may be rapid and may make it impossible to take rings off after a short time. The ring will act much like a tourniquet and will worsen the damage.

3. **Stay calm and limit exertion.** Remind yourself that the odds are on your side, that you will get through this. If you have to walk to a car, take the shortest route; if possible, have someone bring the car to you. Muscle activity and exertion increases the venom's spread within your body.

4. **Call the national Poison Control phone number: 1-800-222-1222.** Write that number somewhere and keep it with you in the field (or use the SnakeBite911 app—see below). This 24-hour toll-free number is staffed by experts who can help you evaluate what symptoms you are having, and chances are that a hospital will consult with them as well.

5. **Get to the hospital as quickly as you can.** Have someone drive you there; if you can get an ambulance or any other emergency responder, do it. Your ability to drive a car may rapidly deteriorate, so driving should be a last resort.

6. **Do not take alcohol or pain killers.** Even aspirin will interfere with blood clotting, so do not take any medicine unless told to do so by a physician.

7. **Once you arrive at the hospital,** you will likely receive an intravenous administration of antivenom, a medicine that binds with snake

venom proteins to inactivate them. Usually an initial dose is followed by additional amounts of antivenom until symptoms are sufficiently improved. In-depth discussion of venomous snakebite effects and treatment is beyond the scope of this book and outside the competency of the authors. The reader may wish to consult Rubio and Keyler's *Venomous Snakebite in the Western United States*.

8. **Beware of folk remedies or outdated procedures** that can actually make snakebite injuries worse. Years ago snakebite kits included instruments for cutting the skin over fang marks so that people could attempt to suck the venom out. Nowadays experts agree that this method does not remove venom and adds needless injury to the bitten area. Previously, some rescuers and physicians recommended packing the bitten limb in ice or immersing it in icewater to slow the progression of the venom. This method has been proven harmful to the patient and is no longer recommended. Recently, there was the suggestion that electric shock can treat snakebite. Jim Harrison, who extracts venom for pharmaceutical and research purposes at the Kentucky Reptile Zoo, told me that this one originated with a podiatrist who was vacationing in Ecuador and witnessed local people applying electric shock to snake bites; the victims survived. "But," Harrison pointed out, "some of the people would have survived anyway from the envenomation," with or without electric shock. Further, not all the snakes were positively identified and some were likely not venomous. The podiatrist came to the erroneous conclusion that the shock enabled victims to recover. The method was not scientifically tested and has since been discredited. "The best first aid for snake bite," Harrison said, "is a car, car keys, and someone to drive you to the hospital."

SnakeBite911

There is an app for smartphones and tablets that could be useful in the field in the event that you or someone with you is bitten by a venomous snake. Called SnakeBite911, it was developed by the company that makes CroFab antivenom. Among the features of the app is a locator to find nearby hospitals and a Get Emergency Support button that walks the user through the things not to do; it can also dial 911, reminds the user to remove rings and other constricting items, and prompts the user to take photos of the bite zone every fifteen minutes to track the progression of symptoms. It can also call the Poison Control Center for additional information while on the way to the hospital.

SnakeBite911 has profiles of the venomous pit vipers of North America with a representative photo of each. It does not include the coralsnake (the developers of the app make antivenom for North American pit vipers but not for coralsnakes), but the recommendations are for the most part relevant for coralsnake bites, and the hospital locator and dialer for 911 and Poison Control would still be helpful. Additionally, coralsnake bites constitute only a small proportion of venomous snakebites.

The app includes a "snake sightings" feature that would enable the user to report a sighting of a venomous snake, but most readers of this book would find the iNaturalist app much more useful and functional.

It's now up to you

We hope that you will get out and explore some of the natural places in Texas and see some of the reptiles and amphibians that live there. These firsthand experiences are valuable, both for you and for the landscapes that we hope to preserve for future generations. Exploring as we have done for many years has been a priceless education; the more we have seen, the more we wanted to understand, and a fascination with a few animals gradually expanded to a desire to understand the whole ecosystem. It has also inspired us to think more deeply about our place within this extraordinary "garden" on earth and about our role as stewards as well as members of the community of living things. Our travels have allowed us to add to the scientific understanding of herps, contributing specimens to scientific collections and submitting citizen-science observations using tools such as iNaturalist. We also have become advocates for saving natural areas and living in ways that have fewer impacts on air, water, land, and wildlife. This book will be successful to the extent that it inspires you to do some of these things. Go out and see the reptiles and amphibians of Texas—we're pretty sure that you'll have a blast!

Afterword:
Copperhead Road for the Generations

Clint King

OPEN FIELDS OF FARMLAND gave way to bluestem prairie, broken up by thick huddles of lush and green deciduous woodland, as my son Zev and I headed south on the little-traveled farm road. Out of the passenger-side window an amber sun hung on the edge of an overcast, dove-gray sky. The ambient air temperature was still holding, refusing to fall even in the face of another impending spring storm. The pavement was smoky gray and slick from recent rainfall. To the northeast a solid wall of dark blue stood like a towering fortress. It was the perfect meteorological recipe for the copperheads to move, and the electricity in the air was equally matched by the static charge of enthusiasm in the truck between my son and me.

We turned west off the farm road onto a paved two-lane county road that cut like a dark scar through impenetrable grapevine and greenbrier. The presence of cottonwoods and willows standing in a line like ranks of soldiers indicated a major tributary to the West Fork of the Trinity River running parallel to the road several miles to the south. The sun was almost gone now, the only remaining evidence of its presence a roseate smudge across the horizon. To the east, the lightning illuminated the center of the storm. As we drove on, dense thickets of cane grew along the roadside in front of thick post oaks standing guard. The presence of prickly pear seemed out of place as Blanchard's cricket frogs and gray treefrogs called from the flooded ditches.

"Are we there yet?" Zev asked me with childlike impatience. "Is this Copperhead Road?"

"Yeah, we're here," I told him.

"Where are all the copperheads you used to see?"

"They're out there," I said, fanning my arm out across the dark fields that lay to our left and right. "Just wait. We'll cross paths with one any minute now."

"Copperhead Road" is more than just a two-lane asphalt trail cut out of the mixed grassland in central Wise County. It is a personal, sentimental path through time to the fields and floodplains of my youth. I had discovered

"Copperhead Road," Wise County

the road in the early fall of my sixteenth year, shortly after acquiring my first vehicle, on an evening not unlike the one I was about to share with Zev. I had set out on my usual weekend road-cruising excursion in search of all things reptilian and had stumbled upon one of those few-and-far-between sweet spots where the habitat is so pristine and untouched by the destructive hand of man that the place literally crawls with wildlife. Within the span of two hours I had found fifteen broad-banded copperheads, not to mention an array of local frog and toad species that had come out to enjoy the rain. From that memorable night on, the road was transformed from County Road whatever to "Copperhead Road." I had driven it many Friday and Saturday nights while my friends and classmates were out partying or dancing or attending sporting events or whatever it was the "normal" kids were doing. The road seldom failed to produce herps, even during unfavorable conditions. Come drought, full moon, wind, water, or unexpected cold front, the road proved itself reptilian-reliable.

Broad-banded copperheads weren't the only serpents that made their brief nocturnal appearances on the roadway between the high grass of the seasonal floodplain and the dense oak groves that grew uphill. Western ribbonsnakes, plain-bellied and diamond-backed watersnakes, and Great Plains ratsnakes were all regulars. In the daytime it was possible to see the lime-green outline of a rough greensnake lying quietly in a patch of dappled sunlight beneath an oak tree whose branches overhung the roadway. Eastern yellow-bellied racers and western coachwhips were liquid blurs of serpentine

A particularly feisty speckled kingsnake

motion as they streaked to the safety of high grass and cacti. One of my fond-est memories is of a beautiful speckled kingsnake lying in a dip in the road on the still-warm pavement one cool September around midnight when all other activity had ceased. But the copperheads were definitely the predom-inant species. On a perfect night, if the humidity, moon phase, barometric pressure, and temperature all lined up in one's favor, one could see a copper-head every 200 feet between dusk and midnight.

As the years rolled on and time stretched out into that mysterious expanse of miles and memories, I graduated high school, moved out of my parents' house, went to college, changed vehicles several times, got married, and had a son. A lot of the areas once renowned for their favorable habitats of mesquite-laced fields and log-strewn riparian bottomland were converted into hous-ing additions, drill sites, and grazed pastures of coastal Bermuda grass and alfalfa, all in the name of human progress. But as my son and I rolled along Copperhead Road in the last lingering moments of dusk, I was happy to see that the scene here had remained virtually unchanged. There were no sub-divisions where open fields had once been, and those long-standing oaks whose boughs have supported countless generations of rough greensnakes and Texas spiny lizards remained unfelled. Not a single car passed us as we cruised slowly, flashlights at the ready and eyes glued to the road surface in front of us.

The sky to the south became enshrouded in an inky indigo blue as night took over. To our north it was pitch black as the storm passed over the prairie. Faint sheets of rain could be seen in the distance whenever lightning illu-minated the sky in a brief flash of brilliance, like a teasing glimpse of some

Broad-banded copperhead

divine still-life painting. Stray droplets of rain began to accumulate in random splatters across our windshield, but these would be no deterrent for the prolific and persistent pit vipers of Copperhead Road. Within minutes every cluster of purple-headed thistle and every bunch of cottony-white bullnettle flowers on either side of the road glistened with fresh raindrops as our headlights struck them. The road was a sheet of reflective black metal. I glanced over at my son, who was leaning as far forward as his car seat would allow, his wide brown eyes straining to see those promised snakes.

The moisture in the air coaxed out May beetles and moths, and they swarmed to the luminescent beams of our headlights. A beautiful luna moth sailed in front of the windshield like a pallid green phantom for a split second, delighting us with its presence as it sought out a mate in the darkness, following some pheromone trail too vague for any creature but it alone to detect. As the air temperature began to cool with nightfall, a misty fog hovered over the pavement and hugged the ground like prairie ghosts from my past. An anuran symphony began to play for us, conducted by the gently falling rain. The entire scene was unfolding so splendidly, almost magically, that for a moment I became lost in thought; my mind traveled away from the physical action of herping and settled on some long-gone season, devoid of drought, climate shift, and adulthood. Luckily, my son's mind was still finely honed on the task at hand.

"Copperhead!" he yelled. The magic word uttered, I broke free from my trance and tapped the brakes. The snake was a species I had encountered

Zev admiring a copperhead

countless times, but here, contrasting against the wet, black tarmac in alternating crossbands of chestnut and mahogany that glowed fluorescent orange in the headlights, with wispy white tendrils of mist curling around it, the broad-banded copperhead was a spectacular sight to behold.

Even better was the look in my son's eyes—that awe-inspired sense of amazement that had always filled my own since childhood as I stood humbled before some spectacular natural wonder. As we stood in the road at a safe distance with our flashlights trained on the little snake in front of us, I could see that he was as totally mesmerized as I had once been.

"It's beautiful, isn't it?" I whispered to him. He responded with a silent nod, his eyes never leaving the copperhead. We watched it as its bright pink forked tongue flicked in and out, testing the humid, scent-rich spring air and extracting our presence from the smells of the rain, warm asphalt, and wet leaves. Evidently it deemed us no threat, nor should it have. We watched it for several minutes, talking about its camouflage, diet, and venom structure before it eventually resumed its wandering and slithered slowly to the shelter of the dense greenbrier and prairie grass at roadside.

Most people would consider the discovery of a venomous snake the last opportunity on earth for a father-son moment. But I could think of nothing better: a weekend drive down Copperhead Road to experience the indescribable fascination and joy of sharing an appreciation of the natural wonders of our world with another generation while there was still something natural left in it to share.

APPENDIX: REPTILES AND AMPHIBIANS IN TEXAS LISTED AS THREATENED OR ENDANGERED

In Texas, species may be listed as threatened or endangered under state law (through the Texas Parks and Wildlife Department) or under the federal Endangered Species Act. Species thus protected either by state or federal law may not be collected, captured, trapped, killed, or taken. In the table below, common and scientific names shown in parentheses are from the names list of the Society for Study of Amphibians and Reptiles.

Reptiles

Common Name	Scientific Name	State Status	Federal Status
Loggerhead sea turtle	*Caretta caretta*	Threatened	Threatened
Green sea turtle	*Chelonia mydas*	Threatened	Threatened
Hawksbill sea turtle	*Eretmochelys imbricata*	Endangered	Endangered
Kemp's ridley sea turtle	*Lepidochelys kempii*	Endangered	Endangered
Leatherback sea turtle	*Dermochelys coriacea*	Endangered	Endangered
Alligator snapping turtle	*Macrochelys temminckii*	Threatened	n/a
Cagle's map turtle	*Graptemys caglei*	Threatened	n/a
Chihuahuan mud turtle (Mexican plateau mud turtle)	*Kinosternon hirtipes murrayi*	Threatened	n/a
Texas tortoise (Berlandier's tortoise)	*Gopherus berlandieri*	Threatened	n/a
Reticulated gecko (reticulate banded gecko)	*Coleonyx reticulatus*	Threatened	n/a
Reticulate collared lizard	*Crotaphytus reticulatus*	Threatened	n/a
Texas horned lizard	*Phrynosoma cornutum*	Threatened	n/a
Mountain short-horned lizard (greater short-horned lizard)	*Phrynosoma hernandesi*	Threatened	n/a

Texas scarlet snake (Texas scarletsnake)	*Cemophora coccinea lineri*	Threatened	n/a
Northern scarlet snake (northern scarletsnake)	*Cemophora coccinea copei*		n/a
Black-striped snake (regal black-striped snake)	*Coniophanes imperialis*	Threatened	n/a
Texas indigo snake	*Drymarchon melanurus erebennus*	Threatened	n/a
Speckled racer	*Drymobius margaritiferus*	Threatened	n/a
Northern cat-eyed snake	*Leptodeira septentrionalis*	Threatened	n/a
Brazos water snake (Brazos watersnake)	*Nerodia harteri*	Threatened	n/a
Smooth green snake (smooth greensnake)	*Liochlorophis vernalis (Opheodrys vernalis)*	Threatened	n/a
Louisiana pine snake (Louisiana pinesnake)	*Pituophis ruthveni*	Threatened	Candidate for listing
Trans-Pecos black-headed snake	*Tantilla cucullata*	Threatened	n/a
Chihuahuan desert lyre snake (Texas lyresnake)	*Trimorphodon vilkinsonii*	Threatened	n/a
Timber rattlesnake	*Crotalus horridus*	Threatened	n/a

Amphibians

Common Name	Scientific Name	State Status	Federal Status
Cascade caverns salamander	*Eurycea latitans*	Threatened	n/a
San Marcos salamander	*Eurycea nana*	Threatened	Threatened
Comal blind salamander	*Eurycea tridentifera*	Threatened	n/a
Barton Springs salamander	*Eurycea sosorum*	Endangered	Endangered
Texas blind salamander	*Eurycea rathbuni*	Endangered	Endangered
Blanco blind salamander	*Eurycea robusta*	Threatened	n/a
Jollyville salamander (Jollyville plateau salamander)	*Eurycea tonkawae*	n/a	Threatened
Georgetown salamander	*Eurycea naufragia*	n/a	Threatened
Salado salamander	*Eurycea chisholmensis*	n/a	Threatened
Austin blind salamander	*Eurycea waterlooensis*	Endangered	Endangered

Black-spotted newt	*Notophthalmus meridionalis*	Threatened	-
South Texas siren—large form (lesser siren)	*Siren* sp. 1 (*Siren intermedia*)	Threatened	-
Houston toad	*Anaxyrus houstonensis*	Endangered	Endangered
Mexican treefrog	*Smilisca baudinii*	Threatened	n/a
White-lipped frog (Mexican white-lipped frog)	*Leptodactylus fragilis*	Threatened	n/a
Sheep frog	*Hypopachus variolosus*	Threatened	n/a
Mexican burrowing toad	*Rhinophrynus dorsalis*	Threatened	n/a

Source: Texas Parks and Wildlife Department, "Federal and State Listed Amphibians and Reptiles in Texas," https://tpwd.texas.gov/huntwild/wild/wildlife_diversity/nongame/listed-species /amphibians-reptiles.phtml, accessed November 30, 2017.

amphibian   a member of the group of vertebrate animals that includes frogs, toads, salamanders, and caecilians. With a few exceptions, they start life in an aquatic, larval form and then metamorphose into an adult, air-breathing form.

amplexus   a position in which a male amphibian uses his front legs to grasp the female and then provides external fertilization of eggs as they are deposited. For example, in many frog and toad species, the male grasps the female just before or behind her forearms. Sitting atop her back, the male can release sperm as the female deposits eggs in the water.

anal plate   in snakes, the belly scale just prior to the tail, that covers the cloacal opening. It is larger than the scales under the rest of the snake's body and may be a single scale or divided into two scales. Knowing if it is single or divided may help in identifying some snake species.

anuran   a frog or toad. The order Anura, comprising frogs and toads, is one of three major groups of amphibians.

autotomy   the loss of the tail by a lizard or salamander as a strategy for avoiding a predator. The severed tail continues to move, distracting the predator and giving the animal a chance to escape. Some lizards have "fracture planes" in the tail that allow for easy separation when the tail is grabbed. The tail is then regenerated, though the length and appearance is different from the original tail.

Big Thicket   an area in southeast Texas with pine forests as well as beech and magnolia trees, bogs with pitcher plants, and sloughs with cypress trees. In some areas the forest and understory growth are nearly impenetrable. A number of areas within the Big Thicket have been set aside as the Big Thicket National Preserve.

Blackland Prairie   a tallgrass ecosystem running roughly north to south in Texas from the Red River to San Antonio. Named for its rich, black soil, it is located to the east of the Cross Timbers and the Edwards Plateau and west of the Post Oak Savannah.

brumation   in reptiles and amphibians, a period of winter dormancy when metabolism and activity are greatly slowed (but some activity, such as periodic drinking, occurs). Proponents of the term note that it is different physiologically from the state of hibernation that occurs in some mammals.

carapace   in turtles, the upper shell, consisting of underlying bone and, usually, a series of scutes composed of keratin. (A few species, such as the softshell turtles, have tough, rubbery skin rather than scutes over the bones of the shell.)

chelonian   a turtle; a member of the reptilian order Testudines, under which turtles are classified.

Chihuahuan Desert   a large ecosystem in northern Mexico and parts of the United States, including Texas west of the Pecos River. Several plant species characterize this desert, such as creosote bush, lechuguilla, and ocotillo. The lower elevations are flat and gravelly, while higher areas support grasslands; several mountain ranges are found in the Chihuahuan Desert region.

cloaca   in reptiles and amphibians (and certain other animals such as fish), the opening at the posterior of the body. Feces and urinary tract materials are expelled from it, and it also serves as the opening for the reproductive tract.

cold-blooded   *See* **ectothermic**

colubrid   a member of the huge snake family Colubridae. Snakes within this family are distributed worldwide; in the United States the group includes most nonvenomous snakes such as kingsnakes, ratsnakes, gartersnakes, etc.

costal groove   one of several vertical grooves along the sides of the body in many salamanders. Counting the number of such grooves is sometimes useful in identifying different species.

cranial crest   a raised ridge on the top of the head of some toad species. Their distinctive shapes and patterns can help distinguish one species from another. Cranial crests are found around, in front of, or behind the eyes of these toad species.

crepuscular   a species that is primarily active during twilight, either near sunrise or sunset.

crocodilian   a member of the reptile order Crocodilia, which includes alligators and crocodiles.

Cross Timbers   a forest, savannah, and prairie ecosystem running from north-central Texas through Oklahoma and into a small area of Kansas. It is dominated by post oak and blackjack oak but also includes prairies such as the Grand Prairie. In Texas it is found east of the Rolling Plains and west of the Blackland Prairie.

cryptic   characterized by coloration, pattern, or form that serves to camouflage an animal in its natural environment.

cut-shining   the activity of shining lights on the exposed rock surfaces of roadcuts in an attempt to find lizards and snakes at night.

desiccation   drying; the removal of water. The skin of some animals offers some protection from desiccation, while other animals (such as amphibians) are much more vulnerable to desiccation.

diurnal   most active during the daytime.

dorsolateral ridges   raised ridges in some frogs, running from behind the head to near where the back legs join with the body. Toxin glands are concentrated in this tissue.

dorsum   the back or upper side of an animal. The adjective form is "dorsal."

ecdysis   the act of shedding the outer layer of skin. In reptiles the shed skin is thin and somewhat translucent, and it retains the form of the scales and a faint image of the pattern. Snakes shed the entire skin at once, rubbing to loosen it around the mouth and then crawling out of it so that it is turned inside out like removing a sock.

ecosystem   a community of living organisms and their physical environment that interact as a system. The organisms and environments in different places can be described as distinctive ecosystems, such as the Blackland Prairie or the Chihuahuan Desert.

ectothermic   animals that do not generate heat through metabolic processes to maintain a specified temperature. Such animals regulate their temperature by shifting between warmer and cooler surroundings.

Edwards Plateau   a broad area of uplift in Central Texas, extending westward to the Pecos River. The western part of the plateau is mostly grassland with scattered trees, while the eastern areas have extensive juniper ("cedar") and oak woodlands and limestone canyons and caves.

endemic uniquely found in a defined area. For example, the Brazos River watersnake is endemic to Texas, meaning that it is found only in that state.

femoral pores a series of openings (with associated enlarged scales) along the ventral surface of some lizards' thighs. The pores may exude chemical cues to mark territory or attract a mate.

frog an amphibian without a tail and with enlarged back legs. The frog group also includes toads, although in common usage a frog often (not always) has smoother skin and longer back legs than a toad.

genus (plural: **genera**) in scientific classification a group of related organisms, ranked above species and below family. A family includes related genera, and a genus includes related species. Organisms are known by two names, the genus and species. For example, the small-mouthed salamander is *Ambystoma texanum*—it is the species *texanum* within the genus *Ambystoma*.

gravid the state in which a female is carrying eggs or embryos.

habitat the ecological area within which a species or subspecies lives and can meet its needs for food, water, shelter, temperature regulation, and other requirements. Habitat that can support a population of a given species might be referred to as "suitable" habitat for that species.

hemipenes the paired copulatory organs of male snakes and lizards. Ordinarily, they are kept inverted within the tail below the cloaca. As a result, the tails of male snakes generally are less tapered than those of females of the same species. In some cases this allows one to determine the sex of the snake with reasonable certainty. During copulation, one hemipenis is everted within the female's cloaca.

herpetofauna reptiles and amphibians, especially those of a particular area (e.g., "the herpetofauna of Texas"). The term is sometimes shortened to "herps."

herpetology the branch of zoology devoted to the study of reptiles and amphibians using scientific methods.

hibernation a winter period of dormancy and lowered metabolism, especially in certain mammals that would otherwise maintain a fairly constant body temperature and metabolism. Some argue that dormancy in herpetofauna during winter is a different process. *See* **brumation**

High Plains an area of relatively flat landscape, short grasses, playa lakes, and relatively sparse rainfall in the western part of the Texas Panhandle.

It starts at the Pecos River and extends northward as part of the Great Plains.

intergrade a transitional form in areas where the ranges of two distinct subspecies meet, having some characteristics of each subspecies.

Jacobson's organ a part of the olfactory system in many animals. In snakes it opens into the roof of the mouth, where it can sense chemical cues picked up by the tips of the tongue. Snakes use this sense in detecting prey or predators, and males use it to track potential mates. Also known as the vomeronasal organ.

keeled having a raised ridge. The dorsal scales of some snakes are "keeled"; that is, a ridge runs lengthwise along each scale on the back from the neck to the tip of the tail.

labial pertaining to the lips. The scales along the sides of the mouth of snakes and lizards are referred to as labial scales.

lizard one of a group of reptiles, closely related to snakes but usually with eyelids, external ear openings, and four legs (there are exceptions, such as the glass lizard). Like snakes, lizards are members of the reptilian order Squamata.

marsh a wetland that primarily contains grasses, reeds, or other herbaceous plants (as opposed to shrubs or trees with woody trunks).

microhabitat a small, localized habitat that is distinct from the surrounding habitat, such as a fallen log or pond margin. These specific places may be key to supporting certain species.

mimicry an evolved resemblance between two species so that a third species responds to the mimic in a similar way to how it would respond to the model. In one type (Batesian mimicry) a harmless mimic looks like another animal that is harmful to a predator, so the predator avoids both the mimic and the dangerous model.

musking a reptile's release or expulsion of a noxious-smelling substance that may secure its release from a captor or predator. In snakes the musk glands are located at the base of the tail, and the semiliquid musk is usually smeared on the aggressor as the snake thrashes its body.

nocturnal primarily active at night.

nuchal pertaining to the back of the neck, such as a "nuchal blotch" (a characteristic pattern on the neck just behind the head) or "nuchal scute" (a small scute at the center and front of a turtle's carapace).

parotoid glands paired glands located around the back and sides of the head of some amphibians, particularly toads. These raised, lumpy glands secrete a milky, irritating, toxic substance that may deter predators.

Piney Woods an ecoregion in East Texas containing loblolly and other pines and mixed hardwood forest with such trees as oak, sweetgum, elm, and ash. It is an area with sandy soil and relatively high rainfall. There are many ponds and other wetlands in parts of the Piney Woods.

pit viper one of a group of venomous snakes in the subfamily Crotalinae; they possess heat-sensitive pit organs on the face between the nostril and the eye. In the United States this group includes copperheads, cottonmouths, and rattlesnakes.

plastron in turtles, the lower shell, consisting of underlying bone and, usually, a series of scutes composed of keratin. This lower shell is attached to the upper shell (carapace), typically by a relatively narrow "bridge" of the same material.

prairie an ecosystem dominated by grasses and forbs (as opposed to woody shrubs and trees), such as the tallgrass prairies once common in the Blackland Prairie ecoregion or the shortgrass prairies of the High Plains.

rear-fanged possessing enlarged teeth toward the rear of the upper jaw. These enlarged teeth or fangs have a groove that facilitates toxins or mild venom entering a prey animal as the snake chews. A bite from a rear-fanged snake in North America (such as a hog-nosed snake or nightsnake) would not be considered medically significant for a human. The technical term for "rear-fanged" is "opisthoglyphous."

Rolling Plains an ecoregion in Texas bordered on the west by the High Plains, on the south by the Edwards Plateau, and on the east by the Cross Timbers. Much of it contains mesquite grasslands as well as juniper, prickly pear, and other plants.

rostral located at the front of the snout or tip of the nose. The rostral scale is located at the very tip of the snout, just above the mouth.

salamander a group of amphibians with tails and generally with four legs (but with exceptions such as sirens and amphiumas). Many have an adult air-breathing stage, but others remain in an aquatic larval stage (described as "neotenic"). Still others, as adults, are land-dwelling but lungless.

savannah a mixed grassland and woodland ecosystem in which the trees are scattered or at least spaced so that the canopy does not close. As a result, there is enough sunlight to maintain a continuous cover of grasses and other herbaceous vegetation.

scales   in reptiles, raised areas of the outer skin made from keratin. They may be bead-like or granular, or may be a series of overlapping shields. In lizards and snakes some of these (especially on the head) may have characteristic positions and shapes such as the "labial" scales bordering the lips.

scutes   in most turtles, the flat, horn-like plates that cover the bony shell. They are arranged in characteristic ways and named (e.g., the vertebral, costal, marginal, and other scutes of the carapace).

snake   one of a group of reptiles, closely related to lizards but without eyelids, external ear openings (but they do have inner ear structures and can hear some airborne sounds), or legs.

species   the biological classification that indicates a particular "kind" of animal. Generally, only the members of a given species can breed and produce fertile offspring. A kind of animal is known by its genus and species names, such as *Thamnophis sirtalis*, the common gartersnake.

subspecies   variations or subtypes within a species that are capable of interbreeding with others of that species, such as *Thamnophis sirtalis annectens*, the Texas gartersnake. Subspecies may be geographic variations, found in different areas, or they may be separated by an ecological niche.

taxonomy   the scientific discipline that classifies and gives names to different organisms. It is a hierarchical classification that branches into successively more specific groups (i.e., class, order, family, genus, species). Modern taxonomic classification is based on the evolutionary relationships between organisms.

thorn scrub (or **Tamaulipan thorn scrub**)   a description of much of the South Texas Plains roughly south and west of San Antonio. It is thought that the area was once dominated by grassland and savannah, but factors such as grazing, fire suppression, and agricultural uses led to dominance by thorny brush and various cacti.

toad   a type of frog, typically with drier, warty skin and smaller back legs for hopping rather than leaping. The term is not very precise, but in the United States it usually refers to various kinds of spadefoot toads, narrow-mouthed toads, and "true" toads.

tortoise   a term for certain turtles; in the United States "tortoise" refers to a genus of land-dwelling turtles (including, in Texas, Berlandier's tortoise).

Trans-Pecos   the part of Texas that is found west of the Pecos River. Although some areas around the Pecos River could be considered a transition from the Edwards Plateau, most of it would be described as Chihuahuan Desert.

turtle   a reptile having a bony or cartilaginous shell covering its body. This protective shell consists of a carapace above and plastron below. Turtles do not have teeth but instead have a hard beak capable of shearing through food.

tympanum   a membrane capable of vibrating and transmitting sounds to other structures involved in hearing. In frogs and toads the tympanum is located behind the eyes on the surface of the head. In certain species of frogs the tympanum of males is larger than that of females.

venom   toxin produced by an animal that can be injected into a prey or predator species, either as a way of subduing it in order to eat it or as a defense. Reptile venoms are variable but are often classified as either hemotoxic (they destroy tissue) or neurotoxic (they disrupt nerve transmission).

vent   the external opening of the cloaca.

ventral   pertaining to the underside of an animal.

vomeronasal organ   *See* Jacobson's organ

Introduction

1. Pough et al., *Herpetology*.

2. Powell, Conant, and Collins, *Peterson Field Guide to Reptiles and Amphibians*.

3. Dixon, *Amphibians and Reptiles of Texas*, 1.

4. Texas Parks and Wildlife Department, Texas Conservation Action Plan: Support Documents and Links, http://tpwd.texas.gov/landwater/land/tcap /documents.phtml, accessed May 14, 2015.

5. US Census Bureau, "Texas: 2016 Population Estimates," https://www.census .gov/search-results.html?q=Texas+population%2C+2016&search.x=0&search .y=0&search=submit&page=1&stateGeo=none&searchtype=web&cssp=SERP, accessed November 11, 2017.

6. David Todd and Jonathan Ogren, *The Texas Landscape Project: Nature and People* (College Station: Texas A&M University Press, 2016).

7. Kauffeld, *Snakes and Snake Hunting*, 256.

8. Crother, *Scientific and Standard English Names of Amphibians and Reptiles*.

Chapter 1

1. Peacock, *Nature Lover's Guide to the Big Thicket*, 5.

2. Al Reinert, "The Big Thicket Tangle," *Texas Monthly*, July 1973, http://www .texasmonthly.com/articles/the-big-thicket-tangle/, accessed November 25, 2017.

3. J. W. Gibbons and M. E. Dorcas, "Defensive Behavior of Cottonmouths (*Agkistrodon piscivorus*) toward Humans," *Copeia* 2002, no. 1 (2002): 195–198.

4. Spearing, *Roadside Geology of Texas*, 15.

5. R. N. Reed, J. Congdon, and J. W. Gibbons. "The Alligator Snapping Turtle [*Macrochelys (Macroclemys) temminckii*]: A Review of Ecology, Life History, and Conservation, with Demographic Analyses of the Sustainability of Take from Wild Populations." Report for the Division of Scientific Authority, US Fish and Wildlife Service. Aiken, SC: Savannah River Ecology Laboratory, 2002.

Chapter 2

1. US Fish and Wildlife Service, "Caddo Lake National Wildlife Refuge, Texas: About the Refuge," https://www.fws.gov/refuge/Caddo_Lake/about.html, accessed November 11, 2017.

2. Harry W. Greene and Roy W. McDiarmid, "Coral Snake Mimicry: Does It Occur?," *Science* 213, no. 4513 (1981): 1207–1212.

Chapter 3

1. Gibbons and Dorcas, *North American Watersnakes*, 69.
2. Ernst and Lovich, *Turtles of the United States and Canada*, 35.
3. Manaster, *Horned Lizards*, 27.

Chapter 5

1. Tipton et al., *Texas Amphibians*, 89, 101.
2. Dodd, *North American Box Turtles*, 159.

Chapter 6

1. US Forest Service, "Caddo-LBJ National Grasslands," http://www.fs.usda.gov /detail/texas/about-forest/districts/?cid=fswdev3_008440, accessed August 22, 2015.
2. H. W. Greene and G. V. Oliver, "Notes on the Natural History of the Western Massasauga." *Herpetologica* 21, no. 3 (1965): 225–228.
3. Werler and Dixon, *Texas Snakes*, 243.

Chapter 7

1. Spearing, *Roadside Geology of Texas*, 15.
2. Texas Parks and Wildlife Department, "Post Oak Savannah and Blackland Prairie Wildlife Management: Historical Perspective," http://tpwd.texas.gov /landwater/land/habitats/post_oak/, accessed May 19, 2015.
3. Jason Spangler, Native Prairies Association of Texas, "Why Protect and Restore Prairie?," http://texasprairie.org/index.php/learn/about_prairies_entry/why _protect_and_restore_prairie/, accessed April 17, 2016.
4. Stebbins and Cohen, *Natural History of Amphibians*, 22.
5. Powell, Conant, Collins, *Peterson Field Guide to Reptiles and Amphibians*, 436–437.
6. C. J. Franklin, "Texas Smallmouth Salamander," *Cross Timbers Herpetologist* 6, no. 9 (2004): 3.
7. Tipton et al., *Texas Amphibians*, 66.
8. R. K. Vaughan, J. R. Dixon, and R. A. Thomas, "A Reevaluation of Populations of the Corn Snake *Elaphe guttata* (Reptilia: Serpentes: Colubridae) in Texas," *Texas Journal of Science* 48, no. 1 (1996): 175–190.

Chapter 8

1. Spearing, *Roadside Geology of Texas*, 355–356.
2. Werler and Dixon, *Texas Snakes*, 259.
3. Manaster. *Horned Lizards*, 71–74.
4. Cornell Lab of Ornithology, "All about Birds: Wild Turkey," https://www .allaboutbirds.org/guide/wild_turkey/lifehistory, accessed November 28, 2015.

Chapter 9

1. Texas Parks and Wildlife Department, "Feral Hogs," https://tpwd.texas.gov/huntwild/wild/nuisance/feral_hogs/, accessed November 26, 2017.

Chapter 11

1. Wauer and Fleming, *Naturalist's Big Bend*, 22–24.
2. Dodson, *Guide to Plants of the Northern Chihuahuan Desert*, 24.
3. Werler and Dixon. *Texas Snakes*, 321.

Chapter 12

1. Spearing, *Roadside Geology of Texas*, 294–296.
2. Arnett and Jacques, *Simon & Schuster's Guide to Insects*, plate 108.

Final Thoughts

1. Naomi Martin, "Snakebites on the Rise—Watch Out, D-FW," *Dallas News*, April 2016, https://www.dallasnews.com/news/news/2016/04/20/snake-bites-on-the-rise-watch-out-dfw, accessed August 6, 2017.
2. Texas Department of State Health Services, Center for Health Statistics, "Texas Population, 2012 (Estimates)," https://www.dshs.texas.gov/chs/popdat/ST2012e.shtm, accessed November 29, 2017.
3. Price, *Venomous Snakes of Texas*, 5.

BIBLIOGRAPHY

Arnett, Ross H., and Richard L. Jacques Jr. *Simon & Schuster's Guide to Insects*. New York: Simon & Schuster, 1981.

Carroll, David M. *Swampwalker's Journal: A Wetlands Year*. New York: Houghton-Mifflin, 1999.

Crother, B. I., ed. *Scientific and Standard English Names of Amphibians and Reptiles of North America North of Mexico, with Comments regarding Confidence in Our Understanding*. 8th ed. SSAR Herpetological Circulars, no. 43. [Topeka, KS]: Society for the Study of Amphibians and Reptiles, 2017.

Dixon, James R. *Amphibians and Reptiles of Texas*. 3rd ed. College Station: Texas A&M University Press, 2013.

Dodd, C. Kenneth. *North American Box Turtles: A Natural History*. Norman: University of Oklahoma Press, 2001.

Dodson, Carolyn. *A Guide to Plants of the Northern Chihuahuan Desert*. Albuquerque: University of New Mexico Press, 2012.

Elliott, Lang, C. Gerhardt, and C. Davidson. *The Frogs and Toads of North America*. New York: Houghton Mifflin Harcourt, 2009.

Ernst, Carl H., and Jeffrey E. Lovich. *Turtles of the United States and Canada*. 2nd ed. Baltimore, MD: Johns Hopkins University Press, 2009.

Francaviglia, Richard V. *The Cast Iron Forest: A Natural and Cultural History of the North American Cross Timbers*. Corrie Herring Hooks Series, no. 43. Austin: University of Texas Press, 2000.

Gibbons, J. W. 1983. *Their Blood Runs Cold: Adventures with Reptiles and Amphibians*. Tuscaloosa: University of Alabama Press, 1983.

Gibbons, J. W., and M. E. Dorcas. *North American Watersnakes: A Natural History*. Norman: University of Oklahoma Press, 2004.

Greene, Harry W. *Snakes: The Evolution of Mystery in Nature*. Berkeley: University of California Press, 1997.

Hibbitts, Troy D., and T. J. Hibbitts. *Texas Lizards: A Field Guide*. Texas Natural History Guides. Austin: University of Texas Press, 2015.

Hibbitts, Troy D., and T. L. Hibbitts. *Texas Turtles and Crocodilians: A Field Guide*. Texas Natural History Guides. Austin: University of Texas Press, 2016.

Jones, Lawrence L.C., and R. E. Lovich, eds. *Lizards of the American Southwest: A Photographic Field Guide*. Tucson, AZ: Rio Nuevo, 2009.

Kauffeld, C. F. *Snakes and Snake Hunting*. Garden City, NY: Hanover House, 1957.

Kauffeld, C. F. *Snakes: The Keeper and the Kept*. New York: Doubleday, 1969.

Klauber, L. M. *Rattlesnakes: Their Habits, Life Histories, and Influence on Mankind*. 2nd ed. Berkeley: University of California Press, 1940.

Manaster, Jane. *Horned Lizards*. Austin: University of Texas Press, 1997.

Peacock, Howard. *Nature Lover's Guide to the Big Thicket*. College Station: Texas A&M University Press, 1994.

Pough, F. H., R. M. Andrews, J. E. Cadle, M. L. Crump, A. H. Savitzky, and K. D. Wells. *Herpetology*. Upper Saddle River, NJ: Prentice-Hall, 1998.

Powell, Robert, Roger Conant, and Joseph T. Collins. *Peterson Field Guide to Reptiles and Amphibians of Eastern and Central North America*. 4th ed. Peterson Field Guide Series. New York: Houghton Mifflin, 2016.

Price, Andrew Hoyt. *Venomous Snakes of Texas: A Field Guide*. Texas Natural History Guides. Austin: University of Texas Press, 2009.

Rubio, Manny, and Daniel E. Keyler. *Venomous Snakebite in the Western United States*. Rodeo, NM: ECO Herpetological Publishing, 2013.

Spearing, Darwin. *Roadside Geology of Texas*. Missoula, MT: Mountain Press, 1991.

Stebbins, Robert C., and Nathan W. Cohen. *A Natural History of Amphibians*. Princeton, NJ: Princeton University Press, 1995.

Tipton, Bob L., Terry L. Hibbitts, Troy D. Hibbitts, Toby J. Hibbitts, and Travis J. LaDuc. *Texas Amphibians: A Field Guide*. Texas Natural History Guides. Austin: University of Texas Press, 2012.

Wauer, Roland H., and Carl M. Fleming. *Naturalist's Big Bend: An Introduction to the Trees and Shrubs, Wildflowers, Cacti, Mammals, Birds, Reptiles and Amphibians, Fish, and Insects*. Rev. ed. Louise Lindsey Merrick Natural Environment Series, no. 33. College Station: Texas A&M University Press, 2002.

Werler, John E., and James R. Dixon. *Texas Snakes: Identification, Distribution, and Natural History*. Austin: University of Texas Press, 2000.

INDEX

Page numbers in *italic* indicate illustrations, and page numbers in bold indicate maps.

pygmy rattlesnakes, 117–19
Pyle, Mark, 81, 82, 84–85, 88, 89–90

Rabb Plantation house, 88
racers (snakes), 33–35, 87, 88, 89–91, 100,
    121
racerunners (lizards), 104, 134
rainbow grasshopper, 166
rainbow trout in McKittrick Creek,
    273–74
ratsnakes: Baird's ratsnake, 96, 256, *257*;
    Great Plains ratsnake, 71, 105, 159, 170;
    Trans-Pecos ratsnake, 239–40, *241*,
    242, 246, 271; western ratsnake, 3–4,
    109, 116, 159
rattlesnakes: eastern black-tailed rattle-
    snake, 103, 226, 250, 268–69; Mohave
    rattlesnake, 229–30, 242; prairie rat-
    tlesnake, 193, 199, 202–3, *204*; rock
    rattlesnakes, 210–11, 214–15, 217, 244,
    258, 260–61; timber rattlesnakes,
    119–20, 122–25; western pygmy rat-
    tlesnake, 117–19. *See also* western dia-
    mond-backed rattlesnake
*Rattlesnakes: Their Habits, Life Histories,
    and Influence on Mankind* (Klauber), 9
red-bordered pixie butterfly, 92
red-eared slider turtles, 39–40, 49, 128,
    170, 172
Red River, 162, 178
red-spotted toad, 140
red-striped ribbonsnake, 99–100
regal black-striped snake, 88
regal ring-necked snake, 222
reptiles, threatened and endangered list,
    299–300
reticulate banded gecko, 236–37, *249*,
    250–51
Rhinoceros beetle, 270–71
ribbonsnakes: arid land ribbonsnake,
    224, *225*; vs. gartersnakes, 145; Gulf
    Coast ribbonsnake, 60, 72, 84–85; red-
    striped ribbonsnake, 99–100; at Sabal
    Palm Sanctuary, 87; western ribbon-

snake, 122, 131, 145
ring-necked snakes, 168, 170, *171*, 222
Rio Grande, 227, 238
Rio Grande Valley: Boca Chica Beach,
    92–93; Hidalgo County irrigation
    canals, 84–87; King's explorations,
    81–84; Sabal Palm Sanctuary, 75,
    87–92; snake hunting in, 76–79
river cooter (turtle), 49, 91, 170, 172
River Road (FM 170), Brewster County,
    239–44
road-cruising, methods and rules, 211–
    12, 224
road hunting rules, 286–87
road-kill specimens, collecting, 110
Roadside Geology of Texas (Spearing), 30
Robinson, Scott, 237–38, 240, 255
Rock Garden Trail, Palo Duro Canyon,
    182–84
rock rattlesnakes, 210–11, 214–15, 217,
    244, 258, 260–61
Rolling Plains: checkered gartersnake,
    163–64, 191; geology and geogra-
    phy of, 161–62; Great Rattlesnake
    Highway adventure, 189–205; Mor-
    ris Ranch, 164–75; Stonewall County
    badlands, 175–77. *See also* Texas
    Panhandle
rough earthsnake, *283*
rough greensnake, 50, 147, *148, 216*
round-tailed horned lizard, 234–35
Roy E. Larsen Sandyland Sanctuary, 30
Ruthven's whipsnake, 92, 112

Sabal Palm Sanctuary, 75, 87–92
Sabine National Forest, *7*, 47–52
salamanders: amphiuma, 20, 21; lun-
    gless salamander, 96; marbled sala-
    mander, 153, 155, 156; mole group, 153;
    searching for in bottomland habitat,
    148–56; small-mouthed salamander,
    149–51, 152; spotted salamander, 153;
    western lesser siren, 87
salt marshes of Brazoria County, 64–67

278

spotted chorus frog, 125, 166

spotted salamander, 153

spotted whiptail lizards, 133–35, 166, 222, 233, *234*

Starr Ranch, 41

Stonewall County, 175–77

Strecker's chorus frog, 125

sun spider, 277–78

Tamaulipan thorn scrub, 75, 76–78, 79–81

tan racer, 33–35

tarantula hawk, 167

Terrell County, 220–22

Texas alligator lizard, 96, 97–98, 101, 102

Texas banded gecko, 230, *231*, 236

Texas brown tarantula, 83

Texas cooter (turtle), 170, 172

Texas coralsnake, 44, 46–47

Texas diamond-backed terrapin, 70

Texas horned lizard, 72–74, 173–74, 175, 187, 198, 225, 234

Texas indigo snake, 79–81, 82, 86–87

Texas lyresnake, 247–48

Texas madrone tree, 272

Texas map turtle, 107–8

Texas nightsnake, 142, 236

Texas Panhandle: geology and geography of, 161; Lake Meredith, 178–82, 186–87; Palo Duro Canyon, *7*, 178, 182–86; prairie rattler search, 202–3

Texas Point National Wildlife Refuge, *6*

Texas spiny lizard, 101, 102, 104, *105*

Texas spiny softshell turtle, 238

Texas spotted whiptail lizard, 133–35, 166

Texas threadsnake, 181

Texas toad, 190–91, 195

Their Blood Runs Cold (Gibbons), 9–10

threadsnake, 181

threatened species, 299–301

Throckmorton County, 194–95

timber (canebrake) rattlesnakes, 119–20, 122–25

toads and frogs. *See* frogs and toads

Trans-Pecos black-headed snake, 218–19

Trans-Pecos ratsnake, 239–40, *241*, 242, 246, 271

Trans-Pecos region: Chisos Mountains, 97, 226, *228*, 229, 253, 255–60; Davis Mountains, 226, 254, 260–71; Dryden area, 221–26; Edwards Plateau, 207; geology and geography of, 227–29, 253; Guadalupe Mountains, 253, 254, 272–80; Juno Road, 207–17; Pandale Road, 217–20; Sanderson area, 220–22. *See also* Chihuahuan Desert

Trans-Pecos threadsnake, 181

treefrogs, 21, *22*, 38–39, 45, 245, 263

tree lizards, 104, 215–16, 222, 264–65, 273, 276–77

Tuff Canyon, 238

Turkey Creek unit, Big Thicket National Preserve, 22–26

turtles: behavior of semiaquatic, 39–40; box turtles, 109–11, 192; cooters, 49, 91, 170, 172; mud turtles, 168, 172; red-eared slider turtles, 39–40, 49, 128, 170, 172; snapping turtles, 31–33, 37, 172; softshell turtles, 172, 238; Texas diamond-backed terrapin, 70; Texas map turtle, 107–8

two-tailed swallowtail butterfly, 257

Val Verde County, 207–20

variable groundsnake, 105, 173, *174*, 181–82, 202

venomous snakebite guidance, 287–91

Venomous Snakes of Texas (Price), 287

vinegaroon, 259–60, 278

walkingsticks, 44

watersnakes: broad-banded watersnake, 26–27, 62, 158; diamond-backed watersnake, 85, 158, 191; Gulf salt-marsh watersnake, 62, *63*, 64; Mississippi green watersnake, 66; plain-bellied watersnake, 108, 121–22,